D0872364

The Mind
of the
Political
Terrorist

The
Mind
of the
Political
Terrorist

Richard M. Pearlstein

A Scholarly Resources Inc. Imprint
Wilmington, Delaware

The paper used in this publication meets the minimum requirements of the American National Standard for permanence of paper for printed library materials, Z39.48, 1984.

Grateful acknowledgment is made for permission to reprint selected material:

With the Weathermen: The Personal Journal of a Revolutionary Woman by Susan Stern. Copyright © 1975 by Doubleday, a division of Bantam, Doubleday, Dell Publishing Group Inc.

In Search of a Sister by Fred Soltysik. Copyright © 1976 by Fred Soltysik. Used by permission of Bantam Books, a division of Bantam, Doubleday, Dell Publishing Group Inc.

My Search for Patty Hearst by Steven Weed. Copyright © 1976 by Steven Weed. Used by permission of Crown Publishers Inc.

Scholarly Resources Inc.
104 Greenhill Avenue
Wilmington, DE 19805-1897

Library of Congress Cataloging-in-Publication Data

Pearlstein, Richard M. (Richard Merrill), 1953–
    The mind of the political terrorist / Richard M. Pearlstein.
      p. cm.
    Includes bibliographical references (p.
    Includes Index.
    ISBN 0-8420-2345-3 (cloth)
    1. Terrorists—Psychology.   2. Narcissism.   3. Terrorists—
Case studies. I. Title.
HV6431.P43 1991
303.6′25—dc20   90-9134
                                            CIP

To my mother,

who taught me love and loyalty

About the Author

Richard M. Pearlstein received his Ph.D. in political science from the University of North Carolina at Chapel Hill, where he also has taught as well as at the University of Connecticut and Marlboro College. The author of several articles on political terrorism and political psychology, he presently serves as the administrative director of the Institute of Social and Behavioral Pathology in Chicago. This is his first book.

Contents

Preface and Acknowledgments

In recent years, political terrorism has emerged as a conspicuously disturbing problem. Yet, despite our increasingly sophisticated grasp of this issue, practical insight into the individual psychological dimensions of political terrorism remains embryonic at best. Although the social psychology of political terrorism already has been rather handsomely explained, the individual psychology of the political terrorist has not yet proved to be a particularly fertile area of understanding.

The purpose of this book is to explore the mind of the political terrorist. Specifically, it attempts to identify, analyze, explain, and illustrate the critical interrelationship between the underlying psychoanalytical bases and inherent psychodynamic "rewards" of political terrorism. My fundamental conclusions are that the individual who becomes and remains a political terrorist generally appears to be psychologically molded by certain narcissistic personality disturbances. These disturbances appear to predispose strongly such individuals toward the intrinsic psychodynamic rewards of political terrorism.

I sincerely wish to acknowledge the invaluable comments, suggestions, and assistance of the following individuals: Lawrence Zelic Freedman, M.D., and Professor Erik Willenz of

ix

the University of Chicago's Institute of Social and Behavioral Pathology; Professors Lewis Lipsitz, Jeffrey Obler, Andrew M. Scott, Robert A. Rupen, Charles D. Phillips, Paul F. Kress, Michael Lienesch, Gordon B. Cleveland, the late James W. Prothro, and the late Frank J. Munger, all of the University of North Carolina at Chapel Hill.

I am also indebted to Dr. Eric D. Shaw of the Cornell University Medical Center; David G. Hubbard, M.D., of the Behavioral Research Center; Professor David J. Garrow of the City University of New York; Professor J. Garry Clifford of the University of Connecticut; Professor Edward E. Azar of the University of Maryland's Center for International Development; Professor Robert G. Picard of Emerson College; Dr. Carolsue Holland of Troy State University; Mr. Thomas Martinez, author of *The Brotherhood of Murder*; Dr. Kleber Masterson of Booz, Allen and Hamilton Inc.; Mr. Christopher J. Grose of Control Risks Limited; Mr. William Vincent of Aviation Security International; Dr. Sanford Sherizen of Secure Data Systems; and the faculty, staff, and students of Marlboro College for allowing me the time to complete the final revisions of this book. I also wish to express my deepest gratitude for the patience, understanding, and support of Mr. Richard M. Hopper and Mr. Philip G. Johnson of Scholarly Resources.

Finally, I wish to acknowledge my appreciation to the respective staffs of Widener Library at Harvard University; the Dewey, Hayden, and Humanities libraries at the Massachusetts Institute of Technology; and the Fletcher School of Law and Diplomacy at Tufts University.

R.M.P.

Foreword

Political terrorism has afflicted the civilized world during the last quarter of the twentieth century. In the United States the presidencies of Jimmy Carter, Ronald Reagan, and now George Bush have been adversely influenced. Worldwide, millions of people have been fascinated, fixated, or frequently terrorized by political events.

Fellows of the Institute of Social and Behavioral Pathology, of whom Professor Richard Pearlstein is a distinguished colleague, have been studying rage, aggression, and violence since the institute's origin at the Yale Medical and Law Schools in 1945. The institute has focused its research on political violence and terrorism during the past quarter century.

Pearlstein's study is an in-depth analysis of persons from various nationalities and socioeconomic status who became political terrorists. He has investigated their cultural-political origins, traced their developmental patterns, and eloquently described their emergent adult personalities.

Furthermore, the author has provided readers with a psychological theory that integrates a multitude of facts and multilevel perspectives. Theory and fact are thus internally coherent and relevant. They both persuasively demonstrate the predisposing and precipitating factors that influenced these people to become political terrorists. Ultimately, narcissistic injury and disappointment led them to narcissistic rage, defense, and aggression.

xi

Pearlstein has constructed a configuration of psychological and psychopolitical factors to produce a syndrome of autocompensatory violence expressed in political terrorism. The self-selection of these men and women is their attempt to assuage the pain and damage inflicted on their vulnerable and depleted selves.

The twentieth-century political terrorism that is described herein has modern predecessors in the nineteenth century. Insurgent terrorism appeared in Russia, culminating in the assassination of Alexander II in 1881. Political terrorism emerged again in 1917 and also following the end of World War I as governments struggled to assert their sovereignty and legitimacy against the outraged claims of ethnic groups and social and economic classes. Its recurrence a century later painfully prefigures its continuous threat to the stability of societies.

This significant work provides us with a better understanding of this acute and chronic societal syndrome. It now joins previous reports of the fellows of the institute as a valuable contribution to this still unresolved social challenge.

Lawrence Z. Freedman, M.D.
Chairman, Institute of Social and Behavioral Pathology
Research Professor Emeritus of Psychiatry
University of Chicago

CHAPTER ONE

The Nature of
Political Terrorism

It is widely observed that political terrorism may be the most difficult problem of our time. Political terrorism, it is argued, is a wholly illegitimate act that violates the most fundamental human rights. Freely granted as well is that it poses a severe danger to democratic rights and values. Indeed, the political terrorist's self-proclaimed "propaganda of the deed" has resulted in brutal abductions and assassinations, wanton bombings of public places and commercial jetliners, bloody skyjackings, and other manifestations of once-astonishing savagery. Equally alarming have been such related developments as calls for media censorship, actual and perceived travel restrictions, house-to-house searches, persecution of legitimate political organizations, and officially abridged rights to an attorney of one's choice.

What is political terrorism? It is, most generally, a form of terrorism whose overt or professed rationale is political. We must therefore define terrorism as a basic concept prior to qualifying the term as (in this case) "political."

Although, as Walter Laqueur points out, "No definition of terrorism can possibly cover all the varieties of terrorism that have appeared throughout history,"[1] we can survey the history of the term "terrorism" itself. According to the *Oxford English Dictionary (OED)*, the word, when first used in 1795, was meant to denote official governmental repression, or "government by intimidation as directed and carried out by the party in power in

1

France during the Revolution of 1789–94; the system of the 'Terror' (1793–4)," rather than civil rebellion. As Edmund Burke stated in 1795, "Thousands of those Hell-hounds called Terrorists . . . are let loose on the people." Yet the term "terror," first employed during the late fourteenth century, generally had implied a "state of being terrified or greatly frightened; intense fear, fright or dread." The *OED* also informs us that by 1866 the political term of "terrorist" more customarily had been applied by William Fitzpatrick to describe "any one who attempts to further his views by a system of coercive intimidation."

Recent efforts to define the term "terrorism" have focused upon increasingly specific manifestations of such coercive intimidation. Frederick Hacker, who views terror and terrorism as twin brothers, states for example that

> terror, which is inflicted from above, is the manufacture and spread of fear by dictators, governments, and bosses. It is the attempt of the powerful to exert control through intimidation. Terrorism, which is imposed from below, is the manufacture and spread of fear by rebels, revolutionaries, and protesters. It is the attempt of the so-far powerless, the would-be powerful, to exert control through intimidation. Terror and terrorism are not the same, but they belong together, indissolubly linked by the shared belief that fear is the strongest, if not the only, effective human motivation and that violence is the best, if not the only, method to produce and maintain fear.[2]

For Edward Hyams, on the other hand, no such distinction between terror and terrorism is drawn. Hence "[terrorism is a] revolutionary or sometimes counterrevolutionary ('police terrorism') method by means of which a population is induced to cooperate."[3] Jordan Paust, in a similar vein, argues that terrorism is the "purposive use of violence or the threat of violence by the precipitator(s) against an instrumental target in order to communicate to a primary target a threat of future violence so as to coerce the primary target into behavior or attitudes through intense fear or anxiety in connection with a demanded power (political) outcome."[4]

Thomas Thornton also neglects to distinguish clearly between the twin brothers of terror and terrorism. Thus, despite his invention of the terms "enforcement terror" (Hacker's "terrorism"), Thornton defines only terror: "a symbolic act designed to influence political behavior by extranormal means, entailing the use or threat of violence."[5] And, like Hyams, Paust, and Thornton, Claire Sterling fails to differentiate semantically between the twins. While she has entitled her account of the terrorist infrastructure of Western Europe *The Terror Network*, she has subtitled it *The Secret War of International Terrorism*. Sterling compounds her semantic imprecision by referring to the leaders of this terror network as the "aristocrats of terror."[6] Even such an outstanding scholar as Paul Wilkinson has fallen into this semantic trap. Indeed, he employs the terms "terror" and "terrorism" almost interchangeably: "For the political terrorist, however, it is a sine qua non that the overriding objective and ultimate justification for terror is the furtherance of his political cause. . . . A major characteristic of political terror is its indiscriminate nature. . . . Political terrorism, properly speaking, is a sustaining policy involving the waging of organised terror."[7]

Clearly, we must be able to draw a sharp and unequivocal distinction between the two terms. For the purpose of this study, "terrorism" shall be defined as a specific form of civil rebellion or civil insurgency in which the use or threatened use of violence is imposed from below against certain symbolic victims or objects in order to coerce a primary target to accept a demanded outcome due to the effectuation of intense fear or anxiety. Such unacceptable acts of political terrorism typically are manifested as assassinations, bombings, kidnappings for ransom or propaganda effect, hostage-takings, skyjackings, torture, and threats of the above.

On the other hand, "terror" shall be defined as a form of intimidation in which the use or threatened use of violence is directly inflicted *from above* rather than imposed *from below*, thereby differing from terrorism in that it represents an official or quasi-official, as opposed to a rebellious, act. Moreover, both terror and terrorism may be considered authentically political in nature only if calls for a demanded outcome are 1) somehow articulated or otherwise conveyed to a primary target, and 2) couched in distinctly political terms.

What are the causes of political terrorism? Attempts to address this issue customarily have focused upon "direct" and what may be termed "structural-permissive" causes.[8] Direct explanations of political terrorism are evidenced most dramatically within the literature of the participants themselves. Typical recent illustrations are such autobiographical accounts as Pierre Vallières's *White Niggers of America*, Leila Khaled's *My People Shall Live*, and Sean MacStiofain's *Revolutionary in Ireland*.[9] Most of these jeremiads are preoccupied with the integral role of political terrorism in amplifying the grievances of the have-nots in nationalist-separatist conflicts. As Vallières writes, "It was as if our entire existence was nothing but a daily obscenity. . . . If a revolutionary army had existed in Quebec it would have found thousands of workers, women and young people ready to take up arms. . . . Nonetheless, from the seeds that rotted in that wretched ground there would one day spring up something stronger than humiliation."[10]

A variation on this theme is the Islamic Shi'ite challenge to the predominantly Sunni Moslem world and the West, examples of which include the Shi'a car bombings of pro-Western targets in the Middle East. These terrorists, regarded as martyrs by their religious compatriots, are motivated by the historically low social position of the Shi'ites, who also are contending against what they perceive as their own have-not social, political, and economic status.

Much attention has been directed recently toward the structural-permissive causes of political terrorism. For example, theories of why political terrorism has become commonplace in liberal democratic societies have, of necessity, augmented the ungarnished postulates of the direct approach to the phenomenon. Liberal democratic societies present particularly inviting targets to political terrorists. As Wilkinson's pioneering *Terrorism and the Liberal State* makes clear, liberal democratic societies are far less well equipped to deter and deal with political terrorism than are military dictatorships or one-party states. Moreover, such acts as hostage-takings frequently have been dealt with in such a manner as to encourage their repetition.[11] It also has been pointed out that political terrorists who function like average citizens within liberal democratic societies derive tangible benefits from constitutional guarantees against unreasonable search and seizure, domestic travel restrictions, and, most critically, press censorship.[12]

As Laqueur points out, liberal democratic authority is also sensitive to the prospect of ex post facto criticism of a hard-line approach to hostage negotiations since, it is presumed, "one should not be generous with other people's lives."[13] Such an approach nevertheless has been suggested all too often due to a widely held belief that one cannot give in to terrorists.[14] Thus, tactical preparations for acts of political terrorism are facilitated by a tolerance for civil liberties. In addition, such acts are often aimed at manipulating the liberal devotion to the sanctity of human—that is, hostage—rights.

Where the structural-permissive approach suffers is in its contention that what in reality are supporting factors are among the "causes" of political terrorism. As is the case with state involvement in, support of, and control of political terrorism, or new technologies and targets in the transportation, communications, and weapons fields,[15] factors such as civil liberties, media access, or humane value systems do not "cause" political terrorism. Nevertheless, all of the above factors do serve to aggravate an overall problem that is itself determined by a complex equation of direct and indirect factors.

What are the psychological determinants of political terrorism? A preliminary analysis of this issue merits an examination of 1) basic theories of aggression, 2) the "personality-and-politics" literature, 3) individual psychological case histories of political terrorists, and 4) psychological studies of nonterrorist violence and nonpolitical terrorism.[16] Most useful to our immediate purposes, however, is a discussion of the basic theories of aggression.

Students of aggression generally have encountered a conflicting approach to the subject. The search for the causes of violence has raised the question: What which is inherent in man leads to aggressive behavior? This line of inquiry also has been directed toward the influence of psychosocial, political, and economic forces upon aggressive behavior. The former has been labeled the "instinctivist" approach and the latter the "environmentalist."[17] The controversy over the psychological causes of aggression has been commonly referred to as the "nature-nurture" debate.

In addressing the issue of the psychological determinants of political terrorism, I shall not be troubled by the instinctivist claim that man is an inherently aggressive being. Although this is not the appropriate forum for this controversy, I shall nonetheless cast my lot with the environmentalists since 1) it is patently absurd to argue that there are "born" terrorists or that virtually anyone is psychologically predisposed toward terrorism, other forms of aggression, or conflict itself;[18] and 2) if, after all, such a predisposition is universal, why would an overwhelming majority of people refrain from aggressive behavior? Why are certain types of aggression engaged in, and not others?[19] Political terrorists are made, not born.

There are many environmentally oriented theories of aggressive behavior, including, for example, the concepts of frustration-aggression, narcissism-aggression, relative deprivation, authoritarianism, obedience to authority, and adolescent rebellion, as well as guilt, sadism, and paranoia. The most systematic and comprehensive of these theories, however, are set forth in the "frustration-aggression" and what may be termed the "narcissism-aggression" theories.

The frustration-aggression theory has played a major role within the terrorism-and-psychology literature. As Joseph Margolin points out, "Much terrorist behavior is a response to the frustration of various political, economic, and personal needs or objectives."[20] Yet the frustration-aggression hypothesis also is made a major object of criticism, if not outright scorn, by many students of aggression. As Albert Pepitone argues, "Not all violent behavior presupposes frustration" and, conversely, "frustration does not necessarily generate violent impulses."[21] Peter Lupsha concurs, stating that "frustration is not necessary for the occurrence of violence."[22] Both Pepitone and Lupsha thus judge this hypothesis to be hopelessly simplistic.

The frustration-aggression theory, as originally stated, takes as its major point the assumption that "*aggression is always a consequence of frustration. . . .* The occurrence of aggressive behavior always presupposes the existence of frustration, and, contrarywise, that the existence leads to some form of aggression."[23] As amended by N. E. Miller, the concept that aggression is determined solely by frustration was deleted and supplanted by the view that frustration could lead to a variety of reactions.[24] Others, such as Arnold Buss, Leonard Berkowitz, Leo Nagelburg, and Hyman Spotnitz, have argued that aggression may be an instrumental act, a means to an end offering inherent reinforcement or rewards.[25]

Does the frustration-aggression hypothesis serve as an effective psychological theory of political terrorism? Or is this approach too simplistic and vague to be of much value to students of political terrorism? Granting that rejoinders to these respective questions must be no, and yes, one proper heir to the frustration-aggression theory might well be the narcissism-aggression hypothesis.

As a general rule, narcissism may be viewed as a range of psychoanalytic orientations, impulses, or behavioral patterns either wholly or overwhelmingly subject to ego concern, as opposed to object concern.[26] Narcissism also might be seen as the manner in which an individual relates to the external, object world, either wholly or overwhelmingly upon the latter's potential capacity to provide that individual with sufficient ego reinforcement, satisfaction, or compensation. For our purposes narcissism should be defined as an internal, intrapsychic, regulatory "tool" that enables the individual to defend the self from damage and harm.

Based upon the case study evidence, the individual psychological bases of political terrorism may be characterized as "narcissistic injury" and "narcissistic disappointment." As the term implies, a narcissistic injury is defined as massive, profound, and permanent damage or harm to an individual's self-image or self-esteem. Narcissistic disappointment shall be defined on two levels of analysis. As an internal, intrapsychic phenomenon, narcissistic disappointment is a psychological disturbance whereby 1) the ego, or self, is unable to measure up to the ego ideal, or positive and desirable standards of conduct, and consequently is punished by the superego, or conscience; or 2) the ego is veritably tyrannized by an overly grandiose ego ideal. On an external, interpersonal level, narcissistic disappointment is defined as 1) profound disappointment in the self prompted by an individual's pronounced inability to measure up to what he perceives as positive and desirable standards of conduct; or 2) harsh disillusionment with individuals or groups that represent or advocate those standards of conduct, and a resultant disappointment in the self for ever having embraced those standards. In brief, in 90 percent of political terrorist case studies, narcissistic injury or narcissistic disappointment plays a critical psychobiographical role.

Why might the practice of political terrorism itself be psychologically attractive to victims of narcissistic personality disturbances? Friedrich Nietzsche once observed that "nothing on earth consumes a man more quickly than the passion of resentment." Indeed, the apparent ease and spontaneity with which the political terrorist qua victim of narcissistic injury or disappointment so defends himself from profound psychic wounds merely serves to reflect that psychological journey typically taken by such individuals. I refer here first to an overall regression, or return to an earlier stage, of normal childhood development. In his discussion of the child's "grandiose self," Heinz Kohut delineates a normal "phase in which the gleam in the mother's eye mirrors the child's exhibitionistic displays, and other forms of maternal participation in the child's narcissistic enjoyment confirm the child's self-esteem and, by gradually increasing selectivity of these responses, begin to channel it in realistic directions."[27] It is to this and even earlier phases of development that the victim of narcissistic personality disturbances retreats. This psychological manifestation thus has been aptly termed "secondary narcissism."

Important, too, are the direct and indirect aftermaths of narcissistic injury and disappointment: narcissistic rage, narcissistic defense, and, all too typically, some form of narcissistic aggression. Taken as a whole, these manifestations of secondary narcissism may be termed the "narcissistic rage-aggression-defense nexus." As Gregory Rochlin puts it: "When narcissism is threatened, we are humiliated, *our self-esteem is injured*, and *aggression appears*. . . . To redress the balance—to restore our self-esteem, assert our value—in the face of this condition, the defensive functions of aggression are invoked. . . . From our earliest years narcissism and aggression are found to be linked in an indivisible bond."[28] For Rochlin, aggression thus results from something far more substantial and fundamental than mere frustration. Like Albert Camus, who maintains that the "rebel" (for example, the political terrorist) "demands respect for himself" since "he is fighting for the integrity of one part of his being,"[29] Rochlin's explanation of aggression centers upon perceived attacks upon the integrity of an individual's self-esteem or self-image.

Finally, political terrorism offers its practitioners certain distinct and powerfully alluring psychic benefits or "rewards."

These psychodynamic rewards may be classified into two fundamental categories. The first is the syndrome of political terrorism as "autocompensatory violence," itself an interrelated cluster of psychological and psychopolitical factors. These include what I have termed 1) the political terrorist's clearly manifested psychic sense of omnipotence; 2) the political terrorist's establishment, assumption, and maintenance of a "new," "as-if other" pseudoidentity; and 3) the indubitable psychological utility of political terrorist group membership.

The second class of psychic rewards, which springs from the contextual justification of political terrorism, actually enables the political terrorist to assume the "mask of omnipotence" yet eschew the "mask of villainy"—that is, the role of political terrorist as a negative identity. These latter indirect psychic rewards may be realized through the contemporary sanctification of political terrorism as a mode of personal liberation and through the seminal writings of German philosopher Max Stirner and Russian anarchist Sergei Nechaev,[30] the brutally egoistic rationalization of contemporary terrorism.

In conclusion, political terrorism therefore is determined, and affected, by a diverse set of factors. The focus of this study is upon the individual psychological and psychopolitical dimensions of political terrorism. Quite simply, we need to know far more about this topic, but a comprehensive analysis of every social or individual factor that contributes to political terrorism is beyond the scope of this book. Not included, therefore, are topics such as the issue of context—that is, that political terrorism has both a psychological and, obviously, a *political* context; the many other causes or determinants of political terrorism; the internal dynamics of the political terrorist organization, group, or cell; or other options or responses, given the presence of those psychological disturbances considered in this study.

It also will not be possible to analyze fully the other personal or biographical factors underlying an individual's decision to become a political terrorist. For the purposes of this work, it will be sufficient to note that such a decision also is conditioned by 1) the biographical presence of certain preterrorist activities—for example, membership in nonviolent, reformist, or radical student groups, common criminal activities, or incarceration; 2) an actual, or perceived, lack of other satisfying options; and 3) the presence of some form of political terrorist recruitment effort. In an overwhelming majority of political terrorist case studies, including those considered here, these additional factors are clearly present.

Now that we understand both what this study is and what it is not, I shall address the central question: What psychological factors appear to help motivate otherwise highly diverse individuals to become, and remain, political terrorists?

Notes

1. Walter Laqueur, *Terrorism* (Boston: Little, Brown, 1977), 7.
2. Frederick J. Hacker, "Terror and Terrorism: Modern Growth Industry and Mass Entertainment," *Terrorism* 4 (1980): 144. See also idem, *Terror and Terrorism* (New York: W. W. Norton, 1976); and idem, *Crusaders, Criminals, Crazies* (New York: W. W. Norton, 1976).
3. Edward S. Hyams, *A Dictionary of Modern Revolution* (New York: Taplinger, 1973), 275. See also idem, *Terrorists and Terrorism* (London: Dent, 1975).
4. Jordan J. Paust, "Some Thoughts on 'Preliminary Thoughts' on Terrorism," *American Journal of International Law* 68 (1974): 502.
5. Thomas Perry Thornton, "Terror as a Weapon of Political Agitation," in Harry Eckstein, ed., *Internal War* (New York: Free Press, 1964), 73 (emphasis deleted).
6. Claire Sterling, *The Terror Network: The Secret War of International Terrorism* (New York: Berkley, 1982), 290.
7. Paul Wilkinson, "Concepts of Terror and Terrorism," in *Political Terrorism* (New York: John Wiley, 1974), 13, 17.
8. For an excellent analysis of this distinction see Chalmers Johnson, "Perspectives on Terrorism," in Walter Laqueur, ed., *The Terrorism Reader* (New York: Meridian, 1978), 267–85.
9. See Pierre Vallières, *White Niggers of America* (New York: Monthly Review Press, 1971); Leila Khaled, *My People Shall Live* (London: Hodder and Stoughton, 1973); and Sean MacStiofain, *Revolutionary in Ireland* (Farnborough, UK: Gordon Cremonesi, 1975).
10. Vallières, *White Niggers*, 111, 114, 119.
11. See Paul Wilkinson, *Terrorism and the Liberal State* (New York: Halsted, 1977).
12. See, for example, Fromkin's observation that "an open society . . . is especially vulnerable to terrorist violence," in David Fromkin, "The Strategy of Terrorism," *Foreign Affairs* 53 (1975): 698. See also David L. Milbank, *International and Transnational Terrorism* (Washington, DC: Central Intelligence Agency, PR 7610030, April 1976).
13. Walter Laqueur, "Terrorism — A Balance Sheet," in Laqueur, ed., *Terrorism Reader*, 259.
14. It should be recognized that political terrorists generally anticipate that their actions will "force hitherto liberal regimes to become repressive" or

"reveal this hidden [terror] to the population at large." See Fromkin, "Strategy of Terrorism," 698. Although such expectations are transformed into reality, only in rare instances (for example, Uruguay and the Tupamaros) does political terrorism tactically succeed "against . . . governments which refrain from responding . . . with equally indiscriminate repression." See Laqueur, "Terrorism," 264.

15. See, for example, Fromkin, "Strategy of Terrorism," 683; Johnson, "Perspectives," 278–81; and Ernest Evans, *Calling a Truce to Terror* (Westport, CT: Greenwood, 1979), 20. See also Amy Sands Redlick, "The Transnational Flow of Information as a Cause of Terrorism," in Yonah Alexander, David Carlton, and Paul Wilkinson, eds., *Terrorism: Theory and Practice* (Boulder, CO: Westview, 1979), 73–95.

16. Those theories of aggression most germane to our purposes are John Dollard et al., *Frustration and Aggression* (New Haven, CT: Yale University Press, 1939); Leonard Berkowitz, *Aggression* (New York: McGraw-Hill, 1962); and Erich Fromm, *The Anatomy of Human Destructiveness* (Greenwich, CT: Fawcett, 1973).

Key sources in the personality-and-politics literature are Harold D. Lasswell, *Psychopathology and Politics* (Chicago: University of Chicago Press, 1977); idem, *Power and Personality* (New York: W. W. Norton, 1948); Fred I. Greenstein and Michael Lerner, eds., *A Source Book for the Study of Personality and Politics* (Chicago: Markham, 1971); Greenstein, *Personality and Politics* (New York: W. W. Norton, 1969); and Jeanne N. Knutson, "Personality in the Study of Politics," in Knutson, ed., *Handbook of Political Psychology* (San Francisco: Jossey-Bass, 1973), esp. 28–44.

Appropriate psychological case studies of nonterrorist violence and nonpolitical terrorism include E. Victor Wolfenstein, *The Revolutionary Personality* (Princeton, NJ: Princeton University Press, 1967); Bruce Mazlish, *The Revolutionary Ascetic* (New York: McGraw-Hill, 1976); Sidney J. Slomich and Robert E. Kantor, "Social Psychopathology of Political Assassination," in Doris Y. Wilkinson, ed., *Social Structure and Assassination Behavior* (Cambridge, MA: Schenkman, 1976), 40–47; David A. Rothstein, "Presidential Assassination Syndrome," in William J. Crotty, ed., *Assassinations and the Political Order* (New York: Harper and Row, 1971), 161–222; Lawrence Zelic Freedman, "Psychopathology of Assassination," in Crotty, ed., *Assassinations*, 143–60; Thomas Greening, "The Psychological Study of Assassins," in Crotty, ed., *Assassinations*, 222–66; David G. Hubbard, *The Skyjacker* (New York: Macmillan, 1971); Kenneth Keniston, *Young Radicals* (New York: Harcourt Brace and World, 1968); and Robert Liebert, *Radical and Militant Youth* (New York: Praeger, 1971).

General works on nonterrorist violence and nonpolitical terrorism include Ted Robert Gurr, *Why Men Rebel* (Princeton, NJ: Princeton University Press, 1970); idem, "Psychological Factors in Civil Violence," *World Politics* 20 (1968): 245–78; Albert Pepitone, "The Social Psychology of Violence," *International Journal of Group Tensions* 2 (1972): 19–32; Peter A. Lupsha, "Explanation of Political Violence," *Politics and Society* 2 (1971): 89–104; and Paul Wilkinson, "Social Scientific Theory and Civil Violence," in Alexander, Carlton, and Wilkinson, eds., *Terrorism*, 45–72.

17. Sigmund Freud and Konrad Lorenz are seminal figures in the instinctivist school of thought. Freud argued that all human behavior, including aggression, is determined by the conflict between self-preservation—that is, the life

instinct—and the sexual/death instinct. See especially Sigmund Freud, *The Ego and the Id* (New York: W. W. Norton, 1960); idem, *Beyond the Pleasure Principle* (New York: W. W. Norton, 1960); and idem, *Civilization and Its Discontents* (New York: W. W. Norton, 1961). Lorenz similarly claims that human aggression is a basic biological drive or instinct programmed into man as part of his basic instinct for survival. See Konrad Lorenz, *On Aggression* (New York: Bantam, 1971).

18. For a critique of the claim that conflict is an inherent mode of human relations see Michael Taylor, *Anarchy and Cooperation* (New York: John Wiley, 1976).

19. See Erich Fromm, "Different Forms of Violence," in *The Heart of Man* (New York: Harper and Row, 1964), 17–34.

20. Joseph Margolin, "Psychological Perspectives in Terrorism," in Yonah Alexander and Seymour Maxwell Finger, eds., *Terrorism: Interdisciplinary Perspectives* (New York: John Jay, 1977), 273–74. See also Gurr's extension of the principle that frustration leads to aggression to the "relative deprivation-violence" relationship, in *Why Men Rebel*, 33–37.

21. Pepitone, "Social Psychology of Violence," 22.

22. Lupsha, "Explanation of Political Violence," 90.

23. Dollard et al., *Frustration and Aggression*, 1 (emphasis in original).

24. N. E. Miller, "Frustration-Aggression Hypothesis," *Psychological Review* 48 (1941): 337–42.

25. See Arnold H. Buss, "Aggression Pays," in Jerome L. Singer, ed., *The Control of Aggression and Violence* (New York: Academic Press, 1971), 7–18. For Berkowitz's views on aggression as a source of pleasure see Berkowitz, *Aggression*, 196–228. See also Leo Nagelburg and Hyman Spotnitz, "Strengthening the Ego through the Release of Frustration-Aggression," *American Journal of Orthopsychiatry* 28 (1958): 794–801.

26. The study of narcissism also has been described as the "psychology of the self." This term was first coined by Heinz Kohut, a psychoanalyst at the University of Chicago. See, for example, Heinz Kohut, *The Analysis of the Self* (New York: International Publishers, 1971); idem, "Forms and Transformations of Narcissism," *Journal of the American Psychoanalytic Association* 14 (1966): 243–72; idem, "The Psychoanalytic Treatment of Narcissistic Personality Disorders," *Psychoanalytic Study of the Child* 23 (1968): 86–113; idem, *The Restoration of the Self* (New York: International Universities Press, 1977); and idem, "Thoughts on Narcissism and Narcissistic Rage," *Psychoanalytic Study of the Child* 27 (1972): 360–400. For a contrasting and less sympathetic perspective on the pathology of narcissistic personality disorders see especially the work of Otto F. Kernberg, most notably his *Borderline Conditions and Pathological Narcissism* (New York: Aronson, 1975). For a superb overview of the basic literature on narcissism see Andrew P. Morrison, ed., *Essential Papers on Narcissism* (New York: New York University Press, 1986).

27. Kohut, "Psychoanalytic Treatment," 96. Kohut describes the grandiose self, one of the central intrapsychic factors in narcissistic personality disturbances, as a "grandiose and exhibitionistic image of the self." See ibid., 86.

28. Gregory Rochlin, *Man's Aggression* (Boston: Gambit, 1973), 1–2 (emphasis in original).

29. Albert Camus, *The Rebel* (New York: Vintage, 1956), 16, 18.

30. See John Carroll, ed., *Max Stirner* (New York: Harper and Row, 1971); and Sergei Nechaev, "Catechism of the Revolutionist," in M. Confino, ed., *Daughter of a Revolutionary* (London: Alcove Press, n.d.).

CHAPTER TWO

The Individual Psychology of the Political Terrorist

During the last decade the psychodynamic interrelationship between narcissism and political terrorism has been suggested by a growing number of observers.[1] In his fine critique of the psychopathology model of political terrorist motivation, Eric Shaw comments that a far more valid "general theme in the childhood and adolescent development of many terrorists involves the occurrence of serious narcissistic damage, as defined as any event interpreted by an individual as critically affecting his view of himself or self-esteem."[2]

The term "narcissism" has been conceptualized elsewhere as 1) a literary motif derived from the ancient Greek legend of Narcissus, the mythological youth whose obsessive fascination with his own exquisite, pond-reflected image ultimately culminates in varying forms of self-destruction, 2) a sexual perversion or dysfunction, and 3) a theory of individual psychological development.[3] To recall our previous discussion, narcissism may be conceptualized here as an internal, intrapsychic regulatory tool that enables the individual to defend the self from profound damage and harm. More concretely, narcissism may be viewed as a mode of object relations—that is, the manner in which an individual relates to the external, object world, either wholly or overwhelmingly upon the latter's capacity to provide that individual with sufficient ego or narcissistic reinforcement, satisfaction, or compensation, given the existence of such damage or harm. Hence, narcissism shall be regarded as a restorative or reparative psychological "device."

It is also relevant to recognize that narcissism has been interpreted elsewhere as a key manifestation of individual development.[4] As we have already noted, the manner in which the political terrorist qua victim of narcissistic personality disturbances defends himself from psychic harm actually serves as a regression to earlier stages of normal childhood development. This psychological manifestation is thus termed "secondary narcissism."

It is generally acknowledged that every individual begins life in a condition of absolute, unfettered, or, in generally accepted psychoanalytic parlance, "primary" narcissism.[5] Sigmund Freud, for example, construed primary narcissism as a more or less normal phase of psychological development during which the infant's libido, or "love instinct," is cathected exclusively or directed upon himself.[6] Thus, the stage of primary narcissism in part is characterized as a period of extreme self-cathexis, or "self-love." This stage also is psychologically characterized by the infant's wholly undifferentiated fusion or symbiosis with his mother. Indeed, the infant's repeatedly demonstrated ability to cause or coerce his mother to respond to his needs and whims has led some psychoanalysts to term this phase as one of "omnipotent symbiosis."[7] During this rudimentary period of individual development, libidinal cathexis upon other objects or individuals and tangible or intangible entities in an individual's environment—that is, object cathexis—has not yet begun.

The infant's normal development into early childhood may be conceived as the period in which primary narcissism is discarded or outgrown. During this phase the child both becomes increasingly able to cathect libidinally with differentiated objects in his environment and becomes progressively more aware of himself as a distinct self. This personality development, which usually takes place between the twelfth and thirty-sixth months of life, thus has been termed the "separation-individuation" phase.[8] As we observed in Chapter 1, it is during this phase that the child seeks "the gleam in the mother's eye [that] mirrors the child's exhibitionistic displays." It is also during the separation-individuation phase that "the child's narcissistic enjoyment confirms the child's self-esteem."[9]

Secondary narcissism implies adolescent or adult regression to the developmental stages of infantile primary narcissism and the subsequent separation-individuation phase of early childhood. Therefore, secondary narcissism may be construed as adolescent or adult libido withdrawal from objects and total or overwhelming libidinal recathexis upon the self. For our purposes, secondary narcissism may be understood as an adolescent or adult individual's unremitting manipulation of objects in order to transform negative self-image or self-esteem into positive self-representation.

We are ultimately concerned with the psychopolitical ramifications of secondary narcissism; thus, narcissism, as it pertains to public or social behavior, may be conceptualized as a mode of object relations. In analyzing narcissism as a developmental concept, we have sought to understand who the victim of narcissistic personality disturbances *is*. On the other hand, when we examine narcissism as a mode of object relations, we seek to analyze what the victim of narcissistic injury or disappointment *does*.

Most relevant to our understanding of narcissistic object relations is the concept of "narcissistic object manipulation."[10] This concept shall be defined as the unmitigated abuse or exploitation of objects whereby any possible conflict between ego satisfaction, reinforcement, or compensation and the real needs, values, and identities of objects is wholly or overwhelmingly resolved in favor of the self. When we speak, therefore, of narcissistic object manipulation, we refer not to normal or healthy narcissism—that is, normal self-concern, self-regard, or self-interest—but rather to extreme or even pathological public, social, or otherwise interpersonal acts.

Psychoanalyst Warren Brodey makes some interesting and, as we shall observe in Chapter 3, pertinent observations about the nature of narcissistic object manipulation. In pointing out that narcissistic object manipulation is actually a means of *non*-reality testing, Brodey claims that such manipulation is intended to make the realities of an individual's existence fit his own expectations, rather than vice versa. These dynamics are learned and inculcated in a stable group, such as the family,[11] and rest upon two closely related ego defense mechanisms, projection and externalization.[12]

According to Brodey, externalization is a combination of projection and the manipulation of reality selected for the purpose of verifying the projection. Moreover, the reality that cannot be used to verify the projection is not perceived. The individual is unable to cathect libidinally with other objects; hence, "ego libido does not become object libido." Rather, ego libido "invades the object world."[13]

For Brodey, this narcissistic "image mode" of object relations is characterized by unbridled self-validation and object manipulation. As he explains:

> What is perceived as reality is an *as-if* reality, a projection of inner expectations. The senses are trained to validate; the intense searching for what is expected dominates and forces validation. It is difficult not to validate an unquestionable conclusion. Each validation makes the conclusion even less questionable. The restricted reality perceived is experienced as though it were the total world. A special kind of learning is needed to hold this restricted world intact. The narcissistic person learns to manipulate reality to conform with his projection. His experiments are designed to make prior conclusions inevitable. Within this framework his world is reasonable. This way of life becomes a system of survival.[14]

As in the Narcissus myth, "the image of himself seen reflected at a distance is called *an as-if other*. . . . An identity grows that is supported from within. The process of externalization verifies this pseudo identity, this *as-if* total person."[15] Thus, for those who dwell within the image mode of object relations, "the identity that is conceived is not continuously reworked. The meaning of any newness that seeps in is retranslated to fit the closed system. Sensations from within or response from outside that would make the pseudo identity an obvious fiction are not skillfully received. They do not refine the image of the self according to the object mode of reality testing."[16] We shall return to the concept of the as-if other pseudoidentity in Chapter 3.

From a psychoanalytical perspective, political terrorism may be regarded as an excellent example of narcissistic object manipulation. Recall that terrorism has been defined (politically, sociologically, and psychopolitically) as a specific form of civil rebellion or civil insurgency in which the use or threatened use of violence is imposed from below against certain symbolic victims or objects in order to coerce a primary target to accept a demanded outcome due to the effectuation of intense fear or anxiety. Recall, too, that narcissistic object manipulation has been defined (psychoanalytically and individually) as the unmitigated abuse or exploitation of objects whereby any possible conflict between ego satisfaction, reinforcement, or compensation and the real needs, values, and identities of objects is wholly or overwhelmingly resolved in favor of the self.

That political terrorism is in part a spectacularly vivid example of narcissistic object manipulation already has been noted by several skilled observers of the phenomenon. As Risto Fried states, "One of the most frightening things about terrorism is the terrorist's willingness to treat his victim as a mere object, not even a valuable but a discardable object." For Frederick Hacker, terrorists transform their victims into mere objects, for "terroristic thinking and practices reduce individuals to the status of puppets."[17] Again, we shall pursue these points in greater detail in Chapter 3.

We thus have considered the political terrorist qua victim of narcissistic personality disturbances from the perspective of what he *is* and what he *does*. Let us now address the central concept of narcissism as an internal, intrapsychic regulatory tool that enables the individual to defend the self from damage and harm. In so doing, it shall be possible to explore the most fundamental issue of why—psychologically speaking—the political terrorist does what he does.

In examining the concept of narcissism as a reparative or restorative device, it is first necessary to consider the interrelationship between narcissism and self-esteem. Robert Stolorow makes several key points about this interrelationship, and about the concept of narcissism as a reparative or restorative device:

> Narcissism, as functionally defined, is not synonymous with self-esteem, which is a complex affective state multiply determined by many factors (not the least of which is the vicissitudes of aggression). Narcissism embodies those mental operations whose *function* is to regulate self-esteem (the affective colouring of the self-representation) and to maintain the cohesiveness

and stability of the self-representation (the structural foundation upon which self-esteem rests). . . . When self-esteem is
threatened, significantly lowered or destroyed, then narcissistic activities are called into play in an effort to protect, restore,
repair and stabilize it.[18]

Hence, narcissism may be viewed as a psychic tool or device that
serves 1) to regulate how an individual feels about his own self-
image—that is, the self as the individual perceives himself to be;
and 2) to maintain the structural integrity or wholeness of that
self-image. A sense of self-esteem—that is, an individual's pride[19]
in himself—rests largely, or even wholly, upon a positive or
favorable self-image.

What typically happens when an individual no longer perceives himself in a positive fashion? What generally occurs when
the structural integrity of his self-image no longer can be maintained? The rejoinder to these critical questions is that the individual has suffered a narcissistic injury, a narcissistic
disappointment, or both. What, then, engenders or precipitates a
narcissistic injury? Generally speaking, such injuries may be
traced to 1) an individual's response to his own objective or
subjective role status, 2) the nature or quality of his actual or
perceived object relations with significant others, 3) his acute
sense of personal failure, or 4) his response to serious physical
injury, illness, or disabling handicap.

A major factor in the emergence of narcissistic injuries is the
individual's response to his own objective or subjective role
status. The terms "objective" and "subjective role status" by no
means denote such discrete phenomena. By "objective role status," "actual role status," or "role status membership," I refer to
an individual's real or concrete social, political, and economic
status or makeup within his society. Relevant examples of objective role status might encompass membership within the
ranks of minority groups, refugees, aliens, prisoners, the poor, or
women.

By "subjective," or perceived, role status, I refer to an
individual's *personal awareness of*, and, most critically, *sensitivity
toward*, his own actual or objective role status. Thus, in perceiving
this subjective role status, an individual, in certain particularly
painful or intense cases, may be led forcefully to reject his own
actual social, political, economic—and personal—niche. This being

the case, minority group members, in certain grievous or profound instances, might perceive themselves to be "oppressed." Refugees might come to view themselves as political refugees or castoffs. Aliens, in certain unpropitious instances, might grow to judge themselves as unwanted and unwelcome strangers, undesirables, or outcasts. Given the presence of radical political indoctrination and the typical vicissitudes of incarceration, many prisoners come to consider themselves to be exploited or abused social rejects.[20] And, given both particularly abject personal and financial circumstances and a lack of any hope for even the most modest social or personal advancement, poor people might be led to view themselves as marginalized persons, victims of poverty, have-nots, or even never-will-haves. Moreover, women, the most numerous of all social groups, in certain extreme or acute cases, might well respond to their individual—and collective—role status by deeming themselves to be mere sex objects, enslaved housewives, or victims of the feminization of poverty.

An individual's subjective, or perceived, role status is therefore predicated upon 1) his own actual or objective role status and 2) his perception and evaluation of it. Should an individual respond to his own overall role status in a severely negative fashion, then he may well suffer a narcissistic injury—that is, massive, profound, and permanent damage or harm to his self-image or sense of self-esteem.

A second major factor in the emergence of narcissistic injuries is the nature or quality of an individual's actual or perceived object relations with significant others. The term "actual object relations" refers to an individual's concrete, objective relationships with either other individuals or organic, inorganic, or intangible objects within his own environment. The term "perceived object relations" refers to an individual's personal and subjective awareness of and sensitivity toward other individuals and organic, inorganic, and intangible objects within his environment. Examples of actual object relations might encompass either formal relationships or informal associations based upon consanguinity, matrimony, vocation, property, or beliefs. An individual's perceived object relations then might involve his personal and subjective evaluations of and attitudes toward his or others' family, family members, employer, employees, material possessions, or abstract beliefs. Perception, therefore, is based to a large extent upon fact. Hence, one's overall object relations are based upon both objective fact and personal evaluation.

The term "significant others" simply refers to those persons within an individual's immediate environment who exert, or should exert, a powerful or potentially powerful emotional influence upon him. These significant others might include an individual's spouse, lover, parents, siblings, and very close friends and associates. Powerful emotional influence infers the presence of either strong positive affect or feelings (such as love or admiration) or powerful negative affects (such as hate, scorn, or contempt). What is most basic and relevant, however, is the strength and degree of influence of individual affect vis-à-vis significant others.

As in the case of perceived role status and role status membership, an individual may construe his overall object relations with significant others in a harshly negative manner. These object relations with significant others, for example, may be viewed as based upon or manifested by manipulation, rejection, actual loss, or even enforced isolation from cherished ones. Should an individual's overall object relations with significant others be so construed, then a narcissistic injury may well ensue.

The role of deeply felt rejection by significant others in precipitating narcissistic injuries has been widely noted.[21] This rejection causes a particularly keen insult to self-image or sense of self-esteem when rejection is accompanied by actual or perceived manipulation by that extremely valued object. Such narcissistic assaults occur because 1) these significant others are perceived as having cruelly manipulated, abused, and, finally, betrayed their privileged and trusted status within an intimate relationship; and 2) a manipulated or rejected individual's self-image or sense of self-esteem may withstand grave damage due to profound regret over having ever foolishly submitted to such a relationship.

We also should consider the probable interrelationship between those narcissistic injuries that may be traced to an individual's response to objective or subjective role status and those narcissistic insults that are predicated upon deeply felt rejection or enforced isolation. For example, a poor person or minority group member may perceive his actual, or imagined, rejection by a more socially or economically privileged lover as based upon their divergent role status. Similarly, a prisoner may view his incarceration and enforced isolation from significant others as the obvious and unjust product of his overall role status—for example, as a poor person or persecuted minority member.

The general "loss"—in the widest sense of the term—of an individual's object relations with significant others has been noted as a major cause of narcissistic injuries by many observers. Stolorow points out that "object relationships can serve (with varying degrees of success) to enhance self-esteem," and that "the loss of object ties can be catastrophic for . . . self-esteem."[22] Gregory Rochlin, who has written extensively on the effects of profound object loss, states that, when such traumas occur, "our narcissism, our sense of self is injured. And such injuries to narcissism tend to turn us back toward the self-contained primary state. . . . The failure of important relationships injures self-esteem and lowers it—often unconsciously; on an unconscious level, narcissism is heightened, and one's self-concern corresponds with a diminishing interest in others."[23]

Although rejection and enforced isolation denote a de facto loss of object relations with significant others, the *actual* loss—that is, in the most narrow sense of the term—of valued objects is a somewhat different matter. The term "actual loss of object relations with significant others" rather implies the actual loss of those cherished ones. The actual loss of object relations with significant others thus centers upon the death, incarceration, or involuntary physical disappearance—through, for example, kidnapping or child-snatching—of significant others.

Narcissistic injuries also may result when an individual experiences an acute sense of personal failure. This particular psychodynamic manifestation already has been noted by a number of skilled observers.[24] As Heinz Kohut states, such narcissistic injuries are particularly prevalent among ambitious, success-driven individuals. In such cases, "if the pressures from the narcissistic self are intense and the ego is unable to control them, the personality will respond with shame to failures of any kind, whether its ambitions concern moral perfection or external success (or, which is frequently the case, alternatingly the one or the other, since the personality possesses neither a firm structure of goals nor of ideals)."[25] Edith Jacobson concurs, asserting that the individual who suffers agonizing experiences of anxiety, shame, and inferiority in the face of personal failure tends to be afflicted by "aggrandized, wishful self images" and "narcissistic-exhibitionistic strivings."[26]

An individual's response to his own serious physical injury, illness, or disabling handicap, in certain additionally unfortunate circumstances, may engender profound damage or harm to his self-image or sense of self-esteem—that is, a narcissistic injury. Again, this specific psychodynamic manifestation already has been noted by a variety of observers.[27] Nathan Segel states, for example, that "narcissistic injury . . . [may originate] in either physical or psychological deprivations or traumas."[28]

As Rochlin points out, "We may make the same observation of young children: they too become highly egocentric when they experience a loss of some functions through illness or accidents."[29] Kohut draws a similar point. Noting Sigmund Freud's observation that "it is usual for mothers whom Fate has presented with a child who is sickly or otherwise at a disadvantage to try to compensate him or her for his unfair handicap by a superabundance of love," Kohut instead cites not-so-uncommon cases of "rejection by [the] proud mother who [cannot] tolerate an imperfect child."[30]

The term "narcissistic disappointment" was preliminarily defined in Chapter 1. Now I shall analyze in greater detail the intrapsychic and interpersonal dynamics, as well as the psychoanalytical structure and causes, of narcissistic disappointment. It is useful to recall that the human psyche may be divided into three fundamental components:

1) *ego*—the self (or sense of self);

2) *superego*—the conscience (or "moral" aspect of personality); and

3) *id*—the "seat" or "location" of the libido

Relevant to any examination of narcissistic disappointment is the introduction of a fourth component, the *ego ideal*. The term may be defined as that portion of the ego which represents or delineates what an individual comes to perceive as positive and admirable standards of personal or interpersonal conduct. The ego ideal, furthermore, is in part comprised of the ego's own identification with those individuals or groups who practice or advocate such standards of personal or interpersonal conduct.

The concept of the ego ideal is a mainstay of psychoanalytic theory. Freud, for example, asserts that, through the ego ideal, "man has set up an *ideal* in himself by which he measures his actual ego."[31] In a further elaboration of these views Freud claims that "it is . . . the vehicle of the ego ideal by which the ego measures itself, which it emulates, and whose demand for ever greater perfection it strives to fulfill. There is no doubt that this ego ideal is the precipitate of the old picture of the parents, the expression of admiration for the perfection which the child then attributed to them."[32]

James Bing, Francis McLaughlin, and Rudolf Marburg jointly offer an extremely valuable glimpse into the psychic interrelationship between the ego, superego, and ego ideal. As they put it:

> The ego ideal represents a composite of one's narcissistic picture of oneself and the idealization of the parental object representations. The picture is then used or misused by the ego. The ego attempts to live up to the picture represented by the ego ideal. The superego in turn may punish the ego for not measuring up to the picture of the ego ideal, or on the other hand the superego may approve of the ego for having achieved its goal. The ego ideal is "anatomically" a part of the ego, conscious or unconscious, whereas the superego has become a structure apart from the ego with functions of its own.[33]

It is important to note that the ego requires the approbation or approval of the superego. This "state of security between ego and super-ego," or "narcissistic equilibrium," as Henry Hart points out, is an ongoing concern of the ego: "This equilibrium is maintained by the relationship of the ego and super-ego. . . . Both ego and super-ego are made up of identifications. Where the latter are harmoniously integrated in the personality we have the state of narcissistic equilibrium. The super-ego does not demand of the ego more than it can produce. The ego is not terrified by the threat of super-ego severity."[34]

For any number of reasons, the ego no longer may be able to measure up to the ego ideal. Such intrapsychic occurrences normally incur the wrath of a harshly and readily punitive superego against the fragile ego, thus upsetting any such state of narcissistic equilibrium. This negation of narcissistic equilibrium, or harmony, may be viewed as one form of narcissistic disappointment.

A disruption of narcissistic equilibrium might occur during childhood, adolescence, or adulthood. The ego ideal, as Freud and Bing, McLaughlin, and Marburg point out, ultimately is based upon the child's idealization either of his own parents or parental substitutes. This form of narcissistic disappointment cannot take place prior to adolescence, since the superego is not yet fully developed in childhood. As Jacobson submits:

> As long as the boundaries between [childhood] self and [the] object [world] are still indistinct, and libidinal and aggressive forces freely move back and forth between self and object image, disappointment and devaluation of objects will impart themselves *immediately* to the self and cause self devaluation and narcissistic hurt. . . . But with superego formation, with the internalization of general ethical and moral commands and standards, [narcissistic disappointment]. . . become[s], in part, transformed into fears of the superego, of not measuring up to the standards of the ego ideal.[35]

The superego is by no means the sole psychic culprit vis-à-vis the onset of narcissistic disappointment. In certain individual instances the very potency of the ego ideal itself is apt to foster a second form of narcissistic disappointment. Given the fragility of the ego and ultimate origins of the ego ideal in early parental identification, a hugely unrealistic or overly grandiose ego ideal may persist even after childhood. In her consideration of these extreme cases, Annie Reich explains:

> Not infrequently, the ego ideal is tinged with features of grandiosity, since it is based upon wishes to identify with a parent who is seen in a very infantile way. In normal development these ideals gradually are modified. With the growing acceptance of reality the image of the parent becomes more and more realistic, superego elements gain in importance and become fused with the ideal, and—most important—ego capacities are developed for the translation of inner demands into organized activities. A persistence of intensely narcissistic ego ideals obviously represents serious pathology. The formation of such ideals is a regular process development; normally, however, they do not endure in their infantile form.

Persistence of. . . [such an] ego ideal is not caused by one isolated traumatic incident but by general weakness of the ego [or other factors]. . . . An over-grandiose ego ideal—combined, as it not infrequently is, with inadequate talents and insufficient ego strength—leads to intolerable inner conflicts and feelings of insufficiency.[36]

Narcissistic disappointment, therefore, may follow two possible intrapsychic patterns. The first, the "superego- induced" form of narcissistic disappointment, implies a disturbance of narcissistic equilibrium created by the ego's own inability to measure up to the ego ideal, thus leading to the punishment of the ego by a demanding superego. The second pattern, termed the "ego ideal-induced" form of narcissistic disappointment, implies the direct psychic tyranny of an overly grandiose ego ideal over an inherently fragile ego.

Although narcissistic disappointment may be conceptualized as a dysfunction of intrapsychic dynamics, the ultimate sources of narcissistic disappointment typically lie within the external realm of object interaction. In analyzing the external antecedents of narcissistic disappointment, the operant questions, therefore, must be: Why is the ego unable to measure up to the ego ideal, thus placing itself at the mercy of a demanding superego? What enables an overly grandiose ego ideal to tyrannize the ego?

In order for the ego to be placed at the mercy of either a demanding superego or a tyrannical ego ideal, the individual must undertake some external interaction with the object world. This may be accomplished in either of two ways. He may suffer from 1) an actual, or perceived, inability to measure up to what he sees as positive and admirable standards of conduct in his own object relations—that is, profound disappointment in himself; or 2) extreme and humiliating disillusionment with individuals (particularly those significant others for whom there is deep object attachment) or groups that represent or advocate such standards of conduct, and a concomitant disappointment in himself for ever having embraced the beliefs or ideals of those formerly idealized, or otherwise trusted, others.[37]

In some depth the individual psychoanalytical bases underlying the decision to become a political terrorist have been discussed. These psychological factors shall be illustrated fully in the individual political terrorist case studies presented in forthcoming chapters. Having now analyzed the nature of narcissism, narcissistic injury, and narcissistic disappointment, it will be possible to examine thoroughly the next question: Why might the practice of political terrorism itself be psychologically attractive to victims of narcissistic personality disturbances?

Notes

1. The psychodynamic interrelationship between narcissism and political terrorism was first suggested in Gustave Morf, *Terror in Quebec* (Toronto: Clarke, Irwin, 1970), 95, 98, 105. Varyingly cursory suggestions of this interrelationship also have been raised in Hacker, *Crusaders, Criminals, Crazies*, 44; Christopher Lasch, *The Culture of Narcissism* (New York: W. W. Norton, 1979), 33–34, 57–58; Risto Fried, "Questions on Terrorism," *Terrorism* 3 (1980): 221–23; H. Jager, G. Schmidtchen, and L. Süllwold, eds., *Lebenslauf-Analysen*, vol. 2 of *Analysen zum Terrorismus* (Wiesbaden: Westdeutscher Verlag, 1981); William D. Davidson and Joseph V. Montville, "Foreign Policy According to Freud," *Foreign Policy* 45 (1982): 148–49, 151–52; Neil C. Livingstone, *The War against Terrorism* (Lexington, MA: Lexington, 1982), 37, 50; André Haynal, Miklos Molnar, and Gérard De Puymege, *Fanaticism* (New York: Schocken, 1983), 39, 41, 60; John W. Crayton, "Terrorism and the Psychology of the Self," in Lawrence Zelic Freedman and Yonah Alexander, eds., *Perspectives on Terrorism* (Wilmington, DE: Scholarly Resources, 1983), 33–41; Frederick J. Hacker, "Dialectical Interrelationships of Personal and Political Factors in Terrorism," in Freedman and Alexander, eds., *Perspectives on Terrorism*, 27; Jerrold M. Post, "Notes on a Psychodynamic Theory of Terrorist Behavior," *Terrorism* 7 (1984): 245, 246, 248; idem, "Group and Organizational Dynamics of Political Terrorism," paper presented at the International Conference on Terrorism Research, April 21–23, 1986, at the University of Aberdeen, Aberdeen, Scotland; idem, "Prospects for Nuclear Terrorism," in Paul Leventhal and Yonah Alexander, eds., *Preventing Nuclear Terrorism* (Lexington, MA: Lexington, 1987), 102–3; Eric D. Shaw, "Political Terrorists: Dangers of Diagnosis and an Alternative to the Psychopathology Model," *International Journal of Law and Psychiatry* 8 (1986): 359–60, 363–67; and Stephen Segaller, *Invisible Armies* (San Diego: Harcourt Brace Jovanovich, 1987), 81–85, 90–91, 101, 117–18.

2. Shaw, "Political Terrorists," 363.

3. For secondary sources on the legend of Narcissus see especially Grace Stuart, *Narcissus* (New York: Macmillan, 1955), 104–11; and Louise Vinge, *The Narcissus Theme in Western European Literature up to the Early Nineteenth Century* (Gleerups, 1967).

On the concept of narcissism as a sexual perversion or dysfunction see, for example, Havelock Ellis, "The Concept of Narcissism," *Psychoanalytic Review* 14 (1927): 129–53; Stuart, *Narcissus*, 25; Sigmund Freud, "On Narcissism," in Morrison, ed., *Essential Papers*, 17; M. Kanzer, "Freud's Use of the Terms 'Autoeroticism' and 'Narcissism,'" *Journal of the American Psychoanalytic Asso-*

ciation 12 (1964): 529–39; Robert D. Stolorow, "Toward a Functional Definition of Narcissism," *International Journal of Psychoanalysis* 56 (1975): 181; P. Elkisch, "The Psychological Significance of the Mirror," *Journal of the American Psychoanalytic Association* 5 (1957): 15–25; H. Lichtenstein, "The Role of Narcissism in the Emergence and Maintenance of a Primary Identity," *International Journal of Psychoanalysis* 45 (1964): 49–56; Annie Reich, "Pathologic Forms of Self-esteem Regulation," *Psychoanalytic Study of the Child* 15 (1960): 215–32; and Kohut, *Analysis of the Self*.

4. Some of the more recent theorists of developmental narcissism have included, for example, M. Balint, "Primary Narcissism and Primary Love," *Psychoanalytic Quarterly* 29 (1960): 6–43; Freud, "On Narcissism"; Edith Jacobson, *The Self and the Object World* (London: Hogarth, 1965); Kanzer, "Freud's Use"; Kohut, *Analysis of the Self*; Margaret S. Mahler and Bertram J. Gosliner, "On Symbiotic Child Psychosis," *Psychoanalytic Study of the Child* 10 (1955): 195–212; Margaret S. Mahler, "Symbiosis and Individuation," *Psychoanalytic Study of the Child* 29 (1974): 89–106; idem, *On Human Symbiosis and the Vicissitudes of Individuation* (New York: International Universities Press, 1975); Sydney E. Pulver, "Narcissism: The Term and the Concept," *Journal of the American Psychoanalytic Association* 18 (1979): 319–41; H. A. Rosenfeld, "On the Psychopathology of Narcissism," *International Journal of Psychoanalysis* 45 (1964): 333–47; James F. Bing, Francis McLaughlin, and Rudolf Marburg, "The Metapsychology of Narcissism," *Psychoanalytic Study of the Child* 14 (1959): 9–28; Warren M. Brodey, "On the Dynamics of Narcissism," *Psychoanalytic Study of the Child* 20 (1965): 165–93; Lichtenstein, "Role of Narcissism"; Alice Miller, *Prisoners of Childhood* (New York: Basic Books, 1981); Burness E. Moore, "Toward a Clarification of the Concept of Narcissism," *Psychoanalytic Study of the Child* 30 (1975): 243–76; and G. H. Pollock, "On Symbiosis and Symbiotic Neurosis," *International Journal of Psychoanalysis* 45 (1964): 1–30.

5. See, for example, Freud, "On Narcissism"; Balint, "Primary Narcissism"; Rosenfeld, "Psychopathology of Narcissism"; and Stolorow, "Functional Definition."

6. Freud, "On Narcissism," 19. As Freud observed, "Thus we form the idea of there being an original libidinal cathexis of the ego." See ibid.

7. See, for example, Mahler and Gosliner, "On Symbiotic Child Psychosis"; Mahler, "Symbiosis"; idem, *On Human Symbiosis*; and Pollock, "On Symbiosis."

8. See especially Mahler, "Symbiosis," 90; and Mahler and Gosliner, "On Symbiotic Child Psychosis," 196.

9. Kohut, "Psychoanalytic Treatment," 96.

10. For an examination of narcissistic object manipulation see especially Pulver, "Narcissism"; Stolorow, "Functional Definition"; Brodey, "Dynamics of Narcissism"; Warren M. Brodey, "Image, Object, and Narcissistic Relationships," *American Journal of Orthopsychiatry* 31 (1961): 69–73; Ludwig Eidelberg, "The Concept of Narcissistic Mortification," *International Journal of Psychoanalysis* 40 (1959): 163–68; and Moore, "Toward a Clarification." See also Erich Fromm's excellent discussion of the exploitative orientation toward object relations in Fromm, *Man for Himself* (Greenwich, CT: Fawcett, 1947), 71–73. As Fromm states, the exploitative personality's "attitude is colored by a mixture of hostility and manipulation. Everyone is an object of exploitation and is judged according to his usefulness." See ibid., 73.

11. Or, to offer an even more relevant example, the political terrorist group. The relevance of Brodey's views on the as-if other pseudoidentity vis-à-vis the political terrorist group member will be explored in greater depth in Chapter 3.

12. See Brodey, "Dynamics of Narcissism," 167, 187, 190, 192; and idem, "Image, Object, and Narcissistic Relationships," 70. Reality-testing, a psychological process that begins during the separation-individuation phase of early childhood development and continues throughout life, shall be defined as the ego's objective appraisal and determination of the external world. Projection shall be defined as the process of attributing to others an individual's own characteristics, beliefs, and shortcomings. Externalization shall be defined as the projection of an individual's own subjective perceptions onto the object world.

13. Brodey, "Dynamics of Narcissism," 167–68, 187.

14. Ibid., 167 (emphasis in original).

15. Ibid., 167, 186 (emphasis in original).

16. Ibid., 187.

17. Fried, "Questions on Terrorism," 232; and Hacker, *Crusaders, Criminals, Crazies*, 162, 163. See also, for example, ibid., 105, 114; Johnson, "Perspectives," 268; H. H. A. Cooper, "The Terrorist and the Victim," *Victimology* 1 (1976): 229–39; and Ezzat A. Fattah, "Some Reflections on the Victimology of Terrorism," *Terrorism* 3 (1979): 81–108.

18. Stolorow, "Functional Definition," 183 (emphasis in original).

19. On the distinction between pride and vanity see, for example, Lois B. Murphy, "Pride and Its Relation to Narcissism, Autonomy, and Identity," *Bulletin of the Menninger Clinic* 24 (1960): 136–37.

20. That the great majority of prisons might well be regarded as veritable factories of narcissistic injuries is already widely granted. It is instructive to point to the case of Raymond Luc Levasseur, a leader of two leftist American political terrorist groups, the Sam Melville-Jonathan Jackson Unit and the United Freedom Front. In the early 1970s, Levasseur, a former (and present) prison inmate, was a leading member of a Maine-based prison-reform group with the revealing acronym of SCAR—for Statewide Correctional Alliance for Reform. See, for example, E. J. Kahn III, "The Last American Revolutionaries," *Boston Magazine* (February 1987): 181–83; and Dennis Bailey, "Underground," *Boston Globe Magazine* (March 26, 1989): 28.

21. See, for example, Arthur P. Mendel, *Michael Bakunin* (New York: Praeger, 1981), 436–37; Lawrence R. Ephron, "Narcissism and the Sense of Self," *Psychoanalytic Review* 54 (1967): 505; and Stuart, *Narcissus*, 22–31.

22. Stolorow, "Functional Definition," 183.

23. Rochlin, *Man's Aggression*, 6. See also Gregory Rochlin, "The Loss Complex," *Journal of the American Psychoanalytic Association* 7 (1959): 299–316; and idem, "The Dread of Abandonment," *Psychoanalytic Study of the Child* 16 (1961): 452.

24. See especially Jacobson, *Self and Object World*; Reich, "Pathologic Forms"; and Kohut, *Forms and Transformations*.

25. Ibid., 254. See also ibid., 254n. In stating that the ambitious, success-driven professional woman is "doubly vulnerable to narcissistic hurt" caused by a need for career-based recognition *and* feminine admiration, Sophie Freud Lowenstein develops this point further. See Sophie Freud Lowenstein, "Narcis-

sism, Self-Esteem, and the Divided Self," paper presented on January 19, 1983, at Newton-Wellesley Hospital, Newton, Massachusetts.

26. Jacobson, *Self and Object World*, 203–5.

27. See, for example, Alfred Adler, *Study of Organ Inferiority and Its Psychical Compensation* (New York: Nervous and Mental Diseases Publishing Company, 1917); Sigmund Freud, *New Introductory Lectures on Psychoanalysis* (New York: W. W. Norton, 1965), 66; Sigmund Freud and William C. Bullitt, *Thomas Woodrow Wilson* (Boston: Houghton Mifflin, 1967); James David Barber, *The Presidential Character* (Englewood Cliffs, NJ: Prentice-Hall, 1972); Alexander L. George and Juliette L. George, *Woodrow Wilson and Colonel House* (New York: John Day, 1964); Kohut, "Thoughts on Narcissism," 372–75; Emil Ludwig, *Kaiser Wilhelm II* (New York: Putnam, 1926); Rochlin, *Man's Aggression*, 6–7; and Nathan P. Segel, "Narcissistic Resistance," *Journal of the American Psychoanalytic Association* 17 (1969): 944–45.

28. Ibid., 944.

29. Rochlin, *Man's Aggression*, 6. In his observation that such ill or disabled children become highly egocentric, Rochlin implies the increasing utilization of the regulatory tool of narcissism to minister to that self-image, or sense of self-esteem, which has been subject to a narcissistic injury.

30. Kohut, "Thoughts on Narcissism," 372.

31. Freud, "On Narcissism," 36 (emphasis in original).

32. Freud, *New Introductory Lectures*, 64–65. For a comprehensive examination of the ego ideal see especially John M. Murray, "Narcissism and the Ego Ideal," *Journal of the American Psychoanalytic Association* 12 (1964): 477–511.

33. Bing, McLaughlin, and Marburg, "Metapsychology of Narcissism," 26. That the ego ideal is first developed during childhood is widely recognized. See, for example, Murray, "Narcissism"; and Annie Reich, who states that "as his sense of reality grows, the child, recognizing his own weakness, endows his parents with the [infantile] omnipotence he has had to forego. From this time on, desires set in to become like the glorified parent. The deep longing to become like the parent creates a constant inner demand upon the child's ego; an ego ideal is formed." See Annie Reich, "Narcissistic Object Choice in Women," *Journal of the American Psychoanalytic Association* 1 (1953): 29. Hence, for Reich, the parents are those original object representations comprised within the ego ideal.

34. Henry Harper Hart, "Narcissistic Equilibrium," *International Journal of Psychoanalysis* 28 (1947): 107.

35. Jacobson, *Self and Object World*, 105–6, 104.

36. Reich, "Narcissistic Object Choice," 30.

37. Note the degree of similarity between narcissistic injuries caused by rejection or manipulation by significant others and narcissistic disappointments due to extreme and humiliating disillusionment in trusted and admired others. I shall illustrate the precise, yet subtle, differences between these personality disturbances in the case studies themselves. Note, too, that the specific concept of narcissistic disappointment in others also has been termed the "fallen idol" complex.

CHAPTER THREE

The Violent Defense
of the Self

> With enough money or power, one can endow any
> image with seeming significance and force. With a bomb
> or a gun, the weakest people can see themselves as a
> powerful force in the world. And in fact they are. They
> have a power to destroy that the average person doesn't
> have.
>
> Alexander Lowen
> *Narcissism*

Political psychologist Jeanne Knutson once noted
that "the type of person who occupies a certain role has a good
deal to do with the way the role is performed." More germane to
our purposes, however, is Knutson's companion observation
that "certain people do seem to occupy certain roles."[1] Let us first
transform her assertion into a general query: Why do certain
people seem to occupy certain roles? More specifically, why
might victims of narcissistic personality disturbances gravitate
toward the role of political terrorist? And why might the practice
of political terrorism itself be psychologically attractive to victims of narcissistic injury and disappointment?[2]

I already have broached these questions in Chapter 1. My
purpose here will be to offer a far more comprehensive analysis
of 1) the direct and indirect aftermath of narcissistic injury and
disappointment—narcissistic rage, narcissistic defense, and, all

too typically, some form of narcissistic aggression; and 2) the distinct, powerful, and unusually alluring psychodynamic rewards of political terrorism. We should not be very surprised by the specific intrapsychic and interpersonal aftermath most typically experienced by victims of narcissistic injury and narcissistic disappointment. I refer here to narcissistic rage, the necessity for some form of narcissistic defense of the self and, all too frequently, some form of narcissistic aggression. To reiterate, these psychodynamic manifestations of secondary narcissism may be termed the "narcissistic rage-aggression-defense nexus."

It is widely recognized that the single most common and immediate psychodynamic reaction to narcissistic injury and narcissistic disappointment is the emotional state or condition of narcissistic rage.[3] Unlike more focused and structured emotions, such as anger or frustration, narcissistic rage should be regarded as exceedingly diffuse and unspecified in nature. Thus, Alexander Lowen distinguishes between blind or unbounded rage and the more focused or directed emotion of anger.[4] To comment, therefore, that an individual flew into a rage is to imply that he is so far overhead of reality as to have a necessarily unfocused perception of reality. Hence, we differentiate between rage or fury, on the one hand, and mere anger or frustration, on the other. For a substantial number of individuals, the psychic toll of narcissistic injury upon self-image or self-esteem engenders narcissistic rage. Heinz Kohut thus delineates a specific personality type, "the shame-prone individual who is ready to experience [life] setbacks as narcissistic injuries and to respond to them with insatiable rage." Gregory Rochlin similarly refers to those victims of narcissistic injury who believe that these "assaults on their being . . . constituted injuries to [their] self-esteem." These narcissistic injury-engendering events lead to "rage at deprivation with heightened demands for restitution."[5]

The psychic damage wrought by narcissistic disappointment upon self-esteem or self-image also tends to culminate in narcissistic rage. In his comments, for example, on the loss of the ego ideal, John Murray states that, when "harmonious living and creating [within] the framework of the ego ideal" are no longer possible and "with the [ego] ideal now lost [and] its validity and sense of imminence gone, nothing [may be] left but disillusionment, despair, and ineffectiveness."[6] Clearly, there is a firm and crucial psychodynamic interrelationship between narcissistic injury and disappointment, on the one hand, and narcissistic rage, on the other.

What are the direct, and indirect, psychodynamic consequences of narcissistic rage? Such rage generally predisposes an individual toward some form of aggressive—albeit not necessarily destructive or otherwise violent—behavior. Thus, aggression may fulfill a defensive function vis-à-vis the regulation or, more properly, restoration or reinforcement of self-esteem or self-image. The relevant literature is clearly replete with detailed references to the overarching raison d'être of narcissistic aggression—that is, narcissistic, or ego, defense.[7] For our purposes the related terms (narcissistic defense, ego defense, and the defense of the self) all pertain to one vital, unifying concept: the shielding or protection of the ego or self from damage, harm, guilt, or shame through 1) the veritable unleashing of heretofore-repressed[8] narcissistic rage, 2) the energizing of regulatory narcissism, and 3) an accompanying regression to some manifestation of secondary narcissism. This process, which might result in an extensive range of behavior, would culminate ideally in the restoration or reinforcement of wounded self-esteem or damaged self-image.

The complex interrelationship between narcissistic rage, narcissistic aggression, and narcissistic defense already has been either wholly or partially set forth by a wide assortment of observers.[9] Chief among these are Kohut, who skillfully delineates the relationship between narcissistic rage and narcissistic aggression, and Rochlin, whose superbly comprehensive and pioneering study, *Man's Aggression: The Defense of the Self*, constitutes the finest work on the relationship between narcissistic aggression and narcissistic defense. Rochlin's most pertinent contribution to the narcissistic rage-aggression-defense thesis actually expands upon Kohut's more narrow categorization of narcissistic rage as a mere type of aggression. Thus for Rochlin, narcissistic aggression *is* the narcissistic defense. Hence, "to redress the balance—to restore our self-esteem, assert our value . . . the defensive functions of aggression are invoked."[10] Kohut, who draws a neat line through narcissistic rage and aggression, also lays the basis for a further view, that there is actually a property or quality inherent in narcissistic rage that predisposes an individual toward aggression as a defense of the self.

Political terrorism, a specific form of narcissistic aggression, also might be regarded as an excellent example of what may be termed "autocompensatory violence" and "compensatory narcissism." The latter may be defined as the violent taking of remuneration or reparation for those psychic damages typically incurred by victims of narcissistic injury or narcissistic disappointment. The use of the prefix "auto"—that is, "by oneself"—indicates not solitary or isolated behavior but rather that such action, even if taken in conjunction with one's fellow political terrorists, symbolic victims, primary targets, audiences, or the news media, is first taken by oneself. Thus, from a purely psychological perspective, the individual who commits terrorist acts takes such action to compensate himself for the psychic damages of narcissistic injury or narcissistic disappointment.

The concept of compensatory narcissism already has been considered by a wide range of psychoanalysts and social scientists.[11] In his discussion of narcissistic equilibrium, Henry Hart describes compensatory narcissism as "an ego deficiency in which the narcissism is reparative." Lowen, in a more forceful and specific statement, argues that "the narcissistic character . . . is able to compensate for narcissistic injury by gaining power in the world." Indeed, this "striving for power and control characterize all narcissistic individuals."[12]

Manifestation of compensatory narcissism within a wide range of power-seeking or power-wielding behavioral displays also have been discussed in the social science literature. The first, and certainly most notable, observer of compensatory power was Harold Lasswell, whose seminal work, *Power and Personality*, strongly suggests that the political personality or power seeker reaches for force or influence in order to compensate for deprivations that have resulted in diminished self-image or self-esteem.[13] As Lasswell stresses, "The power seeker . . . pursues power as a means of compensation against deprivation. *Power is expected to overcome low estimates of the self*, by changing either the traits of the self or the environment in which it functions."[14] He states, moreover, that

> the accentuation of power is to be understood as a compensatory reaction against low estimates of the self. . . . [The exercise

of power] occurs when opportunities exist both for the displacement of ungratified cravings from the primary circle to public targets and for the rationalization of these displacements in the public interest; and, finally, when skills are acquired appropriate to the effective operation of the power-balancing process.[15]

As Lasswell properly argues, such compensatory narcissism might manifest itself in a "public redress of private grievances" or, more generally, in the "displacement of private affects upon public objects."[16]

The fundamental concept of political terrorism as a manifestation of compensatory narcissism also has been suggested somewhat vaguely by observers of political terrorism.[17] In his analysis of the psychopolitical dynamics underlying the individual gravitation toward a terrorist identity—a point that we shall examine shortly in greater detail—Frederick Hacker argues that

the recognition of jointly suffered oppression welds isolated, impotent individuals into a potentially powerful unit capable of combating the injustice to which they have been subjected. This, in turn, affects the individual's self-esteem and self-understanding. The old (powerless) self, "me," discovering that just rights have been unjustly withheld, becomes a demanding "me, too" that, in order to acquire the denied rights, produces a new "we" awareness. . . . Through the new "we" feeling, a new individual personality is created, a more powerful and richer "me."[18]

Jerrold Post concurs with Hacker's analysis, arguing that, "especially for those [political terrorists] with damaged self-esteem and weak ego boundaries, there is a tendency to merge themselves in the group." For Risto Fried, there is an appropriate term for the establishment and adoption of this new identity—"compensatory grandiosity."[19]

The syndrome of political terrorism as autocompensatory violence may be regarded as an interrelated cluster of psychological and psychopolitical factors, including: 1) the psychic sense of omnipotence; 2) the establishment, assumption, and maintenance of a new pseudoidentity; and 3) the psychological utility of political terrorist group membership. The doctrine that political terrorism is, above all, an act of power over other objects is well-established. As V. I. Lenin reminded his Bolshevik followers,

"The purpose of terrorism is to terrify." Brian Jenkins, in a frequently quoted aphorism, has claimed correctly that "terrorism is violence for effect," while Jan Schreiber has offered an even more extreme characterization of terrorism as the "ultimate weapon." Certainly, too, we are increasingly aware of the fact that the more centralized, urbanized, and industrialized the contemporary world has become, the more vulnerable it is to this ultimate weapon. What is less well understood, however, is precisely how this awful power is perceived by the individual who ultimately becomes the political terrorist.

Although not in fact omnipotent or all-powerful, the political terrorist's psychic sense of omnipotence enables him to perceive himself as if he were omnipotent. The core of this grandiose self-image is the political terrorist's demonstrated ability to manipulate powerful objects through 1) his own powerless victims and 2) uniquely immediate, widespread, and intense media coverage. To recall Warren Brodey's delineation of the two fundamentally distinct forms of object relationship, what the political terrorist qua psychological entity actually does is to abandon the normal object mode of reality testing in favor of the narcissistic image mode of self-validation and severe object manipulation. Therefore, by perceiving himself as if he were omnipotent, "what is perceived as reality is an 'as-if' reality, a projection of inner expectation."[20]

This as-if world of self-omnipotence serves as natural and welcome compensation for the political terrorist qua victim of narcissistic injury or narcissistic disappointment. Although a psychic sense of omnipotence cannot unmake an individual's wounded sense of self-esteem or damaged self-image, it can enable him to compensate for or help make suitable payment to himself for the psychic damages associated with narcissistic injury or narcissistic disappointment. The political terrorist is able to achieve this psychic sense of omnipotence through the establishment, assumption, and maintenance of a new pseudoidentity. Brodey's theories on the as-if other image mode of object relations and this pseudoidentity, which grows from within and is verified through externalization, already have been discussed in the previous chapter.[21] I shall attempt here to apply Brodey's theories to a specific type of as-if other pseudoidentity—that of political terrorist.

In many respects, the fateful decision to become a political terrorist constitutes a firm rejection of an individual's old, weak, and psychically discredited self or identity through the establishment, assumption, and maintenance of a new, omnipotent, as-if other self. By resorting to an autocompensatory act of behavior such as the practice of political terrorism, the victim of narcissistic injury or narcissistic disappointment therefore is able to create not only an as-if reality but also an as-if pseudoidentity which, in effect, is defined by that process of externalization and self-validation. Hence, in acting out his narcissistic personality disturbances through the creation, adoption, and preservation of a specific direct action—as-if other pseudoidentity—the political terrorist might be said to don a mask of omnipotence. The violent defense of the self that is, psychologically speaking, political terrorism constitutes not a mere narcissistic defense of the old self but rather the veritable *replacement* of an old, feckless identity by a new and grandiose one—the omnipotent political terrorist. This change will be illustrated in the forthcoming case studies.

The autocompensatory rewards of political terrorism encompass what may be called the psychological utility of political terrorist group membership.[22] This fairly straightforward point already has been suggested by Hacker.[23] In a later essay, he is even more forceful: "The unifying identity conferring worth, belonging, and meaning to the individual is the group, under the cover of which the terrorist can gratify his most elementary, infantile, and grandiose desires for omnipotence, omniscience, narcissistic satisfaction, and aggressive release."[24]

Post concurs with Hacker, stating that "insofar as the individual psychosocial identity is incomplete or fragmented, the only way the member feels reasonably complete is in relation to the group. Belonging to the terrorist group becomes for many the most important part of their psychosocial identity."[25]

Again, these points will be made in the case studies. Having theoretically considered the individual political terrorist's direct narcissistic defense, it now will be possible to examine that same individual's secondary or auxiliary self-reinforcement through the philosophical *justification* of political terrorism.

Although the autocompensatory rewards of political terrorism are the most direct and dramatic psychic rewards available to the political terrorist qua victim of narcissistic personality disturbances, they by no means constitute the only such psychic benefits. Nor, given both the brutally violent nature of political terrorism and the specific type of individual who becomes a political terrorist, can these rewards alone be regarded as entirely sufficient. Quite simply, it is almost universally recognized that the commission of violent aggression in and of itself is a wholly unacceptable phenomenon. Acts of aggression, and particularly violent aggression, therefore must be justified, defended, or otherwise rationalized.

The need to justify acts of narcissistic aggression is particularly well granted. As Rochlin points out, "Aggression must have its justification" regardless of narcissistic injury, narcissistic disappointment, and the need to defend the ego against assaults to self-esteem or self-image; "without justification it is *not* condoned." Indeed, Rochlin stresses that "before the threats of injury to our narcissism may be relieved . . . the ensuing aggression must be justified."[26]

If it is true that narcissistic aggression must be justified, then it is proper to observe that political terrorism somehow must be defended, or rationalized, as well. The overall issue of the justification, rationalization, or rhetorical defense of political terrorism already has been covered elsewhere; therefore, it is not necessary to mount any comprehensive analysis of this topic within these pages.[27] What must, however, be carefully considered are 1) the issues of why, from a psychological perspective, acts of political terrorism must be justified; and 2) the idiosyncratic style in which that justification is packaged.

For the vast majority of people, the very term "terrorist" conjures up all kinds of highly pejorative or negative images. It is, therefore, not particularly rewarding for an individual to assume the negative identity of political terrorist. Moreover, for the individual who already has suffered serious insults to his self-esteem or self-image, the self-perceived assumption of a new such identity might itself constitute an additional source of narcissistic injury or narcissistic disappointment.

The psychoanalytic term "negative identity" may be traced in part to Sigmund Freud's essay, "Taboo and Emotional Ambivalence." For him, the basis of taboo is a prohibited action, and "anyone who has violated a taboo becomes taboo himself."[28] Erik Erikson offers the classic analysis of the individual-as-taboo—

that is, the concept of negative identity: "On the whole, [certain individuals'] . . . conflicts find expression in a more subtle way than the abrogation of personal identity. They chose instead a *negative* identity, i.e., an identity perversely based on all those identifications and roles which, at critical stages of development, had been presented to them as most undesirable or dangerous."[29] Might, then, the decision to become a political terrorist signify the willing assumption of a negative identity?

The concept that the political terrorist consciously assumes a negative identity already has been suggested by Knutson. For her, negative identity is thus actually selected by the political terrorist.[30] I would posit, however, that the political terrorist qua victim of narcissistic personality disturbances would seek vigorously to refute or otherwise dispel any perception of himself as a political terrorist cum negative identity. To fail to do so might cause a further, and perhaps devastating, accumulation of narcissistic injuries or narcissistic disappointments resulting from that individual's 1) highly negative response to his own objective or subjective role status as political terrorist cum negative identity, a major categorical determinant of narcissistic injury; or 2) direct disappointment in himself, a major external antecedent of narcissistic disappointment. It is clear that, for both political terrorists and other individuals, the conscious assumption of a new, negative identity is not a means of mounting a successful narcissistic defense.

Although it is psychologically rewarding for the political terrorist to assume a new, as-if other, omnipotent pseudoidentity, the parallel assumption of a negative identity must be avoided at all costs. Indeed, if the political terrorist is compelled to assume a negative identity, then all of his subsequent autocompensatory psychodynamic rewards might well be neutralized. Hence, some psychopolitical compromise must be arranged. That compromise—the rhetorical justification, rationalization, or defense of political terrorist acts—actually enables the political terrorist to assume the mask of omnipotence but not (albeit if only from his own perspective) the mask of villainy. Instead, the political terrorist is able to eschew the mask of villainy in favor of what is, in fact, the mask of rhetoric.

Precisely how does the justification of political terrorism facilitate this avoidance of negative identity? John Crayton has suggested that the "meaningful high ideals" of the political terrorist group "protect the group members from experiencing shame,"[31] and it is true that the expressed philosophy of any given political terrorist group functions to support not only the group itself but also the individual member who otherwise might brave the psychodynamic liabilities of a violently negative identity.

The actual psychopolitical dynamics inherent in this evasion or circumvention of negative identity are illustrated in George Orwell's characterization of political writing and speech as "the defense of the indefensible." Thus, through the promiscuous, yet careful, utilization of murky euphemism, the political terrorist is—again, from his own perspective—able to deflect ultimate responsibility for his own actions or, preferably, to assume a positive identity. In so doing, political terrorism becomes, to recall a familiar military dictum, "what the other guy does." At the same time, the political terrorist both perceives and publicly portrays his craft as a defensive us-against-them response to the other guy's actions.[32] Thus, through heavy rhetorical stress upon the frequently vague idealistic ends—rather than the all-too-evident means—of political terrorism and the generally euphemistic portrayal of bona fide political issues, the political terrorist skillfully pursues the latter pose of Walter Laqueur's now-familiar adage, "one man's terrorist is another man's freedom fighter." These points will be illustrated in subsequent chapters.

The fact that the political terrorist rhetorically justifies his deeds is of tremendous psychological significance, yet heretofore largely overlooked is precisely how that justification takes place. I speak here of the political terrorist's warnings of acts to come and claims of responsibility for acts that already have taken place. By warning of acts to come, the political terrorist tacitly communicates several psychologically significant messages. He is able to use such occasions not only as another opportunity to deliver a conventionally rhetorical message but also to assert, "You've been forewarned that, what, and where, I will strike, and I therefore bear no responsibility for any casualties; I am capable of such spectacular acts *precisely because I am omnipotent*." By claiming responsibility or credit for acts that already have taken place, another excellent opportunity for delivering sheer rhetorical messages, the political terrorist also is able to affirm that his accomplishment is legitimate and defensible precisely because he can establish such responsibility. "I am indeed omnipotent because I can both commit such spectacular acts and possess the quintessential capability to claim credit for—indeed, boast of— having done so."

I have discussed the issue of why political terrorism must be justified and also have considered those psychopolitical dynamics inherent in this psychologically necessitated, rhetorical justification of political terrorism. It now will be possible to focus upon an even more fascinating issue: the nearly perfect psychophilosophical congruity between the specific psychological predisposition of the political terrorist and the distinctive contemporary philosophical packaging of political terrorism.

Although the philosophical consideration of violence is nearly as old as Western civilization itself, the concept of personal liberation through violence, a theme central to the philosophical justification of political terrorism, is relatively new. For most premodern political thinkers, violence stemming from individual motivation was either unknown or morally repugnant. Heroic and, frequently, violent acts rather were viewed as signs from the gods. Thus, although, as Homer affirms in *The Iliad*, man may choose to author heroically violent acts, he must encounter whatever ultimate destiny or fate has been preordained for him by the gods. Sacrificial or conventional violence also was accepted; as Aeschylus suggests in the *Oresteia*, Orestes' act of matricide, despite its element of revenge, was based ultimately upon moral and legal justice. Plato, Aristotle, Thucydides, and, much later, Saint Thomas Aquinas all theorized that acts of violence and warfare must be undertaken solely for heroic or moral purposes, and never for mere greed or individual ambition.[33]

It was not until the advent of modern, and particularly contemporary, political philosophy that twin notions—the sanctification of political violence itself and the individual utility or value of that glorified, instrumentally justified violence—were first set forth. This philosophical trend is most dramatically evidenced in the writings of such nineteenth- and twentieth-century theorists as Georges Sorel, Albert Camus, Jean-Paul Sartre, and Frantz Fanon. Indeed, what most tightly binds men such as these four together is a mutual hostility to the modern bourgeois state and, even more immediately relevant, a shared faith in personal liberation through violent action. For Sorel, dedication to the small group that is sworn to legitimate political violence is personally liberating because it creates a "new man."[34] For Camus, rebellion by its very nature implies a dualistic "no" to enslavement, and an emphatic "yes" to an individual's own personal worth. As he puts it, "With rebellion, awareness is born. . . . From his very first step, [the rebel] refuses to allow anyone to touch what he is. He is fighting for the integrity of one part of his being."[35]

We also might note Sartre's preface to Fanon's classic treatise, *The Wretched of the Earth*. For Sartre, political violence—in this case, of the anticolonialist genre—generally must be viewed as a process of "man recreating himself."[36] For theorists such as Sorel, Camus, Sartre, and Fanon, therefore, one of the most fundamental aspects of political violence is its liberating, cathartic, or cleansing effect upon every individual who participates in it.

Of even more direct relevance to the central focus of this study, however, is the exceptional conceptual congruence between narcissistic personality disturbances, particularly the energizing of regulatory narcissism, and subsequent regression to secondary narcissism on the one hand, and the blatantly egoistic philosophical wellsprings of contemporary political terrorism on the other. This is a startling philosophical relationship that demands further examination.

The major philosophical forefathers of twentieth-century political terrorism are two nineteenth-century figures: the German philosopher, Max Stirner, and the Russian anarchist, Sergei Nechaev. What fundamentally binds Stirner to Nechaev is not a devotion to political terrorism, ideologically or otherwise, but rather a shared faith in what may be termed "ruthless egoism." Thus, although Stirner himself never takes up the cudgels for political terrorism per se, Nechaev's essay, "Catechism of the Revolutionist," faithfully, albeit subtly, pursues Stirner's essential vision of "a new, ruthless Ego" dedicated, in Nechaev's case, to political terrorism.[37] However, it is Stirner, and not Nechaev, who first and most comprehensively introduces the brutally frank and ruthlessly egoistic philosophy that so reigns over Nechaev's later efforts. A brief discussion of Stirner's own work, therefore, is in order.

Max Stirner's nihilistic opposition to the state, society, and conventional morality was based exclusively upon his ultraindividualistic, brutally egoistic, and, ultimately, solipsistic philosophy.[38] For Stirner, only the self, and the needs, beliefs, and knowledge of the self, are of any importance. Hence, "one must carry *in himself* the law, the statute; and he who is most legally disposed is [therefore] the most moral."[39]

As R. W. K. Paterson points out, this "calculating, self-conscious egoism" has important implications for its ultimate practitioners.[40] In his discussion of "The Unique One," Stirner's own characterization of the absolute egoist, Paterson comments that

> . . . Stirner's portrait may be said to illustrate three main and recurring themes. First, it depicts the metaphysical solitude of the total egoist, his utter detachment from others in the self-sufficiency of his enclosed and reticent being. Secondly, it illustrates the specifically ethical posture of the egoist, his deportment towards those others whose claims he begins by repudiating, and his rejection of every moral and social absolute that seeks to establish its alien authority over his person, aims, or conduct. Lastly, Stirner's portrait of The Unique One describes the egoist's fundamental existential project, his modes of subjugating those contingent, transient objects which he arbitrarily chooses as the materials of his [ruthlessly egoistic endeavors].[41]

From our perspective it must be evident that Stirner's philosophical depiction of the egoist resembles nothing so much as the individual who has regressed to a level of secondary narcissism. In particular, Stirner's egoist manifests three of the clearest indications of secondary narcissism: 1) a profound libidinal withdrawal from the object world, 2) an unmitigated manipulation of other objects whereby any possible conflict between ego needs and the values and identities of those objects is wholly or overwhelmingly predetermined in favor of the needs of the self, and 3) the forceful manipulation of the object world so as to fit the egoist's own as-if expectations. *The Ego and His Own*, therefore, is only an elaborate philosophical apologia for a supposedly legitimized regression to secondary narcissism. And, in light of later philosophical and practical applications of Stirner's arrantly egoistic philosophy—such as Nechaev's own essay, "Catechism of the Revolutionist"—we are compelled to conclude that political terrorism is not only a stunning manifestation of, but is also *actually justified or otherwise rationalized by,* an ostensibly legitimized regression to secondary narcissism. In this chapter I have examined the question of why the practice of political terrorism itself might be psychologically attractive to victims of narcissistic personality disturbances and have analyzed the typical intrapsychic and interpersonal consequences of narcissistic injury and narcissistic disappointment— narcissistic rage, narcissistic aggression, and narcissistic defense. I have also asserted that political terrorism offers its practitioners certain powerfully alluring psychodynamic benefits or rewards. I now shall analyze, in even greater depth, nine case studies of individuals who dealt with the decision to become a political terrorist.

Notes

1. Knutson, "Personality," 28.
2. Or, to pose the question somewhat differently: Why might political terrorism help to represent what Harold Lasswell has termed the "public redress of private grievances," or, more generally speaking, the "displacement of private affects upon public objects"? See Lasswell, *Psychopathology and Politics,* 39, 53. It has been observed that contemporary society in part has been distinguished by its privatization of the public realm, or, more broadly speaking, by its blurring of the traditional conceptual boundaries between the public and private realms. One of the underlying premises of this chapter is that the social and psychological distances between public and private have largely disappeared. This contemporary blurring of the two realms already has been superbly addressed. See, for example, Hannah Arendt, *The Human Condition* (Garden City, NY: Doubleday, 1958), esp. 23–69; Marshall Berman, *The Politics of Authenticity* (New York: Atheneum, 1970); Richard Sennett, *The Fall of Public Man* (New York: Knopf, 1977), esp. 259–68, 313–36; Erving Goffman, *The Presentation of Self in Everyday Life* (New York: Overlook, 1973), esp. 252–55; Joseph Bensman and Robert Lilienfeld, *Between Public and Private* (New York: Free Press, 1979), esp. xi, 8–9, 15–16, 76–79, 94–98, 107–9; and Stanford M. Lyman and Marvin B. Scott, *The Drama of Social Reality* (New York: Oxford University Press, 1975), esp. 101–14. In their fundamental contention that "the private and public are inextricably intertwined and interlaced" in contemporary society, Bensman and Lilienfeld argue that "the individual [in contemporary society] is indivisible. . . . [Thus,] his public and social roles can only be understood in relation to his private, intimate, personal and psychological existence. This in no way denies what must be regarded as the overwhelming importance of public and social roles. But we would argue that to understand the dynamics of public and social roles, one must understand their relationship to the self as a totality." See Bensman and Lilienfeld, *Between Public and Private,* 182, 8.

3. See especially Kohut, "Thoughts on Narcissism"; Alexander Lowen, *Narcissism* (New York: Macmillan, 1983), 140–41; and Murray, "Narcissism," 488, 493.

4. Lowen, *Narcissism*, 93.

5. See Kohut, "Thoughts on Narcissism"; and Rochlin, *Man's Aggression*, 141.

6. Murray, "Narcissism," 486, 488.

7. See, for example, Anna Freud, *The Ego and the Mechanisms of Defense* (New York: International Universities Press, 1946); Heinz Hartmann, *Ego Psychology and the Problem of Adaptation* (New York: International Universities Press, 1958); Murray, "Narcissism," 177; Kohut, *Restoration of the Self*; idem, "Thoughts on Narcissism," 384; idem, "Forms and Transformations," 248; Rochlin, *Man's Aggression*, 1–9, 14–15, 94, 119, 216, 241, 253; Stolorow, "Functional Definition," 183; H. G. van der Waals, "Problems of Narcissism," *Bulletin of the Menninger Clinic* 29 (1965): 297; Moore, "Toward a Clarification," 270–72; Thomas Freeman, "Narcissism and Defensive Processes in Schizophrenic States," *International Journal of Psychoanalysis* 43 (1962): 415–25; idem, "The Concept of Narcissism in Schizophrenic States," *International Journal of Psychoanalysis* 44 (1963): 299; Murphy, "Pride," 137; Segel, "Narcissistic Resistance," 949; Eidelberg, "Concept of Narcissistic Mortification," 166–67; Ephron, "Narcissism," 505; and Karl M. Abenheimer, "On Narcissism," *British Journal of Medical Psychology* 20 (1945): 324.

8. The term "repression" shall be defined as the energetic self-removal of unpleasant or otherwise painful experiences or perceptions from an individual's own consciousness.

9. See especially Kohut, "Thoughts on Narcissism," 377–98; Lowen, *Narcissism*, 75–100; and Rochlin, *Man's Aggression*, 1, 68–69, 83–84, 90–91, 108, 120, 128, 154–79, 185, 204, 239–41, 253–58. See also Stuart, *Narcissus*, 104–11; Moore, "Toward a Clarification," 254–57, 270–72; Segel, "Narcissistic Resistance," 944–49; Abenheimer, "On Narcissism," 323–25; Rochlin, "The Dread of Abandonment," 458–59; and Reich, "Narcissistic Object Choice," 43–44.

10. Rochlin, *Man's Aggression*, 1 (emphasis added). For Kohut's views on narcissistic rage as a type of aggression see Kohut, "Thoughts on Narcissism," 380.

11. See, for example, Hart, "Narcissistic Equilibrium," 107; Van der Waals, "Problems of Narcissism," 309; Kohut, "Forms and Transformations," 248; idem, "Psychoanalytic Treatment," 89; and Lowen, *Narcissism*, esp. 75–100.

12. See Hart, "Narcissistic Equilibrium," 107; and Lowen, *Narcissism*, 79, 75.

13. See Lasswell, *Power and Personality*, 39–58.

14. Ibid., 39 (emphasis in original).

15. Ibid., 53. The term "primary circle" may be defined as each individual's own group of significant others—for example, his own family or very close friends or associates. The term "displacement" may be defined as the shifting of affect or emotional feeling from one appropriate object to another surrogate object.

16. See ibid. The concept of compensatory political behavior therefore is introduced quite early in the development of the personality-and-politics literature. Moreover, this theme has emerged as an enduring motif of many subsequent works, such as Erik H. Erikson, *Gandhi's Truth* (New York: W. W. Norton, 1968); Barber, *Presidential Character*; Michael Paul Rogin, *Fathers and Children* (New York: Vintage, 1975); George and George, *Woodrow Wilson*;

Alexander L. George, "Power as a Compensatory Value for Political Leaders," *Journal of Social Issues* 24 (1968): 29–49; and Bruce Mazlish, *In Search of Nixon* (Baltimore: Penguin, 1973).

17. See, for example, Hacker, *Crusader, Criminals, Crazies*, 39–44, 74–75; Fried, "Questions on Terrorism," 223; Adolphe D. Jonas, "Introduction," *Terrorism* 3 (1980): 259–61; Crayton, "Terrorism," 33–41; and Post, "Notes," 241–56.

18. Hacker, *Crusaders, Criminals, Crazies*, 42.

19. See Post, "Notes," 250; and Fried, "Questions on Terrorism," 223.

20. Brodey, "Dynamics of Narcissism," 187.

21. See ibid., esp. 167–68, 186–87, 190, 192; and Brodey, "Image, Object, and Narcissistic Relationships," 70.

22. I do not refer here to the erroneous and highly contradictory notion of social narcissism or group narcissism—a concept that has been introduced by an otherwise impressive population of observers. See, for example, Sigmund Freud, *Group Psychology and the Analysis of the Ego* (New York: W. W. Norton, 1959), 1, 9–10, 16–17, 34–35, 55–56; Fromm, *Heart of Man*, 71–116; Bing, McLaughlin, and Marburg, "Metapsychology of Narcissism," 17–18; Kohut, "Thoughts on Narcissism," 397–98; and Crayton, "Terrorism."

23. Hacker, *Crusaders, Criminals, Crazies*, 42.

24. Hacker, "Dialectical Interrelationships," 27.

25. Post, "Group and Organizational Dynamics," 7. See also idem, "Prospects," 94; and idem, "Notes," 250.

26. Rochlin, *Man's Aggression*, 190, 256 (emphasis in original). For more on his assertion that narcissistic aggression must somehow be justified, see ibid., 204, 216, 259.

27. See especially Yonah Alexander, ed., *Terrorism: Moral Aspects* (Boulder, CO: Westview, 1980); Moshe Amon, "The Devil's Righteousness," paper presented to the Conference on the Moral Implications of Terrorism, March 14–16, 1979, at the University of California at Los Angeles; idem, "Terrorism: Problems of Good and Evil," paper presented to the Conference on Psychopathology and Political Violence, November 16–17, 1979, at the University of Chicago; D. J. C. Carmichael, "Of Beasts, Gods, and Civilized Men," *Terrorism* 6 (1982): 1–26; idem, "Terrorism: Some Ethical Issues," *Chitty's Law Journal* 24 (1976): 233–39; Martha Crenshaw, ed., *Terrorism, Legitimacy, and Power* (Middletown, CT: Wesleyan University Press, 1983); John Dugard, "International Terrorism and the Just War," *Stanford Journal of International Studies* (Spring 1977): 21–38; Fred Ermlich, "Ethical Implications of Terrorism," paper presented to the Eighteenth Annual Convention of the International Studies Association, March 16–20, 1977, at St. Louis; Richard Falk, *Revolutionaries and Functionaries* (New York: E. P. Dutton, 1988), 70–94; R. Higgins, "Can Terrorism Be Justified?" *Listener* 99 (1978): 558–59; Jeanne N. Knutson, "The Terrorists' Dilemmas," *Terrorism* 4 (1980): 195–222; Post, "Notes"; David C. Rapoport, ed., *Inside Terrorist Organizations* (New York: Columbia University Press, 1988); David C. Rapoport and Yonah Alexander, eds., *The Morality of Terrorism* (New York: Pergamon, 1982); Rapoport and Alexander, eds., *The Rationalization of Terrorism* (Frederick, MD: University Publications of America, 1981); Richard E. Rubinstein, *Alchemists of Revolution* (New York: Basic Books, 1987); John Stevens, "Ideology and Ethics of Terror," in Michael Stohl, ed., *The Politics of Terror* (New York: Marcel Dekker, 1977); Robert Young, "Revolutionary Terrorism, Crime and Morality," *Social Theory and Practice* (Fall 1977): 287–302; G. C. Zahn, "Terrorism for Peace and Justice,"

Commonweal, October 23, 1979, 84–85; and Ciro Zoppo, "The Moral Factor in Interstate Politics and International Terrorism," paper presented to the Conference on the Moral Implications of Terrorism, March 14–16, 1979, at the University of California at Los Angeles.

28. Sigmund Freud, *Totem and Taboo* (New York: W. W. Norton, 1950), 32.

29. Erik H. Erikson, *Identity* (New York: W. W. Norton, 1968), 174 (emphasis in original).

30. Knutson's own term. See Jeanne N. Knutson, "Social and Psychodynamic Pressures toward a Negative Identity," in Yonah Alexander and John M. Gleason, eds., *Behavioral and Quantitative Perpectives on Terrorism* (New York: Pergamon, 1981), 112. See also ibid., 110–11, 113–15; and Knutson, "Terrorists' Dilemmas," 196–200.

31. Crayton, "Terrorism," 38. It also might be useful to consider Sandra J. Ball-Rokeach's statement that violence-prone individuals "may have to find a way to justify their behavior to themselves." See Ball-Rokeach, "The Legitimation of Violence," in James F. Short, Jr., and Marvin E. Wolfgang, eds., *Collective Violence* (Chicago: Aldine, 1972), 105.

32. On this point see especially Maurice A. J. Tugwell, "Guilt Transfer," in Rapoport and Alexander, eds., *Morality of Terrorism,* 275–89.

33. See especially Homer, *The Iliad* (Garden City, NY: Doubleday, 1974); Aeschylus, *The Orestes Plays* (New York: Mentor, 1962); Plato, *Statesman* (Indianapolis: Bobbs-Merrill, 1977); Aristotle, *The Politics* (London: Oxford University Press, 1977); Thucydides, *The Peloponnesian War* (New York: Modern Library, 1951); and Saint Thomas Aquinas, "The Summa Theologica," in Dino Bigongiari, ed., *The Political Ideas of St. Thomas Aquinas* (New York: Hafner, 1953), 3–172.

34. Georges Sorel, *Reflections on Violence* (London: Collier, 1969). One particularly striking, practical exemplification of political terrorism in the guise of personal liberation is Dr. Wolfgang Huber's Socialist Patients' Collective (SPK), an organized group of West German psychiatric patients whose "violent attack on 'society' [was intended] . . . to cure their personal mental disorders." See Jillian Becker, *Hitler's Children* (Philadelphia: Lippincott, 1977), 230. As Becker comments, "In his group therapy sessions, Dr. Huber propagated the view that 'the late-capitalist performance society of the [West German] Federal Republic' was sick, and was therefore continually producing physically and psychologically sick people, and that this could only be altered by a violent revolutionary change of society." See ibid., 227, 228–29. The SPK, or IZRU (Information Center Red People's University), as it was eventually renamed, was responsible for bombings, shootings, kidnappings, and other acts of political terrorism during the early 1970s and also was loosely linked to certain members of the Baader-Meinhof Gang/Red Army Faction. On this point see ibid., esp. 275, 278. On the SPK/IZRU see also Jillian Becker, "Case Study 1: Federal Germany," in David Carlton and Carlo Schaerf, eds., *Contemporary Terror* (New York: St. Martin's, 1981), 122–38; and Jane Kramer, "A Reporter in Europe," *The New Yorker* (March 20, 1978).

35. Albert Camus, *The Rebel* (New York: Vintage, 1956), 15, 18. For more on his views on violence and personal liberation see his *Resistance, Rebellion, and Death* (New York: Vintage, 1960).

36. Jean-Paul Sartre, "Preface," in Frantz Fanon, *The Wretched of the Earth* (New York: Grove Press, 1963), 21.

37. Hyams, *Terrorists and Terrorism*, 26. For an excellent secondary discussion of Nechaev see ibid., 18–30. For the full text of Nechaev's own treatise see, for example, Nechaev, "Catechism."

38. The term "nihilism" may be defined as the philosophical belief that all political, social, and religious authority is illegitimate in the face of the far superior and legitimate authority of scientific thought. In certain cases, such as that of the nineteenth-century Russian terrorist group, the People's Will, nihilistic thought led to violent action. In certain other cases, such as that of meek scholar Max Stirner, nihilistic thinking produced only highly controversial treatises on the subject. The term "solipsism" may be defined as the belief that only the self is of any philosophical or practical significance, for the self is the only knowingly conscious entity in existence.

39. Carroll, ed., *Max Stirner*, 66 (emphasis in original).

40. R. W. K. Paterson, *The Nihilist Egoist* (London: Oxford University Press, 1971), 252.

41. Ibid., 253.

CHAPTER FOUR

Weathering the Storm: Susan Stern and Diana Oughton

> The sociological imagination enables the possessor to understand the larger historical scene in terms of its meaning for the inner life and the external career of a variety of individuals. . . . The sociological imagination enables us to grasp history and biography and the relations between the two within society. . . . It is the capacity to range from the most impersonal and remote transformations to the most intimate features of the human self—and to see the relations between the two. . . . That is its task and its promise. To recognize this task and this promise is the mark of the classic social analyst.
>
> C. Wright Mills
> *The Sociological Imagination*

It is difficult to deny that social and political analysis remains a mere abstraction without clear and direct reference to the human element. Any theory of man's behavior, therefore, must be firmly rooted in man, regardless of the novelty, sophistication, or methodology of theory. Hence, in order to understand fully the individual *psychology* of the political terrorist, it is essential to understand the *individual political terrorist*. This may be accomplished only through a careful application of the case-study method of analysis. For the purpose of validating the theoretical bases of this book, I shall focus upon nine persons: Susan Stern, Diana Oughton, Donald DeFreeze, Patricia Soltysik, Victor Gerena, Thomas Martinez, Ilich Ramírez Sanchez, Ulrike Meinhof, and Renato Curcio.

These particular individuals have been selected for a number of reasons. First, in each of these nine examples a variety of unusually detailed accounts pertinent to the secondary construction of psychological case studies already has been generated. Second, I am concerned that my choice of case studies be as substantial, diverse, and representative as possible. In concentrating upon this case-study sample, I am able to focus upon individuals whose personal attributes vary on the bases of nationality, gender, and socioeconomic status. Thus, five of the nine—Stern, Oughton, DeFreeze, Soltysik, and Martinez—are Americans, while the remainder are Puerto Rican (Gerena), Venezuelan (Ramírez), West German (Meinhof), and Italian (Curcio). Five are men (DeFreeze, Gerena, Martinez, Ramírez, and Curcio), and four are women (Stern, Oughton, Soltysik, and Meinhof). Stern, Oughton, and Ramírez are from backgrounds of extreme wealth. Soltysik, Meinhof, and Curcio are from middle- or upper-middle-class families; and DeFreeze, Gerena, and Martinez grew up in lower-class surroundings. With these preliminary points addressed, let us turn to the first of these nine case studies.

Like so many "first generation" American and West European political terrorists, Susan Stern's political involvement and psychopolitical development may be traced to the university activism of the Vietnam War era.[1] Her participation in the militant Weathermen, a splinter group of the radical-reformist organization, Students for a Democratic Society (SDS), centered chiefly upon her role as a coconspirator in a number of violent events: the Days of Rage disorder, The Day After disturbance, and violent attacks upon a U.S. Air Force Reserve Officer Training Corps (ROTC) center at the University of Washington at Seattle. In comparison to the scope and magnitude of political terrorist "propaganda of the deed" since the early 1970s— kidnappings and assassinations of prominent figures, brutal bombings of public places, and other acts of mass atrocity—these are relatively low-level acts of violence.[2]

Still, the case of Susan Stern is an invaluable one, for she made a highly conscious and unusually revealing decision to go underground as a political terrorist. As she characterizes that decision in her memoirs, *With the Weathermen: The Personal Journal of a Revolutionary Woman*:

> Going underground was not just a wild gambit for me. It was all that was left before death. All my fears, my anxieties about going underground paled beside the specter of living out my life untrue to my revolutionary visions, simply for the sake of living. Life was not that appealing to me. It never had been. Its loss could mean little, if in the process something better for humanity could be born. . . . I sat . . . and tore up my life. All the photos of my youth taken out of my album, one by one, torn up and into a big garbage can. Then my scrapbooks. . . . All traces of Susan Harris Stern shredded and into a foul garbage can. . . . Then I took the rest of my money, about a hundred dollars, and went to meet a man who dealt in unregistered firearms. He sold me an Ithaca model double-barrel shotgun and a .38 caliber handgun. I went to the sporting goods store and bought a supply of bullets. . . . That was it. I was ready.[3]

Stern's case also is invaluable because she is one of the few political terrorists who has written an autobiographical account that transcends mere rhetoric.[4] Instead, *With the Weathermen* concentrates upon the key and, at times, most intimate themes of her personal life and the nature of her psychological and psychopolitical evolution. She then honestly and successfully attempts to unify her personal life and political beliefs.[5]

Born Susan Harris on January 31, 1943, in Brooklyn, New York, Susan Stern was raised in what she describes as very wealthy surroundings. However, her childhood and adolescence were miserable, as she states in her autobiography:

> My parents divorced when I was three, and at the age of nine, after years of brutal courtroom battles, I went to live with my father and brother in New Jersey. My father, unstable and insensitive, loved me compulsively. . . . My mother, beautiful and childlike, remarried when I went to live with my father, and devoted the next ten years of her life to the dashing, tumultuous man she could not live without. She loved my brother and myself, but she loved her husband more.[6]

The narcissistic injuries surrounding Susan's upbringing bore heavily upon her sense of self-esteem and self-image from adolescence onward. As she writes, "I grew up terribly shy and introverted and convinced of my inferiority to everyone around me. By the time I entered Syracuse University at the age of eighteen, I was a slight, sallow girl with sad dark eyes, short, unstyled hair, and large black-rimmed glasses. I always half-dreamed of suicide as an alternative to a drab, meaningless, and miserable existence."[7]

Thoughts of suicide troubled her throughout a great deal of her life. For example, shortly after being asked to leave a Weathermen collective, Susan once again entertained the notion of taking her own life. At this juncture, she bemoaned her anxiety that she "was at the age of twenty-seven, still as emotionally unequipped to deal with myself as I was at thirteen." She reveals, moreover, that she had first attempted suicide at thirteen: "My father slapped me because he thought he had seen me driving in a car with my lovely mother, and I told him I hadn't seen her for months, but he wouldn't believe me, and at thirteen it's a long time to go until you're free from that much oppression, like not being allowed to see your own goddam mother when you want to. And so I had swallowed several bottles of pills, and puked until I almost did die."[8] Unsuccessful even at suicide, Susan sought to escape what she characterizes as "the odyssey of my adolescence" through her poetry, the "panic scribbles of those endless, sleepless nights of my youth." She also confesses that, even later in life, the only sentiments that she possessed for anyone in her family were hostility and disgust.[9]

During her senior year at Syracuse University, Susan began to live with Robby Stern, a prelaw student. They were married six months—and one abortion—later. Not long after her enrollment at the University of Washington at Seattle, she briefly dropped out of graduate school and became involved in various civil rights groups. During this period she also taught in a black ghetto school but was thrown out of a local teaching program because her methods were deemed too radical. She then set up a Peruvian Peace Corps library. Influenced strongly by one of her husband's more radical friends, who had burned his draft card and gone to prison, Susan swung sharply to the left.[10]

Although she was stirred politically by a number of her husband's friends, her marriage to Robby was nearly as miserable as her childhood and adolescence. Most striking is the fact that her low self-esteem and highly negative sense of self-image deteriorated even further when contrasted with what she, at least, perceived as her husband's own positive qualities. As Susan puts it, "He was so exciting compared to me and my own lackluster life that I was grateful to him for having chosen me from all the other women he could have had."[11]

As Susan recalls, she had pinned her hopes on the couple's move to Seattle: "He would go to law school, and I would go to the School of Social Work, and somehow, everything would work out and our marriage would be saved. We had told each other we were leaving the East to escape my family and the strangling hold of my miserable childhood. But I knew we were running in desperation from the unhappy rut of our life together."[12] The move west, however, proved to be no escape from her earlier narcissistic injuries. Rather, it served only to reaccentuate her low self-esteem and negative sense of self-image. She resented having to perform all the housework while her husband occupied himself with more pleasant matters, and she became nervous and morbid. As Susan puts it:

> I would go on long crying jags before Robby ever came home, and fly into a rage the minute he entered the apartment. I found fault with everything he did, and would accept no criticism from him concerning anything I did. The more miserable I made our home, the more insecure I became. The more Robby withdrew from me, the more I craved his love. Although I was among the top students at the School of Social Work, I compared myself to Robby and convinced myself that I was stupid. I compared myself to Robby in all ways and always came out inferior. But I had grown up thinking I was stupid and ugly. I had grown up lonely and envious of people like Robby to whom friends and grades came so easily.[13]

Indeed, in summarizing the state of her marriage and the narcissistic injuries of her childhood and adolescence, Susan admits that

> Robby and I were never happily married. Neurotic, depressed, insecure, and totally dependent on Robby, I demanded constant attention. Comparing myself to him endlessly, and always finding him superior, I hated and resented him for the very qualities that made me love him: his charm, brilliance, robust handsomeness, and charismatic appeal. . . . The scars of my

childhood stood between me and the ability to simply slide soundlessly into the niche the system had provided for me.[14]

Without some alternative to this miserable relationship, however, she remained terrified whenever she considered a life without Robby. She thus stayed with him for another two years.[15]

During her attendance at the School of Social Work in Seattle, Susan was exposed further to radical politics as well as to the hippie subculture and the feminist movement. Although recognized early on only as Robby Stern's wife to campus activists, her membership in SDS and a feminist organization, Radical Women, proved to be a turning point in her life. Susan and Robby had attended the New Politics Convention in Chicago in August 1967; both joined SDS in the fall of that year.[16]

By early 1968, Susan's marital problems were reaching a climax. At about this time, she attended a Radical Women demonstration at the University of Washington, where several feminists were assaulted by a group of counterdemonstrators. Susan was dragged off stage and thrown down a small flight of steps. This initial taste of violence dramatically transformed her. As she writes in *With the Weathermen*:

> Now, for the first time in my life I had something to talk about, and people listened to me, especially women. . . . I felt a new sense of pride which quickened my step, raised my head more firmly in the air, and gave my voice a resonance and force that had never before been there. . . . I developed my Style. Zip, zap, I was a new Susan Stern, and honey, when I walked, I threw back my head, and moved with determination. People moved out of my way as I strode through them. When I entered a room, I did so with a flourish, and people looked at me, and God damn it, when I talked, they listened, finally they listened.[17]

Shortly afterward, Susan asked Robby to move out of their apartment. Just prior to her decision to ask him to leave, his unfaithfulness was becoming blatant. Robby was having an affair with one of the Radical Women, Beth Allworth. Susan writes that "it was nothing serious, but while it lasted, I suffered. One night we all went to a party together after an SDS meeting. I asked Robby to dance with me, but he said he was too tired. Dejected, I went into another room to get something to drink, and when I returned Robby was dancing a slow dance with Beth. Choking back tears, I hitchhiked home."[18]

While working on her master's thesis in the spring of 1968, Susan turned her attention to the first regional meeting of the Seattle SDS. The original purpose was to have been the development of a strategy to deal with the issues of racism and the Vietnam War. The women at the meeting decided to call a general assembly to discuss women's liberation, and Susan was selected as chairwoman. As she recalls:

> When I stood to speak, I waved a clenched fist in the air, spit as I spoke, and hardly pausing to catch my breath, I put my hopeless marriage and its demise on a silver platter and danced around and around with it. Startled by the force of my language, and the rage that accompanied it, the restless movement of the men stopped. When Robby had heard enough and couldn't take it anymore, for he was no worse than any other man, he attempted to interrupt me, and backed by three years of bitterness and frustration I screamed, "Fuck you—sit down and shut up, it's my turn now." He sat down stunned, and I felt a surge of power in my body that I had never felt before. And that was the very first moment of my life![19]

Susan left Seattle for Berkeley, California, one week later. There, she led a lethargic existence, tagging along to political rallies while trying to find a niche. She decided to seek employment and, on a friend's recommendation, took a position as a topless dancer since she was utterly titillated by the prospect. She also toyed with the idea of becoming a prostitute. Tiring of her newfound employment, she soon left Berkeley for Los Angeles.[20]

While based at the Los Angeles regional SDS office, Susan participated in demonstrations against the Vietnam War and the 1968 Democratic Convention in Chicago. Her emotional reaction to the police riots at Chicago's Grant and Lincoln parks vividly illustrates the powerful psychological rewards that radical political action held for her:

> This was my first street action and I was nervous. . . . But I felt *good*. I could feel my body supple and strong and slim, and ready to run miles, and my legs moving sure and swift under me, and the hot sun growing pale as night came on cooling my sweat and fanning my perfume into my nose. I was ready to riot. . . . Once a pale and terrified pig raced up to me, and for a second his club hovered in the air, and he stared at me, and then, screaming wildly, he backed away. Did I look like a witch, blood-spattered, with vomit hanging from my mouth in

mucous streams, dirt-smeared, tears streaming down my face, hot, sweaty, and angry beyond despair? I wanted to kill. . . . A new feeling was struggling to be born in me. It had no name, but it made me want to reach beyond myself to others who were suffering. I felt real, as if suddenly I had found out something true about myself; that I was not helpless, that life meant enough to me to struggle for it, to take chances with it, to thrust out and wrestle with it. I thought about all the years I had been strangling my misery as I turned my cheek. Now it would be different; now I would fight.[21]

After the Democratic Convention in Chicago, Susan was invited to a national meeting of SDS officers in rural Indiana. Quite striking was her sentiment that her compensatory needs would be well served at this conclave, and afterward. As she puts it, "I was going to mingle with the stars. . . . I felt I was part of a vast network of intense, exciting and brilliant people."[22]

In April 1969, in New York City, Susan participated in the Columbia University SDS chapter's seizure of Philosophy Hall. For the first time, she was on the other side of physical violence. Upon injuring a policeman with a thrown bottle, Susan felt exhilarated and "stayed in front of the action."[23] By June, SDS had split into rival factions, the most significant and violent of which, the Weathermen, effectively took over the national office of SDS. Recruited successfully by this group, Susan, along with seven others, formed a Seattle chapter. As she recalls, "I was as over-zealously aggressive and abandoned as a Weatherman as I had been timid and frightened prior to it. I was intent on being as outrageous as possible. . . . I couldn't resist their appeal. Their flagrant arrogance, their contempt for everyone around them. I thought they were remarkable; I knew I belonged there."[24] It is interesting to note that Robby Stern, Susan's former emotional adversary, was unalterably opposed to the Weathermen and vainly attempted to convince her to leave the group.[25]

The first major radical action in which Susan participated was the Weathermen-sponsored Days of Rage disorder, which took place in Chicago on October 8–11, 1969. She recalls that, while on a crowded microbus on the road to Chicago, she thought about how much she resented the fact that her father "had tormented me for the first twenty years of my life"; her father, Susan surmised, personified all that was wrong with America.[26]

Upon arrival, Susan and her fellow Weathermen, dressed in heavy protective clothing and helmets, stormed Chicago's fashionable Gold Coast. In a particularly vivid passage, she writes: "I passed one man in a restaurant with a luscious piece of steak on the end of his fork. . . . I swung at the restaurant window with my iron pipe. . . . The window shattered, and I felt high as a motherfucker. Boy, did that feel great. . . . I ran down the block as fast as I could chopping at every window, watching them shatter and fall like glaciers falling over mountains. A literal rain of glass. I loved it."[27] She ultimately was arrested, jailed, and bailed out by her father. She expressed great pride in her role at the Days of Rage disorder, which resulted in the injury of hundreds of police personnel and the physical paralysis of Richard Elrod, chief counsel to Mayor Richard Daley. As Susan writes, "I had a right to walk with my head held high; I had done my share."[28]

Toward the latter part of 1969 and early 1970 the Weathermen began to make plans to conduct overt acts of political terrorism. At a war council held in Flint, Michigan, in late December 1969, the group decided to go underground in order to

> . . . make bombs. See big buildings topple. IBM got it last week—how about AT&T next? Who owns Standard Oil anyway? Let's get his kids, his wife. Get a racetrack, like they did in the battle of Algiers. Pour acid in the water supply of Shaker Heights, Ohio. Go out on sniping raids and kill pigs. Bomb a pig station—avenge Fred Hampton. Get your local draft board, your nearest military installation, your campus ROTC building, your high school principal's office. The possibilities were inexhaustible. There was a history for us to follow. . . . The topic was not approached lightly; it was a deadly serious meeting. Everyone knew the implications for even talking about terrorism. And we were discussing what would be necessary to actually *do it!*[29]

On January 17, 1970, two Weathermen were arrested for attempting to bomb the Air Force ROTC building at the University of Washington. On January 20, Susan and several members of the Seattle Liberation Front led a violent attack upon a U.S. Marine recruiter's office and were arrested and jailed. Yet, due to her "bourgeois, sexist, and individualist habits," she was asked to leave the Weathermen and then joined another radical group, the Sundance Collective. She participated in The Day After disturbance and, for similar reasons, was asked to leave the Sundance Collective as well.[30] Shortly after these events Susan made the conscious decision to go completely underground as a political terrorist.[31]

Susan Stern was named as a coconspirator in charges stemming from the Days of Rage disorder and the organization of The Day After disturbance. She also was arrested and indicted for attacking the University of Washington's Air Force ROTC center. Upon learning of her status as an unindicted coconspirator in the Days of Rage indictments, Susan recalls that she was flattered by the news. As she puts it, "I was threatening. Someone was taking me seriously." In reference to the Seattle Seven trial, she writes that "suddenly I was someone. I knew I was someone because there were so many people hanging around me, asking me questions, looking to me for answers, or just looking at me offering to do things for me, to get some of the glow from the limelight. . . . Wherever I went the people loved me. . . . Everybody was mightily impressed with me."[32]

After separate trials, she served one month in jail for assault charges resulting from the Days of Rage, and three months for her role as a member of the Seattle Seven.[33] During her jail term at Washington's Purdy State Prison for Women, Susan wrote a letter to a close friend that succinctly depicts her personal motivations toward political terrorism:

> Still, I am unhappy in my role as revolutionary, because it is not enough for me; I want to stand out in the history I am trying to make. My existence will have meaning only if lots of others know about it. Call it fame, immortality, call it what you will, until I have it, I will always be unhappy. I guess that's the saddest thing about me, my fatal flaw. In a real sense, then, I exploited the revolution for my own personal ends. . . . My desire for immortality, my need for fame is perhaps the essence of my life; it alone can give meaning to my existence. I am helpless in the face of it.[34]

Several years after the publication of *With the Weathermen*, Susan was found dead in a Jacuzzi. An autopsy determined that she had died from an overdose of drugs and alcohol.[35]

The case of Susan Stern is clearly manifested by a long string of narcissistic injuries. Her parents divorced when she was only three, and, after years of courtroom battles, custody of the then nine-year-old girl was awarded to her "unstable and insensitive" father. Susan's mother then remarried and henceforth had little more to do with her daughter because, as Susan painfully recalls, "she loved her husband more." To make matters worse, Susan's father forbade her, upon pain of clearly humiliating physical and emotional abuse, from even attempting to see her mother. In condemning her father—and mother—for having tormented her, Susan articulates bitterly the narcissistic injuries resulting from her being rejected by and forcibly isolated from a significant other: her estranged mother.

Susan's adult life proved to be as humiliating and wretched as her childhood and adolescence. She deeply resented her perceived role status vis-à-vis the exciting and charismatic Robby Stern who, in turn, began to withdraw affection and attention from his troubled wife. He commenced upon a series of extra-marital affairs, and Susan was again forced to endure the terrifying rejection of a significant other. She also suffered an acute sense of personal failure when she was expelled from a ghetto teaching program. Finally, we must take note of her ejection from both the Weathermen and the Sundance Collective. Susan, therefore, sustained a wide variety of narcissistic injuries during her adulthood, including those resulting from her 1) perceived role status, 2) rejection by significant others, and 3) acute sense of personal failure.

Clear manifestations of narcissistic rage also may be discerned in Susan's autobiographical account: she would "go on long crying jags" before her husband returned home and would "fly into a rage" when he entered their apartment. Yet, it was during her speeches to feminist audiences that her narcissistic rage became most evident. Susan's public humiliation of Robby is a particularly conspicuous demonstration of her as-yet diffuse and unfocused fury against her tormentors and, indeed, her own self-perceptions. Finally, it might be useful to consider Susan's well-conveyed ecstasy in her participation in the Days of Rage.

Susan Stern exemplifies splendidly the concept of the as-if psychic sense of omnipotence exhibited by so many political terrorists. One example is her vivid self-perception during her first violent action, the 1968 Democratic Convention rioting in Chicago. There, she felt "good," "strong," and "ready to run miles." A similar sense of omnipotence emerged from her exhilarating participation in the seizure of Columbia University's Philosophy Hall. A distinct sense of omnipotence may be discerned, too, in Susan's recollections of the Days of Rage.

The establishment, assumption, and maintenance of an as-if other pseudoidentity also may be clearly evidenced in this case study. For Susan, the decision to become a "new Susan Stern," to become "someone," and, above all, to become a political terrorist was predicated upon a conscious rejection of her old self. Hence, Susan tore up her old life.

In essence, then, Susan Stern exemplifies the individual who, psychoanalytically shaped by multiple narcissistic injuries, demonstrates a clearly powerful attraction to the inherent psychodynamic rewards of political terrorism. I shall examine next a very different type of individual, the political terrorist who is psychically subject to a somewhat more diverse set of narcissistic personality disturbances: another member of the Weathermen, Diana Oughton.

Like Susan Stern, Diana Oughton was an active member of the Weathermen and participated in the violent events surrounding both the 1968 Democratic Convention in Chicago and the Days of Rage. Diana's personal background also was one of considerable wealth and excellent education. And, similarly, she voluntarily embarked upon a short-lived career of political terrorism. Unlike Susan, however, Diana's posture as a political terrorist was prematurely terminated by death rather than by prosecution. She therefore leaves no autobiographical statement for students of political terrorism to scrutinize.

Available for case-study analysis, nevertheless, is Thomas Powers's Pulitizer Prize-winning biography, *Diana: The Making of a Terrorist*. This superb work is based upon both the public record and exhaustive interviews with those in a position to have known Diana most intimately: her family, closest friends, and political confreres. The following analysis of her psychological metamorphosis is based largely upon Powers's study.

Diana Oughton was born in January 1942 to one of the leading families of Dwight, Illinois, a small town located in the plains country south of Chicago. Her father, a high-ranking executive in the family bank and owner of large tracts of farmland and other properties, is characterized by Powers as a strong-willed, intelligent man.[36] The Oughtons were distinguished by a long history of philanthropy and civic achievement. The family had built practically all of Dwight's public works. One of Diana's great-grandfathers had founded the town's famed Keely Institute, the first hospital to treat successfully the disease of alcoholism, and another great-grandfather had founded the Boy Scouts of America.[37]

Diana's childhood was clearly one of gracious, and uneventful, comfort. She joined the 4-H Club and Dwight Congregational Church and performed admirably in school. As Powers learned, Diana, who adored her father,

> ... never caused trouble at home. ... She was generous, loving and strong. She was a perfect child, considered by many the "prize of all the girls," and was constantly held up to her sisters as an example. Astonishingly, her sisters seemed to share in the general admiration of Diana. Years later she told her sister Carol she wished she had resisted more as a child. Carol seemed the one always being scolded or punished, but, looking back on it, Diana felt Carol had been the lucky one; she had learned how to defend her independence.[38]

Such resistance would have been difficult for Diana, however, since her father dominated the family. As Powers points out, James Oughton made all the important decisions, while Diana's mother was a "loving presence who remained, somehow, always on the edge of things."[39]

Diana never was able to accept the social, and particularly economic, status of her wealthy family. Her friends and class-mates were invariably far less privileged than she. As Powers learned:

> In school the other children sometimes teased her by calling her "Miss Moneybags." When she was six she asked her nanny, Ruth Moreheart, "Ruthie, why do we have to be rich?" On another occasion, when money problems forced a girl friend to move away, Diana went to her father in tears and asked, "Why can't we be ordinary like them?" When she was a little older, Diana quietly wondered if her uniformly good marks in school had anything to do with the fact that several of her teachers rented houses from her father.[40]

Diana left Dwight, a wholly white, middle-class, peaceful midwestern town, a place in which "the United States presents a smiling, but placid, face," at a relatively early age. At thirteen, she was sent to Madeira, an ultraconservative girls' boarding school in McLean, Virginia. Diana then entered Bryn Mawr, an elite women's college with much more liberal views on the role of upper-class women. According to Powers, at the time of her matriculation at Bryn Mawr in the fall of 1959, Diana considered herself a midwestern Republican, or something approaching a right-wing conservative to her college classmates. Diana's friends were horrified to hear her find fault with the Social Security system, or to support Richard Nixon, rather than John Kennedy, during the 1960 presidential election.[41]

During her senior year at Bryn Mawr, Diana became involved in a remedial reading program for black ghetto children in nearby Philadelphia. After discovering that her pupils could not read at all, a shocked and chastened Diana tripled her work load and began to commute to Philadelphia twice per week. She also read John Howard Griffin's remarkable account of a white writer who masquerades as a black man, *Black Like Me*, and worked in a black voter-registration campaign in Maryland. These experiences gave her valuable insight into American racial problems.[42]

Unlike the vast majority of her graduating class, who went on to graduate school, marriage, or a big-city career, Diana signed on with the Voluntary International Service Assignments (VISA) program and was assigned to work in Guatemala. After her VISA training, which included one week in New York City's Spanish Harlem, Diana flew to Guatemala. She spent some time during her two years in the capital, Guatemala City, but lived chiefly in Chichicastenango, a poverty-stricken, isolated, Indian market town. She settled rapidly into its tranquil pace and became involved with nutrition programs and a newspaper financed by the Guatemalan Army and U.S. Military Assistance funds. She also established reading classes in a remote village near Chichicastenango.[43]

Diana's response to the plight of the impoverished Guatemalan Indians paralleled her efforts on behalf of Philadelphia's black ghetto children. She worked long, hard hours and learned more and more about the miserable, grinding lives of the people. Quite clearly, her social and political perspectives were undergoing profound transition. As Powers remarks, "The more Diana learned about the hard life of rural Guatemala, the more she reflected on the affluence of the United States. . . . In Chichicastenango, Americans seemed almost an alien presence, the fact of their wealth almost an insult to the impoverished Indians."[44]

As time wore on, the one-time midwestern Republican, whose height and long blond hair drew American tourists to her, grew almost ashamed of her U.S. citizenship. She became aware of the existence of a highly privileged Guatemalan upper class, of guerrilla warfare in Guatemala's eastern mountains, and, most significantly, of the fear, envy, and hatred that divided the country's upper and lower classes. As Powers learned, Diana also could not help noticing that most of the simple wooden boxes sold as coffins in the local market were child-sized.[45]

Her reaction to this misery was to shun whatever small comforts, such as electricity or running water, that she had allowed herself previously. She also ended her escapes to the Mayan Inn, a tourist hotel with a distinctly Spanish colonial atmosphere. During this same period, she met Alan Howard, a Fulbright Scholar who was conducting research on Guatemala's federal prison. Howard disdained reformist programs like VISA which, he claimed, served only to dampen the political rage that precipitates revolution. He thus emphasized to Diana that she was "only delaying the revolution."[46]

She came to embrace Howard's view that the best way to improve the plight of the poor was to overthrow the capitalist system itself. Powers recounts one particularly vivid episode in Diana's psychopolitical evolution: "Out walking with Howard on one occasion, she stopped by a stream used by the Indians for drinking. Diana pointed to the ascarid worms in the water and began to cry. All the doctors in America might come to Guatemala, but the Indians would have to go on drinking the water. It was wrong, she felt, and when things were wrong they had to be changed."[47] She began to question the role of the United States in fostering neoimperialism through the support of a distinct comprador, or commercial, class and alleged Central Intelligence Agency involvement in a 1954 coup, which toppled an elected leftist government.[48]

The outlines of Diana's emerging sense of narcissistic disappointment may be observed when her family visited Guatemala during early 1964. As Powers reports, she demanded that they stay at a cheap hotel rather than at the Mayan Inn. She worried about the visit for weeks in advance and dreaded the image that her wealthy family might convey in Chichicastenango. During their stay, her newfound political views collided with those of her father.[49]

A short time before leaving Guatemala in 1965, Diana received a job offer from an Agency for International Development (AID) official impressed by her fluent Spanish. Although flattered by the overture, she demurred, for at this juncture in her life she "felt [that] it was senseless to help the victims of a cruel system when the system itself might be changed. . . . She had lost her old conception of herself, but had not yet replaced it with a new one. She returned to America disillusioned, but still unformed."[50] Upon her return to Illinois, her family and friends detected a marked change in her temperament and mood. She seemed to have both saddened and matured, and she was nervous about living in her parents' mansion. Clearly, Diana's experience in Guatemala had had a profound effect upon this once-faithful daughter of privilege.

After a brief visit to Philadelphia, where she first had been startled by the realities of America's social ills, Diana enrolled in a graduate program in education at the University of Michigan. She soon became acquainted with members of the Ann Arbor SDS and, in the summer of 1966, returned to Guatemala for a brief visit. Through the assistance of Alan Howard she met with leaders of the guerrilla group, Fuerzas Rebeldes Armas (FRA), which, somewhat ironically, was financing its efforts through the kidnappings of the wives and children of wealthy families. This secret meeting suggested to Diana that future relationships between American and Guatemalan revolutionaries might serve a useful purpose.[51]

In the fall of 1966, Diana began to teach at the Ann Arbor Children's Community School (CCS). It had been founded upon generally permissive principles: children were allowed to do as they pleased, and learning was based upon spontaneity rather than competition. It was at CCS that Diana met her longtime companion and lover, Bill Ayers, who, like Diana, had begun to reject his highly privileged background. The pair was strongly committed to progressive education and CCS and worked many extra hours with its children. As Powers comments, Diana's two years at CCS "were among the happiest of her life," for she and Bill believed that they were a part of a new generation that would revitalize their society.[52]

Like her experience in Guatemala, however, Diana became bitterly disillusioned with the overall logic and morality of what she was doing. The school had been burdened from the start by official harassment and by opposition from those black parents whose children had failed to learn to read while attending CCS. Diana and Bill blamed not these parents but rather the public officials who had held the school to an unusually strict standard of accountability. As Powers observes, the "bitterly frustrating experience" that Diana had endured in Guatemala reappeared at CCS. The result was that she and Bill came to focus their mutually shared narcissistic disappointment upon "*the system* . . . which had created things as they were and which had to be torn apart." The two became even more intensely active in SDS and alienated from their families.[53]

The year 1968 was one of intense radicalization for Diana and Bill. Although only peripherally involved with SDS for two years, they attained cadre status in the organization by the conclusion of that tumultuous year. The issue of the Vietnam War, a primary impetus toward violent confrontation at the Chicago Democratic Convention, had become an obsession of the New Left after the bloody but inconclusive Tet offensive of early 1968. The more militant faction of SDS, led by Bill, Diana, and others, argued in favor of radical action rather than theories of reform. The fiery events in Chicago tended to buttress this stand, for, as Powers reports, the rioting there "permanently changed the political attitudes of Bill and Diana." After Bill was clubbed severely by police, Diana called her sister to tell her that she and Bill had to leave Chicago. As Diana put it, "It's getting too rough."[54]

Her emerging militance was strengthened further when a massive occupation of the Michigan State University administration building, which she had helped organize, was ended upon the intervention of the East Lansing police. Only days later the joint office of the Radical Education Project and SDS in Ann

Arbor was burglarized. Diana and Bill felt strongly that this break-in was an official act and that repression was finally beginning.[55]

The birth of the Weathermen in the spring of 1969 coincided with the deterioration, and eventual demise, of Diana's relationship with Bill. The latter, a habitual womanizer, long ago had rejected what he and many other Weathermen deemed—perhaps conveniently—the "bourgeois trait of monogamy." At about this time, Ayers had begun to spend more and more time with Bernardine Dohrn, a hard-nosed Weathermen member quite unlike the gentle Diana. According to Powers's interview with a close female friend of Diana's, Diana had related to her that she had left Ann Arbor for several days. When she returned, Bill "calmly told her he had slept with a different girl every day she had been gone." Diana then confessed to her friend that she "tried to convince herself it didn't matter, but that the thought hurt anyhow."[56] Hence, "for Diana . . . the revolution had replaced everything else. She rarely saw her family; she had abandoned teaching; she had little in common with her old friends; Bill was drifting away. Politics was Diana's life. Having so little that was her own, she was prepared to give everything for the revolution."[57] By this point, her political discussions with her father and old friends had become extremely acrimonious.[58]

Her revolutionary zeal was reinforced even further by events throughout 1969. These included her attendance at a summer meeting between the Weathermen, other American radicals, and Communist representatives from North and South Vietnam in Cuba, her participation in a march on a Chicago draft board, and the Days of Rage disorder. Diana was arrested by Chicago police for her part in the march and was bailed out by her father; as for the Days of Rage, she was elated but frightened.[59]

She then left for Dwight and arrived at her parents' home with one of her fellow Weathermen. There then occurred a cryptic and telling exchange between Diana and her mother: "In her loving but politically inarticulate way [Mrs. Oughton] tried to talk Diana into leaving the organization. 'But honey,' she said, 'you're only going to make things worse. You're only going to get yourself killed.' Diana did not want to argue the point. 'It's the only way, Mummy,' she said firmly. 'It's the only way.' "[60] Her visit to Dwight during Christmas 1969 would be the last time she saw her family.

On February 4, 1970, Diana made a court appearance stemming from her arrest during the Days of Rage. When her name was called out, the judge turned around and asked: "Are you related to Jim Oughton, the legislator?" As Powers reports, Diana, with a smile of amusement, admitted the relationship. She was then fined $450 and released. That same day she met an old friend, Karin Rosenberg, who later would describe Diana's appearance to Powers: "Karin had grown accustomed to seeing Diana thin and weary, but this time she was drawn to the point of illness, her cheekbones painfully high, her long fingers almost skeletal, her hair a dead, dirty blond. Diana looked not just tired, but on the edge of exhaustion; not just underfed, but starved."[61]

Like Susan Stern, Diana soon made the decision to go underground and become a political terrorist. And, like Susan, she effected a profound—albeit not quite so dramatic—wrenching and irrevocable rejection of her old identity. She sent her sister Carol a large envelope marked N'OUVREZ PAS (Do Not Open): "Inside were letters from old friends, including the priests she had known in Guatemala; an address book; pages from a 1969 appointment book; documents about the family farm corporation; scraps of paper with names and addresses; everything, in short, which conceivably could have been used . . . to identify her."[62] She then traveled to a New York City townhouse apartment owned by the father of Cathy Wilkerson, a member of the Weathermen. On March 2, 1970, another Weathermen member delivered 100 pounds of dynamite to the apartment. According to Powers, Diana and Terry Robbins, also a Weatherman, began to construct bombs. Either Diana or Robbins then placed a wire in the wrong place. Diana, Robbins, and a third man, Ted Gold, died in the massive explosion. Four pipe bombs, each twelve inches in diameter and packed with dynamite, were later uncovered by detectives working at the scene. Six days later, nearly simultaneous bombings rocked corporate offices in three New York City locations.[63]

Thomas Powers, in a trenchant summary of Diana's tragic decision to become a political terrorist, observes that "in Dwight, Diana had hated being rich; in Guatemala, she had hated being an American; in the Weathermen she finally came to hate herself.

How else could she have tried so desperately to destroy everything that she was?"[64] Why, indeed?

Unlike Susan Stern, Diana Oughton's psychological predisposition toward political terrorism appears to have been fostered
by a combination of narcissistic injury and narcissistic disappointment. The overriding psychoanalytical factor underlying
Diana's brief career as a political terrorist, however, seems to
have been a deep-seated narcissistic disappointment in her family and, by extension, herself. I shall consider first the nature and
sources of her narcissistic injuries.

Those narcissistic injuries endured by Diana seem to have
resulted from her object relations with a significant other, her
longtime companion and lover, Bill Ayers. Although Ayers
endeavored to rationalize his many affairs as a rejection of
"bourgeois monogamy," Diana perceived his inveterate womanizing as a rejection of her. Indeed, her decision to go completely
underground came very shortly after her conclusion that Ayers,
her one truly intimate companion, had left her for Bernardine
Dohrn.

The most critical psychoanalytic factor in Diana's embrace of
political terrorism, nevertheless, seems to have been her profound narcissistic disappointment in her family and, by extension,
herself. This narcissistic disappointment was clearly engendered
by her extreme and humiliating disillusionment with 1) those
previously respected and trusted others whose standards and
beliefs had helped comprise her own ego ideal, and 2) herself, for
ever having embraced those standards and beliefs.

It is clear that Diana had come to internalize very strongly her
family's standards, beliefs, and sense of social conscience as her
own. This process was initiated both by her father's strong-
willed presence and what the Oughton family as a whole had
long stood for—generations of generous philanthropy and civic
achievement. The young Diana was thus a "perfect" child, an
unfailing model for her sisters to emulate. By her early college
years, she had become a staunch midwestern Republican, a
devoted Nixon supporter, and an outspoken critic of the Social
Security system.

Gradually, however, Diana began to shed her social and
political beliefs, if not her firm sense of social conscience. She

became involved in an urgently needed remedial reading program for black children in the Philadelphia ghetto, worked in a black voter-registration campaign in Maryland, and read John Howard Griffin's powerful book, *Black Like Me*. What most thoroughly transformed Diana Oughton, however, was her VISA work in Guatemala, for it was there that she, through both her own observations and the relentless tutelage of Alan Howard, came to the startling conviction that U.S. political and economic interests were chiefly responsible for the frightful impoverishment of the Third World. Proceeding further, Diana was compelled to draw an obvious connection between the miseries of the Third World, her own nation, her social class, her family, and herself.

It was thus in Guatemala that Diana, horrified that the recipients of her beneficence held such hatred for *yanqui* wealth and power, first began to suffer a sense of disgrace at being an American citizen. Indeed, it was on the banks of a worm-infested stream used by the Indians for drinking that her narcissistic rage first manifested itself. Yet, ironically, the tyrannical dictates of her overly grandiose ego ideal would cause her to spurn and discredit nearly everything else that her nation, her class, her family, and she herself had embraced. Such ego ideal-induced narcissistic disappointment was clearly evident in Diana's extreme self-denial.

Her narcissistic disappointment intensified following her return to the United States. Moreover, her involvement with the Ann Arbor Children's Community School enabled her to focus her narcissistic disappointment upon a larger object—society and the system. That narcissistic disappointment would be manifested not only by Diana's leadership in SDS and the Weathermen but also by an almost complete rejection of the family and social class that she had come to perceive as the very bedrock of that system.

Like Susan Stern, Diana Oughton's establishment, assumption, and maintenance of a new, as-if other pseudoidentity was evident in a willful rejection of her old self. Thus, shortly after making her fateful decision to go underground and become a political terrorist, she sent her sister, Carol, a large envelope containing anything that might be used to identify her.

Notes

1. Many analysts of political terrorism try to differentiate between "first," "second," and even "third" and "fourth generation" political terrorist groups. For more on the first-generation political terrorism of the Vietnam War era see especially Laqueur, *Terrorism*, 205–13; Stephen Goode, *Affluent Revolutionaries* (New York: New Viewpoints, 1974), 1–8; Stephen Spender, *The Year of the Young Rebels* (New York: Random House, 1968); Jane Alpert, *Growing Up Underground* (New York: Morrow, 1981); and Ellen Frankfurt, *Kathy Boudin and the Dance of Death* (New York: Stein and Day, 1983).

2. The Weathermen ultimately changed their name to the Weather Underground, due to the perceived sexist connotations of the term "Weathermen." The Weather Underground underwent several of the generational transformations noted above.

3. Susan Stern, *With the Weathermen* (Garden City, NY: Doubleday, 1975), 240, 243–45.

4. Other such autobiographies might include, for example, Vallières, *White Niggers*, and Michael Baumann, *Terror or Love?* (New York: Grove Press, 1977).

5. Unlike Vallières, for example.

6. Stern, *With the Weathermen*, 100–101.

7. Ibid., 101.

8. Ibid., 223–24.

9. Ibid., 244, 147, 148.

10. Ibid., 101.

11. Ibid., 1.

12. Ibid., 2.

13. Ibid., 3.

14. Ibid., 101–2.

15. Ibid., 9.

16. Ibid., 3.

17. Ibid., 11.

18. Ibid., 12.

19. Ibid.

20. Ibid., 13–16.

21. Ibid., 23, 24–25, 27 (emphasis in original).

22. Ibid., 32, 40.

23. Ibid., 49.

24. Ibid., 72, 87.

25. See ibid., 90–93.

26. Ibid., 128.

27. Ibid., 134, 135. Additional accounts of this final rampage through the streets of Chicago may be found in Goode, *Affluent Revolutionaries*, 55–56; and Tom Thomas, "The Second Battle of Chicago," in Harold Jacobs, ed., *Weatherman* (Palo Alto, CA: Ramparts Press, 1970), 201–4.

28. Stern, *With the Weathermen*, 148.

29. Ibid., 204 (emphasis in original). Fred Hampton and Mark Clark, two members of the radical Black Panther party, were killed under mysterious circumstances during a predawn police raid in Chicago on December 4, 1969.

30. See ibid., 173–252.

31. See ibid., 240–45.
32. See ibid., 255, 262.
33. Ibid., 227–359.
34. Ibid., 354, 355.
35. See Robin Morgan, *The Demon Lover* (New York: W. W. Norton, 1989), 237.
36. Thomas Powers, *Diana* (Boston: Houghton Mifflin, 1971), 11.
37. See ibid., 10–11.
38. Ibid., 12–13.
39. Ibid., 13.
40. Ibid.
41. Ibid., 14, 15, 21.
42. Ibid., 26.
43. See ibid., 30–35.
44. Ibid., 35.
45. Ibid., 38, 39.
46. Ibid., 40–42.
47. Ibid., 43.
48. See ibid., 44–45.
49. Ibid., 46.
50. Ibid., 54.
51. Ibid., 56–59.
52. Ibid., 63. Ayers's father was chairman of Commonwealth Edison of Chicago and also a trustee of Northwestern University. For more on Ayers's background see ibid., 60.
53. Ibid., 72 (emphasis in original).
54. Ibid., 84.
55. Ibid., 107.
56. Ibid., 74.
57. Ibid., 117.
58. See ibid., 94–100.
59. Ibid., 130, 157–58.
60. Ibid., 158.
61. Ibid., 175.
62. Ibid., 179.
63. Ibid., 3, 183.
64. Ibid., 182.

CHAPTER FIVE

"I'm that Nigger":
Donald DeFreeze

Donald DeFreeze and Patricia Soltysik represent two of the best-known members of the Symbionese Liberation Army (SLA), a California-based political terrorist group whose kidnapping and recruitment of heiress Patricia Hearst in 1974 received enormous media attention. As Walter Laqueur laments, the SLA "attained worldwide notoriety." And indeed, the activities, rhetoric, and motivations of the SLA have been the object of extensive academic, journalistic, and governmental interest. Hence, the case-study literature on the membership of the Symbionese Liberation Army represents a virtual embarrassment of riches.[1]

In his study of the terrorist organizational profile, Thomas Strentz asserts that Donald DeFreeze represents the very prototype of one kind of political terrorist: the opportunist. Strentz suggests that the opportunist is typically a product of both early childhood and family experiences and the prison subculture, which make him—for the opportunist role is typically populated by males— "oblivious to the needs of others and unencumbered by the capacity to feel guilt or empathy." What were DeFreeze's early childhood, family, and prison experiences like? What effect did his personal background and psychological evolution have on his ultimate decision to become a political terrorist?[2]

Donald David DeFreeze was the oldest of eight children born to an aspiring black couple, a toolmaker and a nurse, in the mid-1940s in Cleveland, Ohio. According to Les Payne and Tim

75

Findley, the upwardly mobile DeFreeze family was deeply riven by the alcoholism, impatience, violent abusiveness, and "rowdy rages" of the father, Louis. As Payne and Findley observe, "Louis was one of the many black men who, finding themselves powerless in the larger society, vent their rage on their families; rabbits in the outside world, but lions at home."[3]

Young Donald was the most common target of his father's rampages. Due to the many scars of these sessions, the boy frequently would absent himself from school. Payne and Findley offer a portrait of a solitary, sensitive, moody youth who "passed scarcely noticed on the black mean streets of Cleveland." Indeed, DeFreeze's primary-school teachers and fellow pupils have very little recollection of the troubled adolescent.[4]

Despite an otherwise low social profile, DeFreeze was in nearly constant trouble with the law. Following his arrest for possession of various weapons, including a shotgun, a knife, and a homemade bomb, the then fourteen-year-old DeFreeze revealed his nightmarish family background to a state psychiatrist. In an official report, that psychiatrist verified these complaints: "DeFreeze states father tried to kill him three times. Used to inflict inhuman punishment—hit him with hammers, baseball bats, etc. He shows areas on head where he was struck and had to receive sutures. Every time he went to the hospital, his father told them he just got hurt. The time he was picked up with the gun, he had planned to shoot father who had been mistreating him."[5] The teenager also reported that his father had broken his arm three times. He was ultimately assigned to a long string of foster homes, reform schools, city jails, and state prisons. By age seventeen, DeFreeze was a boys' school dropout with fifteen felony arrests.[6]

Later, in 1970, in a rambling letter to California State Supreme Court Judge William Ritzi that was intended to help him to avoid another return to prison for parole violations, DeFreeze presented the following extraordinary account of his life:

> I am going to talk to you truthfully and like I am talking to God. I will tell you things that no one has ever before know.
> To Start a story of a mans life you can start at the end, but at the start, this start will begin at the age of Sixteen.
> At that age, I had Just gotten out of a boys school in New York after doing 2 1/2 years for braking into a Parking Meter

and for stealing a car, I remember the Judge said that he was sending me to Jail for boys because he said it was the best place for me. I was sixteen at the time and didn't have a home, life in the little prison as we called it, was nothing but fear and hate, day in and day out, the hate was madening, the only safe place was your cell. . . . I had only two frights, if you can call them frights, I never did win. It was funny but the frights were over the fact that I would not be part of any of the gangs, black or white. I wanted to be friends with everyone, this the other inmates would not allow, they would try to make me fright, but I always got around them somehow, they even tried to make a homosexual out of me, I got around this to. After 2 1/2 years I found myself hated by many of the boys there.

When I got out of jail, people just could not believe I had ever been to jail. I worked hard, I didn't drink or any pills nor did I curse. . . . But I was still lonely. I didn't love anyone or did any one love. I had a few girl friends but as soon as there mother found out I had been to Jail, that was the end.

Then one day I met my wife Glory, she was nice and lovely, I fell in love with her I think. . . . We had just met one month before we were married. My wife had three kids already when I met her.

We were married and things were lovely. . . . Then seven months later I came home sooner than I do most of the time from work and she and a old boy friend had just had relations. I was very mad and very hurt. . . . Then one day I found out that none of my kids had the same father and that she had never been married.

I thought that if we had kids or a baby we would be closer, but as soon as the baby was born it was the same thing. I had begun to drink very deeply, but I was trying to put up with her and hope that she would change.

But as the years went by she never did and she told me that she had been to see her boy friend and that she wanted a divorce because I was not taking care of her and the kids good enough, I was never so mad in my life. . . . I could have killed her, but I didn't. I through her out of the house and I got a saw and hammer and completely destroyed everything I ever bought her and I mean everything!

For months later she begged me to take her back and she said she had made a mistake and that she really loved me. I was weak again. . . . I took her back. . . . But I couldn't face anyone any more. I started drinking more and more and staying at my job late. . . . I started playing with guns and firer works and dogs and cars. Just anything to get away from life. . . . I finely got into trouble with the Police for shooting off a rifle in my basement and for a bomb I had made out of about 30 firer works from forth of July.

I told my wife I would forget all that she had did to me. . . . But I was wrong again. I started playing with guns, drinking, pills but this time more than I had ever before did. I was arrested again and again for guns or bombs. I don't really understand what I was doing. She wanted nice things and I was working and buying and selling guns and the next thing I knew I had become a thief. . . .

You sent me to Chino [a California prison] and I lied to them and didn't tell them all the truth. They think I am nuts. . . . But you should not have never sent me back to her. The day after I got home she told me she had had Six relations with some man she meant on the street when I was in Chino. . . .

Sir Don't send me to prison again, I am not a crook or a thief nor am I crazy. I hope you will believe me. . . . Sir, even if you don't ever call me back or want to see me again Thank you for all you have done and all I can say is God Bless you.[7]

Partially on the basis of this letter, Judge Ritzi, deciding that DeFreeze was too emotionally disturbed to remain a free man, returned him to prison.[8]

Many of the basic facts of the letter are correct. However, DeFreeze had failed to mention that, after less than a year of marriage, he had had to make a court appearance to answer a charge that he had deserted his family. Following a reconciliation with his wife, Gloria, in 1965, the DeFreeze family moved to Los Angeles and settled in Compton, a neighborhood south of Watts. That same year, Watts, the major black ghetto of Los Angeles, sustained one of the most severe racial riots in American history.[9]

DeFreeze took full advantage of the widespread white fear that had been aroused by the bloody rioting and its aftermath by leading a double life as violent criminal and opportunistic, manipulative police informant tied to the Los Angeles Police Department's Black Desk and Criminal Conspiracy Section (CCS). On a minimum of six occasions, felony charges stemming from his possession of bombs, handguns, a semiautomatic rifle, an eight-inch dagger, a hand grenade, and a burglary kit were dismissed despite a California Department of Corrections psychiatric report, which characterized DeFreeze as "an emotionally confused and conflicting young man with deep-rooted feelings of inadequacy. . . . He seems to have a fascination with regard to firearms and explosives . . . which makes him dangerous."[10] As David Boulton observes, "With every instance that demonstrated his apparent immunity to the law, DeFreeze's sense of invincibility grew stronger."[11]

He next robbed a woman at gunpoint of a $1,000 check, which he then attempted to cash at a Los Angeles bank. After shooting a suspicious teller, who had sounded an alarm, DeFreeze again was arrested. The Los Angeles Police Department finally disowned DeFreeze, who threatened to reveal the operations of the Black Desk and CCS. Nevertheless, he was brought to trial. As Boulton notes:

> A report from the DA's office described him as "a high risk danger to society" who, if given his freedom, "will return to his same violent career." The report ventured the opinion that "this defendant will eventually kill someone," since his actions indicated "a total lack of regard for human life." DeFreeze was dispatched for an indefinite stay in the psychiatric facility at Vacaville. There he gave himself the African name Mtume and wrote long letters to his judges, one of which warned: "You can smile and laugh at me and call me a fool for you think the Power of my Life is in your hands. But your power my God will take. For I am not alone."[12]

The now-discarded police informant's stay at Vacaville, a state medical facility south of San Francisco, served as an incidental means through which DeFreeze would learn to justify his actions, and his perceived exploitation by authorities, through political rhetoric. He participated eagerly in the Black Cultural Association (BCA), a prison program that sponsored semiweekly classes under the direction of Colston Westbrook, black studies professor at the University of California at Berkeley. The BCA's tutorials were very appealing to men like DeFreeze, for they offered a revolutionary context to these black prisoners' own perceived socioeconomic plight. As Boulton explains, the black prisoners' "own violent actions could be rationalised by a theory of black repression and justified as proper retribution against an oppressive white society." Hence, "revolution gave prison life a meaning."[13]

Prison officials allowed the BCA to bring in outside activists to meet with the black prisoners and to conduct frequent study sessions. Among these outsiders were seven future members of the Symbionese Liberation Army: Patricia Soltysik—a Berkeley dropout, bisexual, and daughter of a prosperous California chemist; Camilla Hall—a former student at the University of Minnesota, Berkeley resident, daughter of a Lutheran missionary, and lover of Patricia Soltysik; Willie Wolfe—a Berkeley student of Westbrook, son of a wealthy Pennsylvania anesthesiologist, and committed pacifist; Russell Little—a former student at the University of Florida, son of a retired Navy civilian employee, and Berkeley radical; Bill Harris—a graduate of Indiana University, stepson of a U.S. Air Force colonel, former U.S. Marine, and Vietnam veteran; Emily Harris—an Indiana University graduate, daughter of a wealthy Chicago consulting engineer, radical feminist, and wife of Bill Harris; and Angela Atwood—an Indiana University graduate, daughter of a New Jersey Teamsters Union business manager, and radical feminist.[14]

DeFreeze, who quickly formed his own political clique within the BCA, became a source of intense appeal for the previously sheltered Wolfe and Little, who became leading enthusiasts in DeFreeze's faction, "fascinated by the man's violent rhetoric and defiant, compelling sense of style." DeFreeze dropped the pseudonym "Mtume" and adopted what ultimately became his SLA nom de guerre, "Cinque." He pronounced his new name "sink-you," or "sin" for short.[15]

Following a schism between DeFreeze's own largely white clique and other black inmates, Cinque was allowed to form his own subgroup under the BCA's auspices. That organization, Unisight, actually presaged the formation of the SLA. Unisight examined carefully the terrorist tactics of the Weathermen and preached vaguely of political and racial unity. And, like the SLA, Unisight's official symbol was a menacing, seven-headed cobra.[16]

In December 1972, DeFreeze was transferred from Vacaville to Soledad, a California state maximum-security prison. On March 5, 1973, he somehow escaped. His flight hardly could be considered very long in the planning, for he had been escorted unexpectedly that very day to the prison's abandoned south section. A short time after midnight, DeFreeze's one guard left him alone, and he mysteriously escaped over Soledad's walls.[17]

Sometime during the spring of 1973, DeFreeze moved into a house in Oakland with Patricia Soltysik and Nancy Ling Perry.

Given his previous discussions with other, soon-to-be SLA members Hall, Wolfe, Little, Atwood, and the Harrises at Vacaville, the formation of the group would soon be complete. The stage, therefore, had been set for one of the most extraordinary episodes in the annals of American political terrorism—the formation of the Symbionese Liberation Army, the bizarre assassination of Oakland school superintendent Marcus Foster, and the Patricia Hearst saga.[18]

Following the completion of the SLA's codes of war sometime during the fall of 1973, the group selected its first target and began to go underground. Shortly thereafter, that target, Marcus Foster, was ambushed and shot by Perry, Little, and Joseph Remiro. Foster, who died en route to the hospital, had been fired upon by cyanide-laced bullets. Remiro and Little were arrested for the crime in about two months. Prison escapee DeFreeze would emerge only later, during the Patricia Hearst episode. In the meantime, the group issued two communiqués to the news media in order to justify the attack.[19]

Only a few weeks after the Foster assassination, the arrest of Remiro and Little, and the issuance of the SLA's two communiqués, DeFreeze and several other SLA members put into action the first of a dramatic series of events for which the group is most closely associated—the February 4, 1974, kidnapping of Patricia Hearst, the daughter of wealthy publisher Randolph Hearst. In his memoirs of the kidnapping and its stirring aftermath, Steven Weed, her former fiancé and live-in boyfriend, recounted DeFreeze's role in the event. According to Weed, several SLA members gained access to the couple's apartment when a female member of the group, feigning car trouble, asked to use the telephone:

> Suddenly, two black men with carbines were pushing their way past her, crowding us back into the hallway and ordering us to get down. . . . It was a military maneuver. Unlike a mugging or a robbery, I had a feeling that, given the slightest excuse, they might blow our heads off. . . . I was jolted by a couple of blows, then went face down in the hallway, my head toward the door, as the second man—DeFreeze—pushed Patty into the kitchen. . . . I could see DeFreeze's legs, flashes of Patty's blue bathrobe, and a rope trailing across the floor. "Stop struggling or I'll have to knock you out," I heard him tell her. . . . [Upon leaving the apartment,] DeFreeze . . . let go [a] burst of gunfire.[20]

Soon after the kidnapping the SLA released a communiqué comprised of a cassette recording and a rambling eight-page letter emblazoned by the group's symbol—the seven-headed cobra and the designation "S.L.A."—to Berkeley underground radio station KPFA. On the cassette, DeFreeze identified himself as General Field Marshal Cinque and intoned the SLA watchword, "To those who would bear the hopes and future of our people, let the voice of their guns express the words of freedom." He stated that the Symbionese War Council had ordered him to announce that its prisoner of war was safe, and that the group's sworn goal was to "liberate the oppressed people of this nation." In endeavoring to justify the SLA's specific choice of kidnap target, he then declared that

> Randolph Hearst is the corporate chairman of the fascist media empire of the ultraright Hearst Corporation, which is one of the largest propaganda institutions of this present military dictatorship of the militarily armed corporate state that we now live under in this nation. . . . Mrs. Randolph A. Hearst is a member of the University of California Board of Regents. . . . [The university is] one of California's largest foreign investors [that] supports through its investments the murder of thousands of black women and children of Mozambique, Angola, and Rhodesia, murder designed to destroy the spirit that all humanity longs for.[21]

According to Weed, who listened to the broadcast recording with the Hearst family,

> Cinque stated that before any negotiations for Patty's release took place the Hearsts were to show a gesture of good faith "in the form of food for the needy and unemployed." In closing he added that he too was a father and held a "high moral value to life," but that he was quite willing "to carry out the execution of your daughter to save the life of starving men, women and children of every race. . . . Let it be known," he said, "that even in death we will win, for the very ashes of this fascist nation will mark our very graves."[22]

Then, after a brief message by Patricia Hearst, who maintained that she was not being abused by her captors, came DeFreeze's final warning: "What happens to your daughter will be totally your responsibility . . . her life and the blood of that life will be on your hands only." Weed further relates that the SLA's good-faith ultimatum demanded "$70 worth of food for every person in the state who held a welfare card, social security card, pension card, almost any kind of card." The cost to the Hearsts of this gesture was estimated to be in the hundreds of millions of dollars.[23]

On February 17 a tape recording from the SLA was delivered to the Hearst family. The recorded voice of Patricia insisted that she was "still okay" but that some accession to the SLA's demands was necessary. DeFreeze, alluding to the group's purported beneficence, omnipotence, and omniscience, then added a final warning: "People are awaiting your gesture. You may rest assured that we are quite able to assess the extent of your sincerity in this matter. . . . We are quite aware of the needs of the people."[24]

After extensive consultations, Randolph Hearst offered to donate $2 million to a food-giveaway program administered by the People In Need (PIN) operation. In a February 17 communiqué, DeFreeze angrily rejected the Hearst counteroffer. As Weed recalls:

> Fired with hatred and rage, [Cinque] spat at us and all our efforts, laid waste to any hopes we had. . . . *Cinque* assaulted us directly. He said he knew us and we knew him. His hood had been removed, his picture plastered across the front page of every newspaper in the country, and now, listening to this tape, we were face to face with him. . . . "Greetings to the people," the communique began. "General Field Marshal Cinque speaking." In a controlled voice he announced that the "SLA War Council and the Court of the People" had directed him to clarify "the request of the people." This amounted to a total, across-the-board denunciation of Mr. Hearst's counteroffer.[25]

Excoriating the Hearst empire and Randolph Hearst's "hundreds and hundreds of millions" of dollars, DeFreeze declared that, with friends like Howard Hughes and the shah of Iran, even an accession to the SLA's original ransom demands would create no financial hardship. Endeavoring to justify the SLA's mission, DeFreeze also made the following plea:

> Cry out! Cry out for all the millions of children of all races who are starving and dying now, and not just cry out for the safety of one human being who just happens to be the daughter of an enemy of the People. Fight and cry out in the defense of millions and save the children, and by this action you will save also the life of one who has never seen the robbed or knew that the riches of her life were the spoils of the robber and the murderer.[26]

Then, in a voice betraying his self-righteous rage, DeFreeze began to read, apparently from his own writing, his memorable retort to the news media's disclosure of his old identity:

> You do, indeed, know me. You have always known me. I'm the nigger you have hunted and feared night and day. I'm that nigger that is no longer just hunted, robbed, and murdered. I'm the nigger that hunts you now. Yes, you know me. You know us all. You know me, I'm the wetback. You know me, I'm the gook, the broad, the servant, the spik. Yes, you know me. You know us all and we know you—the oppressor, murderer, and robber. And you have hunted and robbed and exploited us all. And we will not compromise the freedom of our children. . . . Death to the fascist insect, that preys upon the life of the people.[27]

Despite DeFreeze's bitter threats and the SLA's collective wrath toward any compromise with the Hearsts, PIN's food-giveaway program got under way. Formally conceding to the SLA's demands, the makeshift organization announced its distribution sites through both the print and electronic media. Due to administrative problems, one such distribution center, a food bank in East Oakland, suffered a full-scale, bloody riot, and, as Weed reports, "chaos prevailed at other food banks as well."[28]

Although future PIN food giveaways were more successfully accomplished, the SLA maintained its bitter attacks on the program and on the Hearsts' efforts. DeFreeze continued his attempts to justify what the SLA was doing: "I call upon the people to join the Federation . . . answering this call to arms with the sound of your guns and your commitment to save the children." Most disturbing and puzzling, however, were Patricia Hearst's own increasingly accusatory SLA-taped statements against her family and fiancé.[29]

The subject of the next communiqué proved to be the most stunning development in the entire drama. Declaring that she had become a full-fledged convert to the SLA's cause, Patricia Hearst announced that, like every other member of the SLA, she had adopted a pseudonym, "Tania." She denounced her father, whom she characterized as a corporate liar, and praised the SLA's political goals. Included with the taped communiqué was a photograph of the group's latest recruit, dressed as a guerrilla and holding a semiautomatic rifle in a combat stance in front of an SLA flag. Not surprisingly, the SLA's ransom demands ended abruptly.[30]

The group's next act would be a bank assault, a public action right out of Remiro's confiscated copy of Carlos Marighella's famous terrorist handbook, "Minimanual of the Urban Guerrilla." This "expropriation of governmental resources," to use Marighella's own term, was launched against a San Francisco branch of the Hibernia Bank:

> At 9:50 five people ran single file to the bank door, Patty [Hearst] in the lead. . . . Mizmoon [that is, Patricia Soltysik], Camilla Hall, Nancy Ling Perry, and DeFreeze spilled past her. . . . Perry shouted, "SLA! SLA! Get on the floor!" Then Cinque, "First motherfucker doesn't get on the floor gets his head blown off." . . . With DeFreeze covering the door, swinging his carbine back and forth, barking orders, and Patty in the middle and Camilla covering the far end of the bank, Mizmoon and Perry vaulted the tellers' windows and began emptying the drawers of cash. . . . Ducking outside, Cinque fired another burst, hitting a passerby in the stomach.[31]

Shortly after the Hibernia holdup, Patricia Hearst and the Harrises participated in an aborted shoplifting and subsequent kidnapping at Mel's, a Los Angeles sporting-goods store. A parking ticket left in an abandoned van used by Patricia and the Harrises in their flight from Mel's ultimately would spell the beginning of the end for the SLA. According to Weed, an address on the parking ticket eventually led authorities to a yellow stucco house in Compton, the Los Angeles neighborhood to which DeFreeze and his wife had first moved in 1965. That house would serve as the SLA's final hideout.[32]

The last hours of Donald DeFreeze, Patricia Soltysik, and much of the remainder of the Symbionese Liberation Army on May 17, 1974, are described in graphic detail by Weed:

> "I know I'm gonna die," [DeFreeze] told a visitor, while sipping a bottle of Boone's Farm wine, "and all my people know they will too. But we're gonna take a lot of motherfuckin' pigs with us." Tania, he said, was "real bad," but Bill Harris made a "stupid move . . . [by] blowing our cover." One of the SLA women—Cinque's "children" as he repeatedly referred to them—is remembered making sandwiches, "acting like the woman of the house," while Willie Wolfe sat on the bed twirling a pistol on his finger and Camilla Hall prepared

Molotov cocktails. . . . Meanwhile Cinque and his band were growing increasingly nervous. "There ain't that many insurance men do business around here," he was overheard to say, peeking out the window at an unmarked car. "Trish [Patricia Soltysik], we gotta get outta here. It's getting too hot." But they did not get out. When a nine-year-old boy entered the house moments later, Cinque and his comrades were loading their weapons. "Get in the bathtub if you don't want to get killed," Cinque told him.[33]

Outside the house were three eight-member Special Weapons and Tactics (SWAT) teams, armed with the most advanced and lethal weaponry, yet, "incredibly," as Weed comments, "the SLA had them outgunned." Although implored by authorities to surrender, the cornered group let loose with its massive arsenal. The SWAT teams then returned fire, and the largest domestic firefight in U.S. history was under way.[34]

The hour-long artillery battle ended when the house became completely engulfed in flames. Six bodies were recovered from the scene. Dead were Donald DeFreeze, Patricia Soltysik, Nancy Ling Perry, Angela Atwood, Willie Wolfe, and Camilla Hall. According to Los Angeles County Coroner Thomas Noguchi, DeFreeze and his band

". . . died compulsively. . . . They chose to stay under the floor as the fire burned out. In all my years as a coroner I've never seen this kind of conduct in the face of flames." . . . Based upon the concentration of smoke in the singed lungs of Willie Wolfe, Angela Atwood, [Patricia] Soltysik and DeFreeze, it appeared that in their last moments they were actually breathing flames, their gas masks melting on their faces as they burned to death. . . . Because the concentration of smoke was greatest in Cinque's lungs, Noguchi stated that he was probably the last to die, pressing the pistol to his temple and departing this life, as one writer put it, "on a swoon of highest Hitlerian rapture."[35]

In a final communiqué, Patricia Hearst offered a eulogy to each of her six comrades. Of DeFreeze she wrote:

Cinque loved the people with tenderness and respect. Cin knew that to live was to shoot straight. He was in a race with time, believing that every minute must be another step forward in the fight to save the children. He taught me virtually everything imaginable. . . . Most importantly, he taught me how to show my love for the people. . . . On February 4 [the night of her kidnapping] Cinque Mtume saved my life.[36]

The psychological background of Donald DeFreeze is conspicuously distinguished by the most profound narcissistic injuries. The roots of those injuries lie in 1) the nature of DeFreeze's object relations with significant others, chiefly his father and his wife; and 2) his response to his own actual, and perceived, role status as both prisoner and minority group member.

A typical opportunist, DeFreeze endured a nightmarish family background, demeaning marital relationship, and extremely recidivistic criminal record. He clearly suffered severe physical and emotional abuse at the hands of his unstable father, an alcoholic who had attempted to kill him on at least three occasions. DeFreeze then was assigned to a grim progression of foster homes, reform schools, city jails, and state prisons. By age seventeen, he was a boys' school dropout with fifteen felony arrests. In his lengthy, rambling entreaty to Judge Ritzi in 1970, DeFreeze himself detailed the "madening [*sic*]" existence of prison life.

In that same letter DeFreeze addressed the nature of his relationship with Gloria. Shortly after his marriage, he learned of his wife's habitual infidelity and promiscuity; indeed, DeFreeze alludes continually to Gloria's insulting rejection and manipulation of him and to the marital hardships compounded by the enforced isolation of his chronic prison confinement. Finally, DeFreeze's perceived role status as an oppressed, manipulated black ex-convict was permanently cast when the Los Angeles Police Department's Black Desk disowned him as an informant. Given, therefore, both the nature of his object relations with significant others and his reaction to his overall role status, the California Department of Corrections psychiatric report describing DeFreeze as "an emotionally confused and conflicting young man with deep-rooted feelings of inadequacy" comes as a bland understatement.

DeFreeze's narcissistic rage at these assaults to his self-esteem and sense of self-image was clearly manifested on at least three occasions. The first occurred when, at the time of his first arrest, the then fourteen-year-old DeFreeze was apprehended for illegal possession of a gun. The juvenile had planned to use the weapon to shoot his father, who, DeFreeze claimed, had broken his arm for the third time. DeFreeze's narcissistic rage also was evidenced when, after learning of his wife's continuing infidelity, he angrily threw her out of the house and destroyed everything inside. The third and most revealing manifestation of DeFreeze's "self-righteous rage" came in his "You do, indeed, know me. . . . I'm that nigger" SLA communiqué.

As General Field Marshal Cinque, DeFreeze clearly enjoyed many of the inherent psychodynamic rewards of political terrorism. For example, a psychic sense of omnipotence seems to have pervaded each of the members of the SLA. Thus, with the capture of Patricia Hearst, the group felt emboldened to demand an astonishing ransom of hundreds of millions of dollars. This sense of omnipotence—and the supposed contextual justification for the group's actions—is also evident in the SLA's rhetoric. DeFreeze's ominous threats in the group's February 17, 1974, communiqué—"Now we are the hunters that will give you no rest" and the epithetic "Death to the fascist insect, that preys upon the life of the people"—are highly illustrative.

DeFreeze's establishment, assumption, and maintenance of a new, as-if other pseudoidentity is made apparent in his choice of pseudonym: General Field Marshal Cinque. Here I might emphasize Warren Brodey's point that the existence of an as-if other pseudoidentity, which amounts to a closed learning system, must be maintained. Thus, in the SLA's February 17 communiqué, "*Cinque* assaulted us directly," for "his hood had been removed." Hence, DeFreeze, in a desperate attempt to maintain his new, as-if other pseudoidentity, prefaced his statement with the salutation, "Greetings to the people," "General Field Marshal Cinque speaking"; later in the tape DeFreeze would hurl his bitter response to his unmasking by the press: his "You do, indeed, know me," diatribe.

Notes

1. Laqueur, *Terrorism*, 209. The literature on the SLA is extremely extensive. See, for example, Hacker, *Crusaders, Criminals, Crazies*, 137–78; Thomas Strentz,

"The Terrorist Organizational Profile," in Alexander and Gleason, eds., *Behavioral and Quantitative Perspectives*, 86–104; Shana Alexander, *Anyone's Daughter* (New York: Viking, 1979); Marilyn Baker and Sally Brompton, *Exclusive!* (New York: Macmillan, 1974); David Boulton, *The Making of Tania Hearst* (London: New English Library, 1975); John Bryan, *This Soldier Still at War* (New York: Harcourt Brace Jovanovich, 1975); Patricia Campbell Hearst, *Every Secret Thing* (Garden City, NY: Doubleday, 1982); Vin McLellan and Paul Avery, *The Voices of Guns* (New York: G. P. Putnam's, 1977); Murray Miron, "Psycholinguistic Analysis of the SLA," *Assets Protection* 1 (1976); Albert Parry, *Terrorism* (New York: Vanguard, 1976), 342–64; John Pascal and Francine Pascal, *The Strange Case of Patty Hearst* (New York: New American Library, 1974); Leslie Payne and Tim Findley, *The Life and Death of the SLA* (New York: Ballantine, 1976); Robert Brainard Pearsall, *The Symbionese Liberation Army* (Amsterdam: Rodopi N. V. Keizergracht, 1974); "S. L. A. Shoots It Out," *The Economist* (May 25, 1974); Fred Soltysik, *In Search of a Sister* (New York: Bantam, 1976); U.S. Congress, House Committee on Internal Security, *The Symbionese Liberation Army*, 93d Congress, 2d sess., 1974; and Steven Weed, *My Search for Patty Hearst* (New York: Crown, 1976).

2. Strentz, "Terrorist Organizational Profile," 90, 91. For a remarkably similar psychological analysis of a political terrorist "opportunist" see my case study of Giorgio Panizzari in Richard M. Pearlstein, "Lives of Disquieting Desperation," Ph.D. diss., University of North Carolina at Chapel Hill (1986), 302–50, 483–88, 512.

3. Payne and Findley, *Life and Death*, 10.

4. Ibid., 9, 10.

5. Quoted in Boulton, *Making of Tania Hearst*, 31–32.

6. See ibid., 32; Weed, *My Search for Patty Hearst*, 204; Strentz, "Terrorist Organizational Profile," 93; and Alexander, *Anyone's Daughter*, 137.

7. This verbatim excerpt of Donald DeFreeze's letter to Judge Ritzi is quoted in Weed, *My Search for Patty Hearst*, 204–6.

8. Ibid., 206.

9. Boulton, *Making of Tania Hearst*, 32.

10. Quoted in ibid., 33. For more on DeFreeze's work as a CCS agent see Citizens Research and Investigation Committee and Louis E. Tackwood, *The Glass House Tapes* (New York: Avon, 1973).

11. Boulton, *Making of Tania Hearst*, 36.

12. Ibid.

13. Ibid., 25.

14. These biographical data have been culled from various sources on the SLA, including ibid.; McLellan and Avery, *Voices of Guns*; Weed, *My Search for Patty Hearst*; Soltysik, *In Search of a Sister*; and Alexander, *Anyone's Daughter*.

15. Boulton, *Making of Tania Hearst*, 37. DeFreeze's pseudonym, "Cinque," was, as David Boulton states, "borrowed from an African chief who led a slave rebellion in the 1830s and later, ironically, betrayed the cause of freedom by turning slaver himself." See ibid. For more on DeFreeze and the BCA see Alexander, *Anyone's Daughter*, 136.

16. Boulton, *Making of Tania Hearst*, 37–38.

17. Ibid., 38–39. Thomas Strentz comments that DeFreeze had "bargained himself into a soft, trustee-type assignment and walked away" from the maximum-security institution. See Strentz, "Terrorist Organizational Profile," 93. Vin McLellan and Paul Avery concur, asserting that DeFreeze "had been

reclassified as a minimum-security prisoner, 'trusty' status for inmates unlikely to attempt escape." See McLellan and Avery, *Voices of Guns,* 87. For more on DeFreeze's prison status see also Baker and Brompton, *Exclusive!,* 82.

18. See Weed, *My Search for Patty Hearst,* 206, 273; Strentz, "Terrorist Organizational Profile," 89; McLellan and Avery, *Voices of Guns,* 117–26, 174–80; Payne and Findley, *Life and Death,* 67–87; Alexander, *Anyone's Daughter,* 136–37; and Baker and Brompton, *Exclusive!,* 92–93.

19. See Payne and Findley, *Life and Death,* 67; Weed, *My Search for Patty Hearst,* 8; and McLellan and Avery, *Voices of Guns,* 182,512,514. Joseph Douglass, Jr., and Neil Livingstone assert that the SLA's use of cyanide-laced bullets is of particular interest: "Within the United States, the Symbionese Liberation Army flirted with the use of C/B [Chemical/Biological] weapons: The group used cyanide-dipped bullets, and authorities discovered military manuals on biological warfare in one of their safe houses." See Joseph D. Douglass, Jr., and Neil C. Livingstone, *America the Vulnerable* (Lexington, MA: Lexington, 1987), 30. The interrelationship between the individual psychology of the political terrorist and superterrorist scenarios—that is, potential chemical, biological, or nuclear terrorist incidents—will be considered in Chapter 11.

20. Weed, *My Search for Patty Hearst,* 33, 36.

21. Quoted in ibid., 114–15. For a reasonably thorough compilation of SLA statements see McLellan and Avery, *Voices of Guns,* 499–520. For a psychological analysis of these writings see Strentz, "Terrorist Organizational Profile," 89, 94; Miron, "Psycholinguistic Analysis"; and Berkeley Rice, "Between the Lines of Threatening Messages," *Psychology Today* (September 1981). According to both Murray Miron and Thomas Strentz, the many media statements made by DeFreeze were merely parrotings of chief SLA ideologue and former University of California student Nancy Ling Perry's own political rhetoric. For a psychopolitical analysis of Nancy Ling Perry see my "Lives of Disquieting Desperation," 131–49, 173–78, 469–73, 521, 529.

22. Weed, *My Search for Patty Hearst,* 115.

23. Ibid., 116.

24. Quoted in ibid., 130.

25. Ibid., 137–38 (emphasis in original).

26. Quoted in Alexander, *Anyone's Daughter,* 173. See also Weed, *My Search for Patty Hearst,* 138.

27. Quoted in ibid., 139. See also ibid., 138.

28. Ibid., 141–44, 158.

29. Ibid., 159–60.

30. Ibid., 211, 223, 225. It is widely granted that the brutal conditions of Patricia Hearst's confinement, which included weeks of isolation, rape, and relentless brainwashing sessions, were almost wholly responsible for her apparent conversion. Important, too, is the assumed influence of the Stockholm syndrome, a psychodynamic process by which hostages who share a common, perceived, and legitimate sense of danger with, and actually experience profound feelings of gratitude for having been kept alive by, their captors begin to form an emotional bond with their victimizers. For more on Patricia Hearst's experience as a kidnap victim see her autobiographical *Every Secret Thing.* For more on the Stockholm syndrome see especially Thomas Strentz, "The Stockholm Syndrome," *Annals of the New York Academy of Sciences* 347 (June 20, 1980): 137–50.

31. Weed, *My Search for Patty Hearst*, 248–49. For more on Marighella's terrorist methodology see Carlos Marighella, *For the Liberation of Brazil* (London: Penguin, 1971); and idem, "Minimanual of the Urban Guerrilla," *Tricontinental* 16 (1970): 15–56. Those readers who lack access to *Tricontinental*, a Havana journal, may refer to Walter Laqueur's abridged version of Marighella's "Minimanual" in Laqueur, ed., *Terrorism Reader*, 159–68.

32. See Weed, *My Search for Patty Hearst*, 303–10.

33. Ibid., 311.

34. Ibid., 312.

35. Ibid., 318, 320.

36. Quoted in ibid., 338.

CHAPTER SIX

From Mizmoon to Zoya: Patricia Soltysik

Known to her feminist friends as "Mizmoon" and to her Symbionese Liberation Army (SLA) confreres as "Zoya," Patricia Soltysik exemplifies the dedicated minion, rather than the ringleader, of the political terrorist group. Yet, although her informal role status within the SLA seems to have been considerably less prominent than that of Donald DeFreeze or Nancy Ling Perry, she was as zealous, loyal, and brutal as any SLA soldier. Who was she, and what psychological factors helped underlie her fanatical devotion to a political terrorist group such as the SLA?

Patricia Monique Soltysik, the third child—and first of five girls—in a family of seven offspring, was born on May 17, 1950, in Santa Barbara, California. According to the oldest, Fred, who has written a frank account of Patricia's life, *In Search of a Sister*, Patricia's father was one of nine children, only six of whom survived infancy. Her mother had had a brother and sister perish during the Second World War. According to Fred Soltysik, his parents' own, relatively early loss of their siblings played a major role in their decision to have a large number of children. Patricia's father, who became a thriving pharmacist-chemist, was brought up on a farm during the Great Depression. Her mother, a Belgian war bride whose own adolescence had been severely disrupted by the Nazi occupation of Belgium, arrived in the United States after the Second World War.[1]

Fred recalls that the large family lived a confined, tumultuous existence in an innocuously middle-class, four-bedroom house. Indeed, he comments that the family's cramped living quarters, which he termed the "sardine tin," often "simmered like a pressure cooker." Patricia and her younger sister, Susan, who shared a small bedroom with their headstrong Belgian grandmother, were packed in more so than the rest. Yet, despite the obvious need for additional living space, the urgings of Mrs. Soltysik, and the financial resources available, Patricia's father baldly refused to purchase a larger house.[2]

Center stage in the Soltysik household was occupied by the acrimonious, hateful relationship between Patricia's father and his nine dependents. As Fred points out, family meals were punctuated by "the seven children flinching in their chairs if our grumpy father as much as reached for a piece of home-made bread," for Mr. Soltysik's "swift and not so delicate hand had conditioned us all like seven Pavlovian dogs." Moreover, the children's insufferable shortage of living space served only to exacerbate these already unbearable tensions and antagonisms.[3]

Patricia and her siblings naturally craved a reasonable degree of freedom and independence. Fred recalls that he was the first to "flop out" of the "overcrowded sardine tin." Yet Patricia, as the oldest girl, was unable to replicate her brother's desperate exits from home. Her social life was constrained further by the fact that her mother, as a teenager, had not dated at all, since, as Fred points out, her adolescent contemporaries in Belgium were not allowed visits from prospective suitors without a chaperon present. Moreover, Patricia's father did not date until the overripe age of thirty. Although Fred and his younger brother, Steven, were allowed to date, Patricia's parents forbade her that same privilege. She thus had to "negotiate, fight, plead, and, in the end, cry" for permission to go out. Although Mrs. Soltysik, after soliciting Fred's counsel, eventually relented on the matter, Patricia's father withdrew from the debate. As Fred comments, Mr. Soltysik refused to accept his wife's decision to grant Patricia her freedom; indeed, his retirement from the controversy was "accompanied by one of his typical remarks, that Pat would end up at La Mirada, the local female juvenile detention school."[4]

Despite an active social life, Patricia seemed "at odds with herself, lonely, struggling for a much-needed renewal of confidence" during her frequent visits to the apartment that Fred shared with his fiancée. That much-needed confidence would not be discovered, however, during the absence of Patricia's mother in the summer of 1967. Mrs. Soltysik had arranged a six-week trip to Belgium to visit her mother, who had returned to Europe. Fred—who comments that his father already had "physically thrown me out of the house for the second time"— was extremely worried about his mother's absence, because Patricia would be responsible for the household and subject to her father's dictatorial presence. She thus viewed the approaching six weeks with genuine fear and anxiety.[5]

As Fred asserts, Patricia had good reason to dread her father's temperamental outbursts and brooding manner. Added to his unpredictable and terrifying rages was an additional psychological weapon, "the silent treatment," which "created unbearable stalemates" and "years of tense evenings." And, indeed, Patricia did not have to wait long for her father to behave in this fashion. During the hundred-mile drive to Los Angeles International Airport, he maintained himself in complete silence. Then, as Fred reports,

> When my mother and [younger sister] Michelle left to board the flight to Frankfurt, Germany, he said goodbye to Michelle only. Not a word, not a wave, nothing for my mother but her travel money contemptuously thrown to the terminal floor. The airport scene was not the first time [that] Pat witnessed our father humiliate our mother. But now she feared that it presaged her own relationship with him. She was, however, too frightened to discuss the possibility with the silent, brooding man.[6]

After a full month of Patricia, Susan, and younger sister Ninette scrubbing floors, cooking meals, and crying because they were so frightened, their father exploded. Most humiliating for Patricia, that outburst took place in front of her friends. As Fred explains, his sisters somehow had managed to convince their father to serve as chaperon for the first night of a four-day camping trip to El Capitan Beach. When Patricia and one of her friends failed to return to the camp by late evening,

> ... my father decided he wasn't "running a ghost camp" and proceeded to tear down the tent with all the camping gear and

food still in it. Amid screams from the girls present ... he packed up the cooler, the Coleman stove, and all the food he could find. He took my two sisters home and returned to find Pat. [According to Patricia,] "He came in swinging the lantern, looking for me. I ask—what is this—and why? He just said, 'Pack up, we're leaving.' I ask if we're leaving the rest of the girls alone? He shrugs like too bad—and wouldn't leave anything here for them. Had to not only completely give up, but also pack everything—including the food? God, I was pissed!" Pat vomited in her bedroom when we arrived home. And Ninette cried so much that her face was still swollen the next day.[7]

On the following evening Patricia escaped from the side door of the "sardine tin" after her father had gone to bed. Fred offers a particularly compelling account of a teenage sister in crisis. He recalls that Patricia rode her sister's bicycle and then hitchhiked to his apartment. Neither he nor his fiancée, Carol, heard her 2:00 A.M. knock on their door, and Patricia spent a miserable night with a friend: "The following morning she returned to the house and told Dad, 'We're going to the beach.' He replied, 'You either stay or get out!' Patricia said goodbye. Dad responded by viciously kicking her jacket out the door as she and Sue, both caught in the hallway, tumbled out the door to escape the blows."[8] In long discussions with his sister after these traumatic events, Fred remembers that Patricia still "hoped for ... a reasonable man for a father." She also "felt an acute need to examine and reexamine her relationship with our father" and "desperately needed a more understanding father." In expressing what Fred terms her "disappointment," she seemed reconciled to this grim reality. As Patricia wept, "I don't hate him. I feel ashamed of him." She then moved in with Fred and Carol.[9]

Susan wired her mother in Belgium and outlined the situation. Mrs. Soltysik then sent a telegram to her husband that stipulated that Patricia and Susan be at home when she returned. The two older girls, albeit very reluctantly, did come back. For the first time Mrs. Soltysik had dared to demonstrate that, although her husband remained head of the household, he had been proven wrong.[10]

By her senior year of high school, Patricia's deteriorating relationship with her father had convinced her to "search for another family." She spent much of the Christmas season with a friend's family rather than her own, in order to avoid contact with her father. Then came the final, emotional rupture between the two.[11] As Fred puts it, "In April of the last year Patricia was to spend at home, my father's rift with the family focused directly on her." She was hospitalized with a severely ruptured appendix and other complications. Although her mother and older brother behaved admirably throughout the emergency, her father turned in a shockingly neglectful performance. Informed on the golf course that Patricia was in the hospital emergency ward and that her operation was about to begin, Mr. Soltysik dispatched a chilly message: " 'At this point I see no reason for me to come.' Pat turned her head from the slab and spat, 'Well, let him go to hell.' "[12]

Mrs. Soltysik did not return to the house until several hours after Patricia's doctor announced that the operation had been successful. On their way home Fred and his mother agonized over Mr. Soltysik's conspicuous absence, and Mrs. Soltysik revealed that she regarded her marriage as crushing. As Fred states, he and his mother "both knew that my father had simply put Pat out of his mind, finished his nine holes, and returned home just before dark." Once home, Mr. Soltysik played game after game of solitaire, never once asking about his daughter's health. Then, after a particularly difficult day for Patricia, who endured a raging fever and a poorly inserted intravenous needle, Mrs. Soltysik returned, outraged to find her husband watching a television show.[13]

Although Patricia recovered physically from her medical crisis, she was emotionally devastated by the cruel behavior of her father, who had not paid her a single bedside visit. In a letter to Fred during her two-week recuperation at home, she wrote: "I guess, now that I practically died, he doesn't care too awfully much what happens to me, so all I'm ever going to bother him about is money." The fact that Patricia made this point is striking, since she had cried when her father had complained only two years earlier that all she ever approached him for was money.[14]

When Patricia matriculated at the University of California at Berkeley, her mother filed for divorce. Fred affirms that this decision, which was strongly supported by both himself and Patricia, marked his mother's rebirth. As Mrs. Soltysik, with obvious reference to the years of bitter family enmity, declared: "What a weight out of my shoulders." Yet, despite the departure of her father, Patricia's longtime tormentor's narcissistic insults would endure for the remainder of her life.[15]

Patricia then began her studies at Berkeley. She received three merit scholarships and performed fairly well academically. There appears, however, to be some contradiction. Although Fred recalls that his sister performed admirably, Marilyn Baker and Sally Brompton maintain that she "had taken on a battle she could not win," for Berkeley's students were "smarter than she."[16]

Patricia excelled socially at Berkeley. Having decided to live off campus, she quickly met a wide variety of people. Very early during her freshman year she became friendly with Gene McDaniels, a computer-science major from the Midwest. The two soon became nearly inseparable lovers.[17] In her frequent correspondence with Fred, she expressed pride in her relationship with Gene; as she herself put it, "Gene doesn't put me on a shelf." Nevertheless, she suffered severe doubts about her self-esteem and sense of self-image. As Fred comments, "She felt she ate and dressed like a slob. Her own severest critic, she also suffered from an over-sharpened sense of honesty. At this time she wrote, 'I faked everyone out, except myself, by getting into a university. Why is it I am so dissatisfied, uptight, feeling fake to myself?' "[18]

Perhaps following her mother's example, Patricia spent the summer of 1969 vacationing in Europe. She certainly must have recalled her mother's own visit to Belgium and the emotional turmoil that her absence had created. At any rate, Patricia's contact with her father had been minimized after his ignominious exile from the family. Nevertheless, she still made occasional visits to her father's hotel room which, as Fred points out, "were often painful moments": "It was common for him to call her a hippie or simply say, 'What's the use of talking?' However well she understood the reasons for his untactful and bitter remarks, they always jolted her. Hardly a meeting transpired without her crying afterward. And after the tears, she always felt the residual pain of knowing that he wallowed in self-pity and would never change."[19]

The spring semester of Patricia's sophomore year marked the threshold of her political activism. Her introduction to the political maelstrom that was Berkeley came during the famous battle between police and supporters of a university parking lot turned "People's Park." Fred recalls his sister's initial optimism, and subsequent gloom, over this seminal event. Bitterly disappointed by the clash between police and park supporters, which left one person dead and many injured, Patricia termed Berkeley "a very heavy place to be right now." As Fred discerns, this experience provided his once "superstraight" sister with a miniscenario of the protest against the Vietnam War.[20]

Patricia decided to spend the summer of 1970 in Europe despite her learning that several hundred dollars of her scholarship money would not be forthcoming. Her political perspective clearly had hardened when, while writing to her family from Italy, she stated that "we weren't successful in Berkeley and more importantly we haven't been very successful either in ending the [Vietnam] war. When dealing with a crazy man like [President Richard] Nixon and the rabid American military, there seems little we can do in a 'peaceful' sense. They must be stopped."[21] During her stay abroad, Patricia met Mary Maillot, the daughter of a famous World War II Resistance fighter, Jacques Maillot. Patricia had become familiar with Mary through the elder Maillot, a girlhood friend of Mrs. Soltysik. The two might well have married years earlier except for the need to flee a Nazi manhunt prior to the approach of the American army—and Patricia's father. In a prophetic conversation with Mary, Patricia declared that she, too, would be recognized for her role in a larger struggle: "Remember this well. I am going to become famous. I, Pat Soltysik, I shall be known over the entire world. They will speak of me in the newspapers."[22]

In addition to her evolving political consciousness, Patricia also was developing an intense interest in the feminist movement and related social issues. She began to reject her former "before consciousness" identity in favor of a new self. In her continuing correspondence with Fred, she endeavored to delineate what he describes as her "humanistic self-descriptions." As she herself put it, "I wish to make myself happy in any way"; as Fred saw it, this amounted to a "First the self" pronouncement. More significant, in light of Patricia's relationship with her father, was Fred's observation that she would "no longer . . . pander to the expectations of chauvinist males."[23]

In another of her many letters to Fred, however, Patricia revealed a decidedly unfeminist ambivalence toward her relationship with Gene McDaniels: "I'm so frightened that I won't be able to give him all my love, that one day he won't find me 'cute,' that I'll just be stupid." By the end of her junior year she and Gene were having less and less contact with one another. Patricia eventually moved out of their apartment and, in a letter to Fred, proclaimed, "Gene's done. . . . I can't stand him at all and want him and the memories out my door."[24]

Over the next year Fred became increasingly concerned by several alarming transitions in his sister's life-style. First, he was compelled to take note that her previously tentative and thoughtful feminist rhetoric had taken on a far more strident tone. Second, Fred's younger brother, Steven, brought news that she was becoming heavily involved with drugs. Third, in July 1972, Patricia informed Fred that she had legally changed her name to "Mizmoon." And finally, she dropped out of Berkeley during the fall semester of her senior year.[25]

In early 1972, Patricia met future Symbionese Liberation Army confrere Camilla Hall. The two soon commenced upon a stormy and intermittent love affair. In a few months the pair began to live together and became deeply involved in the radical, political, and social movements typical of Berkeley's Channing Way scene. Like Patricia, who had taken a janitorial job at the Berkeley Public Library, Camilla left her position as a social worker to accept a job as a gardener in a public park.[26]

Fred recalls that, upon his return to California in the fall of 1972, "I had to remind myself that I would be meeting a new sister." He discussed the Marxist tone of one of Patricia's recent letters, and her decision to have her name legally changed, with his mother. Their reaction to Patricia's metamorphosis tended to underline the narcissistic injuries inflicted upon her by her father. As Mrs. Soltysik acknowledged to Fred, "I know she's suffered a lot."[27]

Fred was able to meet his "new" sister during her weekend visit to his house. He apparently had some difficulty in addressing Patricia as Mizmoon. He discerned, nevertheless, that "Mizmoon left little doubt that she was perfectly ecstatic with her new self-image. What she thought of the old self, though, I hadn't yet fathomed. And how she viewed herself as Patricia seemed important, for I found implicit in her being able to identify with Mizmoon the suggestion that she hadn't been able to relate to Patricia."[28] A strong curiosity tempted Fred to make some gentle inquiries about Mizmoon's past life. Asked about her relationship with Gene, Mizmoon replied that he had "loved his computers more than he loved me," and that she had failed to receive the kind of loving and attention she needed. Mizmoon then launched into a harshly Marxist-feminist diatribe with a then-pregnant Carol, her sister-in-law. Mizmoon was particularly incensed, Fred recalls, at the "harassed, objectified and oppressed" role of women, particularly in capitalist societies. He recounts one particularly telling statement of his sister's: "We are not anyone's piece of ass, not anyone's chick, old lady, and not anyone's fuck."[29]

Then, in March 1973, less than one year before the Hearst kidnapping, Fred leafed through what he describes as the happiest letter he had received from his sister in several years. In a trenchant postscript Mizmoon recommended "a very good book," *The Angry Book*, by Theodore I. Rubin: "Very elucidating—I saw myself . . . holding back anger and just collecting it." Perhaps in anticipation of her short-lived career as a political terrorist, she also attempted to apply the same theme to an American society that can "suppress anger and direct releases," for, as Mizmoon put it, "a system can control people."[30]

By early 1973, Mizmoon and Camilla had split up over the issue of the former's romance with Chris Thompson, a black radical who would serve as a conduit between Mizmoon (and Camilla, after she and Mizmoon resurrected their relationship), Nancy Ling Perry, and Thompson's housemates, Willie Wolfe and Russell Little. As Mizmoon sighed, in a conversation with her mother shortly after Camilla's departure, "I'm a dazed, left lover." Through her relationship with Thompson, Wolfe, and Little, Mizmoon became involved in two prisoners' movements, including the Black Cultural Association. After Donald DeFreeze escaped from Soledad Prison, Thompson introduced him to Mizmoon, who cheerfully shared her apartment, and bed, with the future SLA leader.[31]

Upon meeting with his sister and "Cin," as DeFreeze was called, Fred found the latter to be the timely answer to Mizmoon's personal and ideological needs. DeFreeze led Fred to believe that he was a reformed pimp from New Jersey. And, indeed, Fred later would admit that his sister, who was awed by DeFreeze's knowledge of the streets, "took a lot of shit and swallowed every word."[32]

By April 1973, DeFreeze felt secure enough to move from Mizmoon's apartment to a hideout in East Oakland. Mizmoon commuted between Berkeley and East Oakland for about four weeks and, in June, rented an apartment in the Oakland ghetto. By August, Nancy Ling Perry joined Mizmoon and DeFreeze in Oakland, and preparations that would result in the creation of the Symbionese Liberation Army were under way. On January 16, 1974, some two months after the shooting of Oakland public school superintendent Marcus Foster, Mizmoon made a long-distance telephone call to her family. In a now-familiar refrain, she pleaded, "Everything I have at the house from ten years ago, tear up and burn and destroy. Everything of mine in the garage, destroy." By the time that Mizmoon had adopted her SLA pseudonym "Zoya"—after a Russian partisan hanged by the Nazis during the Second World War—the perceived, psychic liquidation of "Patricia" was complete.[33]

After Patricia Soltysik's fiery death with her confreres in Los Angeles in May 1974, her poetry became available to those with an interest in members of the SLA. Mrs. Soltysik's judgment of Patricia as the kindest and most caring of her children contrasts with her daughter's eventual perspectives on violence:

My commitment must be total
My pistol aim must bring death . . .
No nice girl
No nice, groovy young woman
An angry, vicious, deadly revolutionary Woman
I am to be feared.
I mean death
To the class who are our oppressors.[34]

A similar motif was evoked when Patricia struggled to tie together her lengthy history of narcissistic injuries and ultimate gravitation toward an almost surreal savagery:

I'm going to machete my way into, thru denied jungle, off this crazy road forced on me, on you, on all of us, yes on the people. We crawl over each other, trample her down and that baby over there got squashed in the mad rush. He exploded, taking many down with him . . . for . . . for . . . nothing. Smashed into one road, forced to beat each other, fenced off from the jungles and forests and fields of our earth and mind—denied, blinded to what is rightfully all ours. So much to share when we take off our blinds, raise up our machetes and smash down together for our freedom, our happiness.[35]

Fred cites another poem, in which his sister delineated her role as an elite member of the SLA vanguard:

In the revolution
I am in the front
my breasts swelling wide
with strength.
But we are many,
we can't all be first
at the head
    of the fifth grade line
    of the atomic blast alert drill line
    of the bus line home
    of the ex-virgin line.
We can't all be first
at the head of the Revolution.
But ours is so wide
so deep, so long so spherical
we are all the firsts to
touch the sky.[36]

As in the cases of Susan Stern and Donald DeFreeze, Patricia Soltysik's personal predisposition toward political terrorism was psychologically predicated upon a long string of narcissistic injuries. The major sources of those injuries lie in the nature of her 1) object relations with significant others, and 2) actual, and perceived, role status. Let us consider each of these factors.

Those narcissistic injuries resulting from Patricia's object relations with significant others may be traced to her father and to her lovers, Gene McDaniels and Camilla Hall. Of these three narcissistic injury-engendering relationships, Patricia's object relations with her father clearly served as the foundation of those assaults to her self-esteem and sense of self-image. Fred Soltysik provides us with an exceptionally insightful and comprehensive account of his father's chronic emotional and physical abuse of

Patricia and how, as the oldest of five daughters, she was often forced to endure the brunt of her father's grossly insensitive behavior.[37]

Patricia was affected most acutely by her father's actions during two particularly vulnerable times in her life: her mother's six-week trip to Belgium, which left her responsible for the household, and her own life-threatening illness. During the first episode, Patricia, thoroughly humiliated by her father's long, manipulative silences and verbal and physical abuse, fled her home in a fury. Her return was secured only after the most persistent maternal coaxing. Those narcissistic insults engendered by her father's inexcusable neglect during her illness were even more psychologically damaging. As Fred points out, Patricia's hospital stay concluded without a single visit from her father. Thus, although she recovered physically from her medical crisis, she was devastated emotionally by what she perceived as her father's absolute rejection of her. As Patricia's own communications with Fred demonstrate, these narcissistic injuries had profoundly negative effects upon her self-esteem and sense of self-image.

Patricia's actual, and perceived, role status served as a second source of her narcissistic injuries. The nature of her overall role status again seems to have been roughcast by her family conditions, beginning with the differential treatment her parents meted out to their sons and daughters. As Fred points out, his own desperate escape from the "overcrowded sardine tin" was exceedingly difficult for his sister to replicate. It was thus in large part due to her actual role status as the oldest girl and moral exemplar to her younger sisters that Patricia assumed her perceived role status to be that of a "harassed, objectified and oppressed female." That perceived role status, reinforced by Patricia's menial employment experience, ultimately would result, in part, in her militant feminist views, political and social activism, and, finally, SLA membership.

The case of Patricia Soltysik also illustrates both the political terrorist's typical sense of narcissistic rage and gratification in the psychodynamic rewards of political terrorism. One of the most striking manifestations of Patricia's narcissistic rage was her explicit devotion to the frankly ventilationist notions of Theodore Rubin's *The Angry Book* and her poetic characterization of herself as an "angry, revolutionary Woman." Her indulgence in the autocompensatory, psychodynamic rewards of political terrorism is also in evidence. Patricia's psychic sense of omnipotence is explicitly manifested in her "I am to be feared" poem. The attempted eradication of her old, psychically discredited identity as Patricia Soltysik and the maintenance of her new as-if other pseudoidentity as Zoya is evidenced by the familiar plea to her family to destroy all of her household belongings. Finally, Patricia's appreciation of the psychological utility of political terrorist group membership is clearly addressed in her poetic "so much to share" statement.

Notes

1. Soltysik, *In Search of a Sister*, 1, 2–3, 6.
2. Ibid., 2.
3. Ibid.
4. Ibid., 2, 3, 6.
5. Ibid., 9, 10. Fred Soltysik's book is also replete with detailed accounts of his father's neglect of, and cruelty toward, himself, his mother, and other siblings.
6. Ibid., 11-12.
7. Ibid., 12.
8. Ibid., 12–13.
9. Ibid., 13.
10. Ibid.
11. Ibid., 15.
12. Ibid., 16.
13. Ibid., 16, 17.
14. Ibid., 18.
15. Ibid.
16. See ibid., 21; and Baker and Brompton, *Exclusive!*, 104.
17. Soltysik, *In Search of a Sister*, 21, 25.
18. Ibid., 25.
19. Ibid., 21.
20. Ibid., 27. Fred Soltysik's use of the term "superstraight" is quoted in McLellan and Avery, *Voices of Guns*, 117.
21. Soltysik, *In Search of a Sister*, 27.
22. Ibid., 1, 51, 164. Some time after the Hearst kidnapping, Jacques Maillot promised Mrs. Soltysik that he would "help in whatever must be" to hide Patricia; as Fred puts it, "if she wanted, where no one could find her." See ibid., 164, 165.
23. Ibid., 27, 28.
24. Ibid., 29, 30.

25. Ibid., 31–33. As Fred Soltysik states, when Patricia was in seventh grade, "she'd toyed with the idea of changing her name to something 'more interesting.' 'Well,' Mizmoon continued, 'I've never grown out of that need.'" See ibid., 36. According to Marilyn Baker and Sally Brompton, Patricia had adopted "Mizmoon" because Camilla Hall had used it in one of her poems. See Baker and Brompton, *Exclusive!*, 103.

26. See Weed, *My Search for Patty Hearst*, 272; and Boulton, *Making of Tania Hearst*, 27, 28. Although Patricia ultimately would end her relationship with Camilla Hall in order to broaden her sexual horizons, David Boulton maintains that the woman whom Camilla addressed as "Mizmoon" was the former's "only love." See ibid., 28. Boulton adds that Patricia's response to Camilla's affections was to change her name legally to "Mizmoon." See ibid.

27. Soltysik, *In Search of a Sister*, 33, 35.

28. Ibid., 36.

29. Ibid., 37, 38–39, 48.

30. Ibid., 52, 53.

31. See Payne and Findley, *Life and Death*, 86, 95, 97; Boulton, *Making of Tania Hearst*, 24–25, 28; McLellan and Avery, *Voices of Guns*, 90, 118; Baker and Brompton, *Exclusive!*, 92–93, 108–9; and Alexander, *Anyone's Daughter*, 136–37, 424. For Patricia's comments to her mother regarding her breakup with Camilla Hall see Soltysik, *In Search of a Sister*, 51.

32. See ibid., 57; and McLellan and Avery, *Voices of Guns*, 119.

33. Ibid., 93–94; Soltysik, *In Search of a Sister*, 86, 107. According to Marilyn Baker and Sally Brompton, the Soltysik family did not obey Zoya's plea. See Baker and Brompton, *Exclusive!*, 210–11.

34. For Mrs. Soltysik's comments see Soltysik, *In Search of a Sister*, 35. Patricia's poem is quoted in Weed, *My Search for Patty Hearst*, 284. Steven Weed notes that this poem was written on August 21, 1973, the date on which the SLA began its formal existence as a political terrorist group. Even Patricia Hearst's eulogy to "Zoya" refers to the latter's "perfect hate reflected in stone-cold eyes." See Payne and Findley, *Life and Death*, 85. In her own account of individual members of the SLA, Patricia Hearst states that "Mizmoon"—whom she singles out for criticism—"detested weakness, in herself or anyone else. She was a difficult person to come to know and even more difficult to like once you knew her. She was cold and cruel and fiercely independent and I soon decided that my own best course was to stay away from her as much as possible." Patricia Hearst also recalls that, at one point during the SLA's ransom negotiations with her parents, "Zoya, the hard one, spat at me: 'Your father better pay or you're dead.'" See Hearst, *Every Secret Thing*, 150, 73.

35. Quoted in Soltysik, *In Search of a Sister*, 228.

36. Quoted in ibid., 201.

37. One of the few shortcomings of Fred Soltysik's *In Search of a Sister* is the absence of any explanation for the origins of his father's obvious emotional problems. Given the central role that Patricia's father played in her own emotional development, this information would be of great interest and significance.

CHAPTER SEVEN

A Sense of *Dignidad*: Victor Gerena

The September 12, 1983, theft of over $7 million from a Wells Fargo depot in West Hartford, Connecticut, constitutes the second largest bank robbery in American history. The Wells Fargo robbery also serves as one of the most spectacular acts of political terrorism recently committed in the United States. Victor Gerena, the subject of this chapter and a prominent member of the Puerto Rican proindependence group, Los Macheteros (the Machete Wielders), was personally responsible for the commission of this political terrorist "expropriation."

Los Macheteros, like its more established Puerto Rican brothers-in-arms, Fuerzas Armadas de Liberación Nacional (Armed Forces of National Liberation, or FALN), has not received extensive academic attention.[1] In addition to the Wells Fargo robbery, Los Macheteros has taken credit for a series of violent terrorist attacks on U.S. military, judicial, and police targets in Puerto Rico. These include: the group's first known public operation, the assassination of a Puerto Rican police officer in August 1978; the December 1979 ambush of a U.S. Navy bus in Sabana Seca, killing two and injuring nine American sailors; the January 1981 destruction of nine National Guard aircraft at Munoz Airport; the October 1983 and January 1985 firings of rockets at federal courthouses in Hato Rey and Old San Juan; and the October 1986 bombings of two American military installations. Los Macheteros is an exceedingly disciplined, tight, and secretive organization that confines its violent activities to

Puerto Rico proper. Demanding total independence for the island, Los Macheteros has declared war on its perceived colonial master, the United States. Following the 1983 Wells Fargo operation, massive raids by the Federal Bureau of Investigation (FBI) and the arrests of a substantial number of its leading members have caused the group to become either defunct or, at most, quiescent.[2]

Los Macheteros' 1983 "expropriation" from the West Hartford Wells Fargo depot represents the high-water mark for the group. The heist was at least partially masterminded, and personally undertaken, by an American-born Puerto Rican, Victor Gerena. In October 1984, Los Macheteros claimed responsibility for the robbery and hailed Gerena's part in the theft. Now underground, Gerena is probably residing in Cuba. Who is Victor Gerena? And what psychological factors helped culminate in his membership in Los Macheteros?[3]

Victor Manuel Gerena was born on June 28, 1958, in the Bronx, New York City. His father, Victor Gerena, Sr., and mother, the former Gloria Ortiz, who by the time of Victor's birth were still recent arrivals from Puerto Rico, were married when Gloria was nineteen years old. The marriage soon produced five children. Victor was the oldest of four boys and one girl.[4] According to Ronald Fernandez's comprehensive study, Los Macheteros, Victor's father, a lifelong housepainter, was a "hardworking, responsible, concerned" and attentive parent. Nevertheless, Victor confided to friend after friend that he and his father had had severe personality clashes. In his interviews with these friends Fernandez quickly learned that, as in the case of Donald DeFreeze, Victor's father "always put him down. The man had a temper, and if he'd had a drink or two, Victor, Sr., could be especially caustic to his namesake, who, as a result of the verbal assaults, always 'felt he had to do something big because of the nasty way his father had treated him.' "[5]

By contrast, Victor adored and deeply honored his mother. Fernandez's interviews with family acquaintances underline the fact that Gloria Ortiz had overcome harsh poverty, and a severe case of asthma, to hold a daytime factory job while completing her high-school education at night. Gloria Gerena's most striking quality, however, was her unflinching dedication to her children's welfare.[6]

By the time Victor was twelve, his parents' deteriorating marriage and financial circumstances had led to his mother's decision to move herself and her five children to Hartford, Connecticut, while her husband remained behind in the Gerenas' grimly decaying Bronx neighborhood. Young Victor and his family relocated to a similarly crime-infested Hartford housing project, Charter Oak Terrace, where he resided for most of the next twelve years. As Fernandez's many interviews with Victor's former friends and acquaintances point out, "the stigma of poverty" clung tightly to him. And, perhaps more than the majority of his cohorts, Victor detested the "everyday slaps in the face" that are the lot of the residents of Hartford's Puerto Rican ghetto.[7]

Gloria Gerena's hard work as both breadwinner and attentive parent continued during her years in Charter Oak Terrace. Despite her brutal schedule, she attended many of her children's school functions and continued to provide an environment in which Victor consistently had self-respect and a sense of *dignidad*. The Spanish term may be construed as individual dignity, or more precisely, socially acknowledged self-respect. More relevantly, *dignidad* may be conceptualized as an individual's self-esteem or sense of self-image, as demonstrated by his immediate or cumulative interpersonal relationships. As Fernandez emphasizes, "*dignidad* is the basis around which [Puerto Rican] life revolves," for the island's longtime and seemingly permanent colonial status has resulted in a fierce sensitivity to even the slightest insult.[8]

Victor Gerena, indeed, received generous allotments of *dignidad* during his early years. In addition to his mother's love and attention, he derived definite psychic benefits from his stature as a responsible role model for his younger siblings. And, despite the sting of life in Charter Oak Terrace and an "earful of negative input" regarding his objective role status as a Puerto Rican, Victor was academically, athletically, and socially successful in high school. As Fernandez notes, Victor was "a winner, whose pleasing personality—everybody at least liked Victor—moved many people to love and respect him."[9]

Advised again and again that he could and should be successful in life, Victor had every reason to believe that, regardless of his family's chronic poverty and his father's taunts, he would, indeed, succeed. During his years at Bulkeley High School, he was accorded great *dignidad* by the school's devoted teachers, counselors, and administrators, and he excelled at nearly every curricular and extracurricular activity he attempted. He received an academic scholarship and a student internship at the Connecticut State Capitol in Hartford. The future Machetero even designed a clever system, still in use today, that enabled state capitol administrators to append amendments to legislative bills.[10]

Although a talented player, Victor left Bulkeley High's football team during his senior year. As Fernandez learned, certain of his teachers believed that Victor's decision showed his Achilles' heel. He had quit the losing team because he had failed to receive the first-string playing time that he thought his substantial athletic abilities merited. As one of Victor's teachers put it, "It seemed like as long as he wasn't going to be on a winner, why stick with it?" Yet, as Fernandez points out, his "real sensitivity to slights rarely had a chance to make an appearance at Bulkeley."[11]

During his internship at the Connecticut State Capitol, Victor came under the wing of Marion Delaney, a state administrator who later would describe him as showing "a remarkable sense of responsibility for a young man." Attempting to encourage Victor to shed his Puerto Rican mannerisms, she insisted that he "knock off the street talk"; "if you don't speak properly you're not going to get anywhere." As she later admitted, she was brutal with Victor, for whom she held genuinely high regard and expectations.[12]

Nevertheless, the best of intentions frequently can yield the worst consequences. Ironically, Marion's attempts to place Victor in a suitable college ultimately would subject him to a long string of extreme and humiliating narcissistic insults. The school that Marion recommended most strongly was her alma mater, Annhurst College, a small, Catholic, once all-women's institution. Although Victor's scholarship only paid a small portion of Annhurst's costly tuition, Marion was able to find additional funds for him. During early 1976, Victor and his mother visited the campus and were pleased with the school. As Fernandez reports, Annhurst, which at that time was in grave financial straits due to its dwindling student body, quickly accepted Bulkeley High School's most promising prospect.[13]

During the summer before his enrollment, Victor was torn in two diametrically opposite directions. On the one hand, he was strongly encouraged by people such as Marion Delaney who wanted him to jettison his Charter Oak Terrace background. Yet Victor, who also was becoming drawn toward the Puerto Rican nationalist movement, found himself being tugged back to his own ethnic roots. He began to cultivate friendships with a number of Puerto Rican nationalists who were, in a sense, attempting to prepare Victor to face the real world. He was introduced to several works of militant nationalist literature, including a treatise written by the Young Lords party. This particular work taught Victor that the "chains that have been taken off slaves' bodies are put back on their minds," and that Puerto Ricans who had emigrated to the American mainland "didn't take long to find out that the American Dream that was publicized so nicely on the island turned out to be the ameriKKKan nightmare." He treasured this tract for years.[14]

In the fall of 1976 a lukewarm, uncertain Victor Gerena matriculated at Annhurst College. From the very beginning, his experience at the school was miserable. The only Puerto Rican there, Victor fit in neither with the school's affluent, prudish women nor with the pampered sons of Venezuelan oil tycoons—typical of Annhurst's male student body—with whom he was literally locked in at night. As one of the school's Catholic nuns, Sister Francis, would later observe, Victor "didn't mix well with those students because their idea of a good time was to spend a thousand dollars on the weekend." Further underlining his sense of ostracism was Annhurst's isolated, rural location in Brooklyn, Connecticut. Finally, Victor's unauthorized long-distance use of an Annhurst office phone to call home, which was soon discovered, led to serious charges of social misconduct and to his being barred from making any more calls to his family.[15]

The contrast between Victor's experience at Bulkeley High School and Annhurst was dramatic. Fernandez presents a compelling portrait of a nightmarish college experience:

> The dorm was bad, but the classrooms were worse because a sensitive kid with no experience of personal failure suddenly found himself exposed to a barrage of criticism and ridicule. At Bulkeley, street-smart teachers told Victor he was a fine, well-prepared student. At Annhurst, professors in spanking-clean

black robes told him he had no business being in college. His knowledge of grammar was weak, and he couldn't even succeed in Spanish because the nuns, in search of a Castilian brand spoken by the "best" people, didn't recognize that Victor spoke a Spanish developed at the "intersections of two nationalities."[16]

Victor, informed that he possessed no language skills at all, grew extremely sensitive to these assaults upon his role status. As Sister Francis, in a vast understatement, later put it, "The poor guy must have felt very inadequate."[17]

Given the cultural context of his upbringing, Annhurst's nuns were thoroughly and savagely robbing Victor of his precious sense of *dignidad*. Refusing to subject himself to his professors' criticisms of his inadequacy, he began increasingly to absent himself from his classes. Without anyone with whom he might relate, he also refused to associate with virtually anyone else at the school. As another of Annhurst's nuns, Sister Muriel Lusignan, would later remember, Victor was more or less a loner. Sister Helen Bonin characterized him as a student who "had a lot of anger in him." And Annhurst dormitory director Donald Caron concurred, labeling Victor an outsider who, feeling that he did not belong, "walked around with a big chip on his shoulder."[18]

As one of his friends later put it, "Victor always feared failure." Caron attempted to counsel him, but he may have lacked the sensitivity to deal effectively with the young man's feelings. Caron later asserted that he and Victor would talk about the latter's problems until late into the night. One of these problems was that Victor "very often . . . accused people of holding being Puerto Rican against him." Although Caron endeavored to reassure him that this was not the case, he recalls that he was shocked to learn that someone had smeared dog feces on Victor's door. This narcissistic insult provoked Victor to sharpen his already growing awareness of Puerto Rican nationalism and of America's imperialistic treatment of Puerto Rico.[19]

Victor's anger and feelings of outrage toward his treatment at Annhurst ultimately led him to resent bitterly those of his high-school teachers whose high regard for his character and abilities had readied him for humiliation. Hence, at Annhurst he was scarred and personally battered. Shortly after remonstrating to a visiting Hartford friend, "I can't take this bullshit," Victor dropped out of college during the middle of his second semester.[20]

Devastated by an acute sense of personal failure, he went back to Charter Oak Terrace. Victor's initial return to Hartford was punctuated by a succession of low-paying menial jobs, including stints as a roofer, a recreational assistant for the Parks Department, and a social service counselor at the city's Community Resources for Justice. He also engaged in a series of casual relationships. One of his girlfriends, Maggie Ruiz, was an attractive, older woman whom he first had encountered during his high-school days. Victor moved in with her, and she soon became pregnant. During this same period he pursued another former high-school girlfriend, Pamela Anderson. In order to escape Maggie and be closer to Pamela, who had enlisted in the armed forces, Victor joined the Connecticut National Guard. Stationed near Pamela's base in Georgia, the pair were married on May 1, 1978. To help supplement their earnings during their brief time together, Victor accepted another low position, this time as a gas station attendant.[21]

During this gloomy period, Victor's abandonment of Maggie seems to have exacerbated his already profound sense of personal failure. Two weeks after the birth of their daughter he returned to Connecticut to visit Maggie and the baby. As his friends would later report, Victor's confusion about his relationships with Maggie and Pamela—who also was pregnant—centered upon the issue that he "knew neither who he was nor what he wanted to do." Following the demise of his relationship with Pamela, he returned to Maggie.[22]

Victor accepted another menial position as a mail clerk at the *Hartford Courant*. He now had four dependents to support. Although he assured Maggie that he wanted nothing so much as to be successful and to make it on his own, his prospects were bleak. The possibility of his returning to college was precluded by his powerfully compelling horror of further personal failure. He settled instead for technical-school training as a certified machine operator, a position that would offer him some degree of economic security.[23] After receiving his certification, Victor operated a lathe at one of Hartford's largest employers, Pratt & Whitney Aircraft. Despite the attractive salary, he despised the boredom of factory work. In September 1980, eleven months after beginning his job, he called Maggie from the factory and pleaded for her to "get me out of here."[24]

The next months proved to be increasingly difficult. Victor and Pamela were divorced in May 1980. His relationship with Maggie ended shortly after he quit his position at Pratt & Whitney, and he accepted a position as a truck driver for a local furrier. Both women insisted that he provide them with adequate child support, and, according to his roommate during this period, Paul Carney, "Victor would often cry for extended periods of time regarding being hassled by Maggie and Pamela."[25]

Victor's days as a trucker ended when he was offered a low-paying social service position at Hartford's Special Education Learning Center. As had been the case during his previous experience as a counselor, he demonstrated genuine compassion for, and skillful effectiveness in dealing with, the city's troubled Puerto Rican adolescents. Highly conscious of his intelligence, teaching abilities, financial constraints, and still-burning ambition to be successful, Victor's colleagues implored their star staffer to reenter college. Although haunted by his persistent fear of failure, Victor fully realized that he bore some responsibility for his chaotic life. As he would acknowledge to a trusted friend, he recognized that he had "let others, and especially his mother, down."[26]

Victor dealt with this dilemma by enrolling at Central Connecticut State University's night school program in the spring of 1982. Compelled by financial circumstances to retain his job at the center, he endured a lengthy bus commute between Hartford and New Britain. Like a terrible echo from his hellish experience at Annhurst, Victor's instructors demanded that he demonstrate the same, still-lacking language skills. Hence, in his final effort to enter the social mainstream, his sense of *dignidad* once again was subjected to grievous insults. A few weeks later he abruptly quit both the program and his position at the center. And shortly thereafter he took the fateful step of accepting a position with Wells Fargo Guard Services.[27]

Since Victor's bitter departure from Annhurst in the spring of 1977, he had begun to acquaint himself with an ever-widening circle of increasingly militant, Puerto Rican proindependence activists. In March 1982, Juan Enrique Segarra, the head of Los Macheteros' Tainos cell, telephoned him from Puerto Rico to discuss Victor's standing pledge to make a preliminary analysis of Wells Fargo's operations. Victor enthusiastically agreed, for, by this point in his life, he again recognized that he "had let people down." As Fernandez discerns, "What the group offered was self-esteem via participation in a meaningful movement" as well as a way to fight back against anti-Puerto Rican prejudice. Thus, "Los Macheteros offered Victor what he genuinely needed: a meaningful way to make up for the past. By joining their organization, he got service in a just cause, a possible place in Puerto Rican history, and escape from a dead-end life of tedium and turmoil."[28]

Soon after making contact with Segarra, Victor began working for Wells Fargo Guard Services as a jumper, a substitute for regular guards who are ill or fail to appear for their shift. In May 1982 he applied for and received a transfer as a guard—a role that afforded the Machetero little in the way of major robbery prospects—to Wells Fargo Armored Services. He continued to work for the security company until his participation in the $7-million depot robbery in September 1983. During his days as a Wells Fargo armored-car guard and Machetero operative, Victor pursued an exceedingly low-profile existence. Yet, overjoyed by his new, true identity and by life with his live-in fiancée, Liza Soto, he exulted to a fellow Machetero, "I really feel good about this. I'm really into this."[29]

Victor's tenure as an armored-car guard paralleled the bulk of his previously menial, tedious, and low-paying jobs. Passed over for the manager's position that Victor—and Jim McKeon, the man who received it—thought, with some justification, he richly merited, Victor surmised that his ethnicity was again the issue. He also continued to be harassed by Pamela and Maggie, both of whom had taken him to court for having missed child-support payments. Indeed, Victor, who was unable even to afford an automobile, had two separate attachments placed on his already paltry salary and was nearly dismissed over this issue.[30]

Throughout his employment at the security firm, Victor complained to his coworkers that he resented Wells Fargo's puny wages and the firm's refusal to grant him any employee benefits. To add insult to injury, he was suspended from work due to a theft of $20,000 from one of his runs. Although he passed a lie-detector test and clearly had nothing to do with the loss, he received a three-day suspension. Yet, for the most part, Victor had little to say about this issue to his coworkers.[31]

Then, on September 12, 1983, Victor put into action Los Macheteros' monumental "expropriation" plan. The Wells Fargo robbery took place at a company depot in fashionable West Hartford. McKeon, Victor's manager, was present during the entire operation. He recalls that during the onset of the robbery, Victor, who had taken his gun from his holster, began to bark orders "like a Mexican bandido"; "it was the tone of voice he'd use in a street fight in Hartford." Victor also warned McKeon, "I'm not fucking around, man. Move and I'll put a bullet in your head."[32]

Victor then ordered a coworker, Tim Girard, to drop his gun. Girard complied; later, referring to Victor's demeanor, he claimed that "the man seemed mad when he was doing the robbery." Girard was assaulted, and Victor again warned that he was not "fucking around." After hog-tying Girard, Victor spat: "Now! Move and you'll strangle yourself." McKeon was bound, gagged, and handcuffed. Addressing his two captives, Victor asserted that, although he held no personal animus toward either man, he was "just tired of working for other people." Then, throwing jackets over each man's head and ordering the choking Girard to be quiet, Victor proceeded to inject McKeon and Girard with a barbiturate solution. The injections, however, failed to incapacitate either captive. Noting that Girard was still moving, Victor, in another gesture that he meant business, hit the guard across the head. With $7,017,152 in cash in his possession, Victor raced away from his coworkers, his unknowing fiancée, and, ultimately, his entire miserable existence in the United States.[33]

Like the Symbionese Liberation Army's spectacular kidnapping of Patricia Hearst, the Big Sleep Heist—as one newspaper characterized the Wells Fargo operation—became a sensational media event. And Victor Gerena, who had become a full-fledged hero in Hartford's Puerto Rican community, clearly reveled in his newly achieved role status. Shortly after the FBI had determined that the robbery had been sponsored by Los Macheteros, Victor sent postcards to several news reporters. These postcards, which showed highly symbolic pictures of the Statue of Liberty, New Hampshire's Mount Washington, and the Manhattan skyline, represented Victor's attempts to justify his role in the Wells Fargo operation. Claiming that he was speaking on behalf of liberty for those Spanish-speaking peoples who "have contributed so much and have received so little" from the United States, Victor closed his brief communiqués with intriguing postscripts. One such postscript directed the news media to "watch out for an important public announcement that I'll soon make. I'll inform you of the time and place at which it will occur." Another advised, "I want you to be attentive to an important public announcement I will soon make. The date and place will be indicated later on." These announcements consisted of proindependence and anti-American statements. It is interesting to note that each of these communiqués was signed "Victor Manuel Gerena Ortiz." As Fernandez points out, Victor's new signature followed the Puerto Rican custom for men to use both their father's father's and mother's father's names. Hence, this signaled an identity change, for the Machetero "now took great pride in his Puerto Rican ancestry."[34]

Victor Gerena, who is believed to be living now in Cuba, eventually received the "distinguished recognition" of Los Macheteros itself. Then, on January 6, 1985, came a bizarre and ironic epilogue to the Wells Fargo robbery. In an incident similar to the Symbionese Liberation Army's food-giveaway program, three Los Macheteros members—dressed as Epiphany's Three Kings—distributed a huge quantity of toys to the children of Charter Oak Terrace.[35]

The case of Victor Gerena is clearly manifested by a long train of narcissistic injuries resulting from 1) his overall role status as a socioeconomically inferior, oppressed minority-group member, 2) his deep sense of personal failure, and 3) his father's early rejection of him. These narcissistic assaults did great damage to Victor's self-esteem and self-image or, taken in a cultural context, his sense of *dignidad*.

Fernandez details the "everyday slaps in the face" and "earful of negative input" that stung Victor while growing up in Hartford's Charter Oak Terrace housing project. The most severe of these narcissistic injuries, however, occurred not in Hartford but during Victor's brief and humiliating enrollment at Annhurst College. There he was subjected to a "barrage of criticism and ridicule"; he was repeatedly informed that "he had no business being in college" and allegedly possessed no language skills at all. To Victor, these narcissistic insults grew out of his perceived role status as an oppressed and degraded Puerto Rican.

Narcissistic insults to his role status continued during Victor's post-Annhurst period, which was punctuated by a series of menial and low-paying jobs. His grim financial situation was compounded by the fact that both his former wife and girlfriend were insisting that he pay child support. Then, during his night-school attendance at Central Connecticut State University, in a repetition of his ordeal at Annhurst, Victor again was forced to endure merciless criticisms about his lack of language skills. Finally, during a period in which he already had begun his tenure as a Machetero, came his employment at Wells Fargo. For, although Victor's interval at Wells Fargo does not seem to have contributed to his decision to become a political terrorist, it is significant that the security firm's negative treatment of him probably reinforced that decision.

His narcissistic injuries also may be traced both to his acute sense of personal failure and to his father's rejection. Victor's early, successfully executed roles as a surrogate parent, high-school student-athlete, and state capitol intern may have created unduly high personal and social expectations. Indeed, prior to his tribulations at Annhurst and his abandonment of Maggie Ruiz, he had had no experience with personal failure and soon developed a pronounced fear of failure. And last, Victor, whose father "always put him down," seems to have sustained an early narcissistic injury based upon his perceived, and actual, rejection by a significant other. Clearly, Victor's immediate response to these insults to his *dignidad* and, above all, to his perceived role status was a profound sense of narcissistic rage. Reference has already been made to his anger and outrage over his hellishly brief undergraduate enrollment at Annhurst.

Victor's need to compensate for these narcissistic injuries first was manifested when, as a child, he had sensed that he had to "do something big" to counteract his father's constant verbal assaults. It was not until he had actually become a member of Los Macheteros, and in the act of committing the Wells Fargo robbery, that he was able to do something big. And, indeed, Victor manifests clearly each of the autocompensatory, psychodynamic rewards of political terrorism. For example, his sense of omnipotence is indicated not only in his savagely arresting remarks and angry behavior toward his fellow guards during the robbery but also in his communiqué postscripts.

During his brief career as an active political terrorist, Victor appears to have established, assumed, and maintained a new, as-if other pseudoidentity—the mask of omnipotence. His actual assumption of that mask is clearly evidenced when, during the preliminary stages of the Wells Fargo robbery, Victor, in a tone of voice that coworker Jim McKeon had never heard before, shouted "like a Mexican bandido." McKeon and Tim Girard also recall Victor's comment that he was "just tired of working for other people." Victor's newfound status as a full-fledged hero to Hartford's Puerto Rican community indicates that he was able to maintain the mask of omnipotence. This maintenance of his new, as-if other pseudoidentity is evidenced in his signing his Machetero communiqués in customary Puerto Rican fashion, Victor Manuel Gerena Ortiz.

Victor also enjoyed the psychic rewards inherent in political terrorist group membership. Indeed, it was as a Machetero that he was able to participate, not in solitary, futile, or otherwise misguided or nonlegitimate acts, but in a seemingly just and widely shared cause. Above all, it was as a Machetero that Victor Gerena was able to carve out a niche for himself as—to some— a heroic *independentista*, and, as Fernandez observes, to eschew a dead-end life of tedium and turmoil.

Notes

1. Los Macheteros also has termed itself the Ejército Popular de Boricua (Boricua Popular Army, or EPB). The best single work on Los Macheteros, and Victor Gerena, is Ronald Fernandez's meticulously researched study, *Los Macheteros* (New York: Prentice Hall, 1987). See also Alex P. Schmid and Albert J. Jongman, *Political Terrorism* (Amsterdam: North-Holland, 1988), 652; and *Terrorist Group Profiles* (Washington, DC: U.S. Government Printing Office, n.d.), 92–94. Victor Gerena, the 1983 Wells Fargo case, and other Los Macheteros operations have received considerable media attention. See, for example, "Puerto Rican Terrorists Claim Responsibility for $7 Million Wells Fargo Case in Conn.," *Boston Globe*, October 21, 1984; "Is $7M Robbery Suspect Tied to Terrorists?" ibid., February 18, 1985; "Warning on US Terrorists," ibid., February 22, 1985; "11 Alleged Terrorists Held in $7M Heist," ibid., August 31, 1985;

"Woman Held Here in Funds Laundering," ibid.; "3 Wells Fargo Suspects Sought in Puerto Rico," ibid., September 1, 1985; "$7M Heist Suspects Reported Extradited," ibid., September 2, 1985; "Kunstler to Defend 14," ibid.; "US Hides 11 in Fargo Case," ibid., September 3, 1985; "Probers Reportedly Link Rockets to Cuba," ibid., September 4, 1985; "Suspected Terrorists Guarded at Appearance," ibid.; "Wells Fargo Heist Takes on an International Flavor," ibid., September 8, 1985; "Suspect in Heist Linked to Terrorist," ibid., September 15, 1985; "Blunted Machetes," *Time* (September 16, 1985); "FBI Says $7M Heist Suspect Is in Cuba," *Boston Globe*, October 14, 1985; "Puerto Ricans Decry Wells Fargo Arrests," ibid., August 31, 1986; "16 to Face Trial in $7M Conn. Wells Fargo Heist," ibid., September 28, 1986; "2 Bombs Hit, Others Defused at US Sites in Puerto Rico," ibid., October 29, 1986; "Defense Objects to Wiretaps in Wells Fargo Case," ibid., May 11, 1987; "Subversive Lists Causing a Furor in Puerto Rico," ibid., August 23, 1987; "Puerto Rican Linked to Heist Sent to NYC," ibid., September 11, 1988; "Conn. Trial Set Today in Wells Fargo Theft," ibid., October 11, 1988; and "Four Convicted in Conn. Heist of $7.1 Million," ibid., April 11, 1989.

2. See Fernandez, *Los Macheteros*, 259–61; Schmid and Jongman, *Political Terrorism*, 652; and *Terrorist Group Profiles*, 93–94.

3. On Los Macheteros' claim of Victor Gerena's membership in the group see, for example, Fernandez, *Los Macheteros*, 102; and "Is $7M Robbery Suspect Tied to Terrorists?"

4. See Fernandez, *Los Macheteros*, 204; and "Is $7M Robbery Suspect Tied to Terrorists?"

5. Fernandez, *Los Macheteros*, 204. Years later, while being questioned by police following the Wells Fargo robbery, Liza Soto, Victor's otherwise unwitting fiancée, acknowledged that "Victor didn't get along well with his father." See ibid., 27.

6. See ibid., 205.

7. Ibid., 205–6. Thus, for Victor Gerena, "the poverty stigma burned." See ibid., 208; and "Is $7M Robbery Suspect Tied to Terrorists?"

8. Fernandez, *Los Macheteros*, 207.

9. Ibid., 208.

10. Ibid., 208–9. See also "Is $7M Robbery Suspect Tied to Terrorists?"

11. Fernandez, *Los Macheteros*, 208–9. See also "Is $7M Robbery Suspect Tied to Terrorists?" Although only five feet six inches tall, Victor played lineman on the Bulkeley football team, often facing opposing players much larger than himself.

12. Fernandez, *Los Macheteros*, 209–10.

13. Ibid. As Fernandez points out, "Although Victor had just made a big mistake, he had no way of knowing it in the spring of 1976"; see ibid., 210. Fernandez also characterizes Victor's decision to enter Annhurst as a colossal mistake; see ibid., 211. See also "Is $7M Robbery Suspect Tied to Terrorists?"

14. Fernandez, *Los Macheteros*, 210.

15. Ibid., 211.

16. Ibid.

17. Ibid.

18. Ibid., 211–12.

19. Ibid., 212.

20. Ibid., 212–13. According to Fernandez, "Under circumstances that included a school visit by Mrs. and Mr. Gerena, Victor left Annhurst on March 10, 1977—his school records say he was dismissed because of 'social misconduct.' " See ibid.; and "Is $7M Robbery Suspect Tied to Terrorists?"
21. Fernandez, *Los Macheteros*, 213–14.
22. Ibid., 214.
23. Ibid., 214–15.
24. Ibid., 215. Victor's personnel records indicate that he was fired due to his poor attendance; see ibid.
25. Ibid.
26. Ibid., 213, 215–16. Paul Perzanowski, Victor's immediate superior, later recalled that Victor had a "burning desire" to "make somebody remember" him; see ibid., 216.
27. Ibid., 216–17.
28. Ibid., 107, 217.
29. Ibid., 6, 218.
30. Ibid., 6–7.
31. Ibid., 6–9. See also "Is $7M Robbery Suspect Tied to Terrorists?"
32. Fernandez, *Los Macheteros*, 14.
33. Ibid., 14–19, 30. See also "Is $7M Robbery Suspect Tied to Terrorists?"
34. Fernandez, *Los Macheteros*, 31, 98–101.
35. Ibid., 101–2, 106–7. The three Macheteros photographed the toy giveaway, and these pictures, accompanied by proindependence statements, later appeared in several newspapers. As Juan Enrique Segarra, who served as one of the Three Kings, later commented, "I felt great there. I felt like a movie star."

CHAPTER EIGHT

"It's Like a Frenzy": Thomas Martinez

The case of Thomas Martinez offers an invaluable counterpoint to the other illustrations considered in this study. First, Martinez's involvement with political terrorism was of a distinctly right-wing, as opposed to a left-wing or nationalist-separatist, nature. Most fundamental, however, is that, although he appears to fit the psychological and biographical profile of the political terrorist almost perfectly, he never was successfully recruited as a terrorist. And finally, Martinez, who has written a fascinating account of his association with the most violent and notorious of American right-wing terrorist groups, The Order, has made himself available for a rare, personal interview with the author.[1]

The subject of right-wing political violence in the United States is a complex and bizarre field of research. In sheer terms of violent, or potentially violent, American right-wing organizations, virtually scores of ultraracist, neo-Nazi, radically antitax, Identity Christian, and survivalist groups and splinter groups have emerged during the 1980s. Major examples of such organizations have ranged from the ultraracist neo-Nazi National Alliance and The Order to secretive, militant, tax-resister groups such as the Sheriff's Posse Comitatus to the survivalist Covenant, Sword, and the Arm of the Lord.[2]

Given this book's specific definition of political terrorism, few of these organizations may be properly categorized as authentic political terrorist groups.[3] One such example, however, is The Order. Although unsuccessfully recruited by this group, Thomas Martinez, the subject of this chapter, was extremely well acquainted with The Order's leaders and activities. Who is Thomas Martinez, and what factors ultimately led him to reject a career as a political terrorist?[4]

Thomas Allen Martinez was born in Philadelphia in November 1955. Tom was, by far, the youngest of three children; his older brother, Harold, was ten years' his senior, while middle brother Lee was seven years older. During the author's interview with Tom, his paramount relationship with Lee is underlined by his characterization of Lee as "my one brother" and as *"the* brother." During our interview Tom painfully recalled his beloved brother's being stabbed by a black youth wielding a pair of schoolteacher's scissors. The attack, which took place on school grounds, occurred when Tom was two years old. Then, a few years later, came the abrupt interruption of Tom's relationship with Lee, an observation that is the first major autobiographical point made in *Brotherhood of Murder*. When Tom was eleven, Lee joined the army and was transferred to Europe. As Tom puts it, "His desertion of me, as I saw it to be, left me with an anger I couldn't express, a desperate longing for his return, and a need, I now think, for someone to replace him."[5]

What were Lee's most outstanding qualities? Unlike Harold, Lee was an extremely intelligent, rugged, and extraordinarily generous individual whom Tom admired greatly. Tom loved to be with Lee and his friends when they were around the house in the evenings; hence, when Lee left, as Tom painfully recalls, "the family left." The day after Lee's so-called desertion, as Tom admits, he cried all day. Tom also avers that, had Lee remained in Philadelphia, he might never have joined either the Ku Klux Klan or the National Alliance.

In his memoirs Tom acknowledges that he devoted a great deal of his childhood attempting to please his father, a strict and verbally abusive disciplinarian to whom his mother unfailingly deferred. Tom's father appears to have been subjected to an agonizing lifetime of what-ifs and might-have-beens. Graduating from Philadelphia's public school for gifted boys, Central High, at the age of sixteen, the senior Martinez was compelled by his own family's poverty to enter the work force after his graduation, and he enlisted in the navy during the Second World

War.[6] In 1957, at about the time of Lee's stabbing, Tom's father became gravely ill with tuberculosis. To Mr. Martinez's shame, the family, who lost their house and all of their savings, were compelled to move to a public housing project. During our interview Tom painfully recalled that such families were pro- hibited from owning even a television set or a dog. In this truly abject period in his life, Mr. Martinez turned, unsuccessfully, to the Catholic church for assistance.[7]

As Tom recalls, his father's poor health persisted until 1960. Mr. Martinez then was able to secure a position as a trucker for a local bakery, and the family moved into a small house in Philadelphia's run-down Kensington section. A workaholic who spent little time at home, he eventually was promoted and became a baker. As Tom put it during our interview, "My father worked so many damn hours as a breadman, eighteen hours a day, that I never really got to know my father, no ball games, no nothin'." Added to this portrait of neglect was the fact that Tom's mother was constantly in the hospital with all kinds of problems.[8]

Until he began junior high school, Tom's public-school edu- cation was largely uneventful. As he pointed out during our interview, race relations between the small number of blacks and the white majority in his elementary school were reasonably pleasant. Then, in 1967, the city of Philadelphia began the busing of black children to its predominantly white public schools. Many white parents, both Catholic and non-Catholic, decided to send their children to the city's parochial school system. White enrollment at Tom's junior high school was cut in half, and the vacant seats were filled by the newly arrived black children.[9]

From that point on, "hatred became the major subject in the curriculum," and Tom's political outlook began to be molded. It was at this time that Tom began to admire George Wallace, the racist presidential candidate who "stood up there for the white person." It was not, however, until Tom was brutally assaulted by a black student during seventh or eighth grade that he actually became a racist. Bloodied by the attack, he recalls vividly that he left the classroom screaming, "Fucking niggers, fucking niggers."[10]

After junior high school, the situation became even worse. Black enrollment at Thomas Edison, his senior high school, stood at nearly 100 percent. As Tom put it to *Philadelphia Inquirer* reporter Murray Dubin,

Edison was a dungeon. . . . Anyone who reads this [article],
and went to Edison then, feels that way today. Taking showers,
they [black students] kidded you about the size of your penis.
I wasn't naked at home in front of anybody, and now I was
taking my clothes off in front of black kids. . . . I didn't learn. It
was a zoo. People pushed you, knocked down your books
because you were white. There were fistfights.[11]

Edison High School spelled the end of Tom's education when,
following the stabbing of a white pupil, a friend of the black
murderer threatened to kill Tom, who fled from the classroom.
That was the last day he ever spent in school. Unsuccessful in his
attempt to hide the truth from his father, who referred to him as
a "lazy bum," Tom recognizes that, "in both my expectation and
then the reality, [my father] had given me a grievance to nurture,
the first in a long line."[12]

Tom, indeed, had grievances. He pointed out during our
interview that "back then I had nothing going for me," and that,
in retrospect, "given the education, and given that chance, I could
have become a successful professional." At this point in Tom's
life, only his relationship with his wife-to-be, Susan, an uncom-
monly mature girl who successfully persuaded him to avoid
drugs and alcohol, provided him with any positive influence.
Susan's parents, however, viewed him as an unfit companion for
their daughter and insisted that she end their relationship.[13]
Unable to endure the sight of Susan dating other young men,
Tom joined the army. After a brief enlistment, which ended
because, in his view, the army had failed to give him the training
that had been promised him, he returned to Kensington. This was
a relatively pleasant period in his life. He commenced upon an
active and independent social life. And then, after some months,
a newly reacquainted Tom and Susan were married.[14]

This happy phase was relatively brief. By age twenty-one,
Tom had quit his job at a local donut shop because of a dispute
over health benefits. Thus began a chronic pattern in his life, a
cycle of menial employment and the temptation, or even necessity, of identifying a scapegoat for his financial predicaments. He
blamed affirmative action and other minority programs for his
plight. As Tom now acknowledges, the true reason for his failure
to find work was the fact that he was a tenth-grade dropout.[15]

It was during this difficult period that Tom first became acquainted with the American racist movement. After seeing former Ku Klux Klan (KKK) leader David Duke on a television talk show, Tom eagerly joined the virulently racist group. What attracted Tom Martinez to the Klan? During our interview he stressed that these racists were "just average, normal, like-minded guys," likable people who cared about the issues. Also significant were Tom's fears that black Americans, who, unlike their white counterparts, were strong and united, might take what little that he and his neighbors had in Kensington.[16] Moreover, the Klan's publications focused on issues such as affirmative action and busing, which Tom was convinced had been responsible for his own failure. As he stressed to the author, "Racism became a frenzy. . . . I lived it day and night." And Duke and the Klan, he concluded, had the courage to articulate publicly those racist views that he previously had shared only with his closest acquaintances.[17]

The Klan, however, ultimately proved to be a keen source of disillusionment. Doubting the group's seriousness, Tom found it to be a "bunch of yappers" who had no program. He soon was introduced to an ultraracist group that seemed to have such a program, the neo-Nazi National Alliance. This organization subscribed to racist views similar to those held by the Klan, yet its membership and devotion to a coherent ideology appeared to Tom to be far more impressive.[18]

Tom generally received great psychic rewards from his membership in the National Alliance. Unlike the Klan, whose members tended to hail from the same lower stratum of society as he did, the National Alliance's membership was drawn from a far broader and more affluent socioeconomic class. Educated professionals were well represented in the organization, and Tom recalls that he, a tenth-grade dropout, was delighted to be welcome in their company. Indeed, in *Brotherhood of Murder*, Tom firmly refers to these emotional rewards: "I had not many friends in the outside world, and these were my friends. . . . I was sitting there with doctors, lawyers, chemists, and engineers." He became well known and respected in the ultraracist organization, which served as his primary support group. As he puts it in *Brotherhood of Murder*, "It was a heady experience: Anonymous corner boy becomes famous."[19]

As had been the case with his membership in the Klan, Tom became bitterly disappointed with the National Alliance. Found guilty of disorderly conduct and of uttering ethnic slurs, he and a friend, Jack Martin, were fined $350 apiece. Tom, tormented as always by his family's desperate financial straits, was outraged that William Pierce, the group's chief ideologist and leader, refused to commit general funds, or even a small amount of his own money, to help pay these fines.[20]

Tom's disappointment in the National Alliance gradually came to equal his disillusionment with the Klan. The everyday facts of his menial employment led him to question the organization's ideological tenets. He observed, for example, that many of the white tenants of the housing project where he was employed as a maintenance man were also criminals, dopers, and welfare bums.[21] Indeed, he was becoming disillusioned not merely with the National Alliance but also with the entire racist movement. After considerable soul-searching, Tom quit. He clearly remembers this period as miserable. Although he already had begun to reject the racist dogma of the neo-Nazis, the psychodynamic rewards of National Alliance membership still held considerable sway. Thus began a period of difficulty and drama in his life.[22]

The next few years centered upon his relationship with Bob Mathews, the eventual leader of The Order. And, indeed, Tom's relationship with Mathews reflects that narcissistic object manipulation frequently inherent in the political terrorist recruitment effort. They met at a National Alliance convention in Arlington, Virginia, in 1981. Rushing up to the onetime street kid, Mathews had great praise for Tom's recruiting efforts in Philadelphia. Mathews's flattery came at a time of great personal and financial hardship; the small house that Tom recently had purchased developed severe structural problems, and, complicating matters further, he had broken his foot at work. To add insult to narcissistic injury, Tom's workmen's compensation checks were arriving at irregular intervals, thus putting him in the humiliating position of having to beg his creditors for additional time in which to pay his long-overdue bills.[23]

The theme of inferiority was touched upon again and again in the author's conversations. During these earlier years in his life Tom had thought that, ultimately, this sense of inferiority derived from the white working class's inability to stand up for its rights: "You feel inferior to the extent where you're at, where you're coming from. . . . I felt that we were inferior to the black people, the way that we were being treated . . . like a minority in our own little shell. . . . I felt inferior in the schools I went to, junior high and *definitely*, high school." Hence Tom, who felt that he was in a weak, humiliating, and failed position, had gone to listen to people who were telling him that he was actually superior.[24]

This theme of inferiority seems, in part, to have driven him to commit a felony on behalf of a nascent political terrorist group. Tom thus recalls that, with his life going nowhere, Mathews, who had traveled from Idaho to Philadelphia, outlined a grandiose scheme to pass thousands of dollars of counterfeit money. The plan was aimed at financing a new, extreme right-wing terrorist group, which would become known as The Order. Tom felt "important again, pleased and proud" that Mathews would travel so great a distance for his assistance. And Mathews, who correctly and cleverly assessed Tom's financial vulnerability and low sense of role status, had little difficulty in convincing the latter to join him.[25]

Against the recommendations of Mathews and others in The Order, however, those bills were passed not in black neighborhoods—an action intended to create racial havoc—or out of state, but in Kensington. The fact that Tom chose to pass the counterfeit money at the scene of his humble origins is, from a psychological perspective, quite revealing. As he writes, he felt exhilarated to be enriching himself in his old neighborhood.[26]

Tom's decision to pass counterfeit money in Kensington was foolhardy enough, but his behavior was compounded further by his going back to many of the same stores in which he already had passed those bills. It was in one of these stores, a local Beerland, that a counterfeit ten-dollar bill was first discovered. Upon his return, Tom was confronted by the outraged store owner, who accused him of having spent a counterfeit bill there. Firmly denying the charge, Tom, who could have walked home, drove instead, which gave the owner an opportunity to write down the license number. That night, Secret Service agents arrested Tom Martinez at his home.[27]

During their lengthy interrogation, the agents assigned to the case were surprised to learn that Tom was not a simple counterfeiter but a trusted colleague in a full-fledged political terrorist group. Tom agreed to cooperate with authorities and to continue to associate with Mathews and other Order members. The Federal Bureau of Investigation (FBI) then was brought into the case.[28] As a direct result of Tom's work as an FBI informant, the bulk of The Order's membership was arrested and incarcerated and the group was effectively eliminated as an active political terrorist organization. Tom, who had been instructed to meet with Order leaders Mathews and Gary Yarbrough in Portland, Oregon, proceeded to lead the FBI to the pair. Although Yarbrough was apprehended, Mathews narrowly managed to escape the same fate. Later, however, Mathews took his own life during a shootout with government agents in Washington State.[29]

As Tom recalls in *Brotherhood of Murder*, this period was a time of deep contemplation and depression for the once-proud racist. He began to realize that he was a weak individual who had earlier perceived himself as a leader, and that he would have followed any group that flattered him. Tom also began to recognize that his weak sense of self had caused him to seek out the comradeship of those who treated him as if he were superior.[30]

The author's conversations with Tom revealed a veritable deluge of information not merely about his own experiences with The Order but also about the group itself. Although he was acquainted with only one half of its membership, Tom eventually encountered the rest of the group at their trial. When queried about possible common characteristics of Klan, National Alliance, and Order members, Tom replied that, based upon conversations that he had had with individuals in the racist movement,

> ... most [members] joined out of past experiences with problems of some sort, for instance, unemployment. Some of the guys I met in the movement could not find a decent job. They blamed the government for that, affirmative action. So here was this organization that was fighting against [the government], for a white man. . . . They wanted to get involved. Some guys got involved in it because they ideologized [*sic*] Adolf Hitler. . . . There's different reasons why people join groups, and want to participate there. The problem is, when you join groups, the majority of people that join get out of them. . . . But, those who do stay in these groups are the weak ones, who are

so damned brainwashed by the propaganda that's fed to them, it's like a frenzy.

Tom and I also spoke at length about his own experiences in the racist movement. "It was a part of *belonging* to something," Tom continually averred. "It was a very important part of my life, being *accepted* by them." And, as for his own behavior? "I was just like a walking time bomb. . . . I wanted to do something." Although not prepared to take violent action, Tom did not know how far he might go. He was, therefore, actually relieved when he was arrested for passing the counterfeit bills, for he already had come to the conviction that, despite the opportunity to do so, he would not go underground with The Order.

What psychological factors might have helped to motivate Thomas Martinez to become a member of a political terrorist group such as The Order, and what factors appear to have militated against that decision? As is the case with many political terrorists, Tom appears to have been subjected to a long string of narcissistic personality disturbances—chiefly, narcissistic injury and, most intriguingly, narcissistic disappointment. Tom's narcissistic injuries appear to have derived from 1) his own response to his overall role status, 2) his actual, and perceived, object relations with significant others, and 3) his acute sense of personal failure.

The issue of his objective, and subjective, role status certainly appears to have gnawed at him throughout much of his life. His humble Kensington origins, nightmarish public school background, and objective role status as a tenth-grade dropout and menial laborer contributed profoundly to his emerging sense of narcissistic injury. Although these factors were personal and biographical in nature, Tom concluded that there was a firm sociological basis for his life experiences. Moreover, his sense of narcissistic rage appears to derive most keenly from his objective, and subjective, role status.

Tom's narcissistic injuries also appear to have resulted from his actual, and perceived, object relations with significant others—his mother, father, and middle brother, Lee. Tom's enforced isolation from his workaholic father and ill mother appear to have had great impact upon his emerging sense of narcissistic injury. Moreover, Mr. Martinez's apparent rejection of his lazy bum of a son, particularly after the latter's forced exit from high school, also appear to have contributed to Tom's ultimately profound sense of personal failure. Yet, as Tom himself recalls, it was Lee's stabbing and enlistment in the army that most disturbed him.

Tom's membership in ultraracist preterrorist groups such as the Ku Klux Klan and National Alliance provided him with firm psychodynamic rewards. Yet, despite his association with The Order, Tom never actually joined. Why, despite a perfect opportunity, and a seemingly powerful set of psychodynamic motivations, to become a political terrorist, did Tom Martinez refuse to do so?

Tom's inhibitions against violence and disillusionment with those ultraracists groups, the Klan and National Alliance, to which he did belong, account for his refusal to become a political terrorist. The author, nevertheless, might reiterate Tom's self-characterization as a walking time bomb and as a man who wanted to do something. Moreover, even before the time of his arrest on counterfeiting charges, Tom had numerous opportunities to commit acts of political terrorism. He now believes, however, that he could not have lived with the guilt that would have accompanied such acts. Indeed, he was shocked at those murders which The Order actually committed, such as the assassination of Denver radio talk-show host Alan Berg, and at the lack of remorse shown by Order members over those acts of violence. For, as Tom emphasized repeatedly, "If I had committed a crime of murder, if I had murdered anyone in, for example, an armed car robbery, I don't think that I could have lived with it, I would have gone crazy, I would have gone mentally crazy, because it's too much guilt." Clearly, and, to his credit, Tom Martinez enjoys and suffers from a strong sense of moral conscience.

Another factor accounting for his refusal to become a political terrorist is that he had become extremely disillusioned with the most fundamental, ideological tenets of the ultraracist movement. By 1983 he was moving away from ultraracist ideology. Noting that many of Philadelphia's white neighborhoods were as poorly maintained as its black ghettos, Tom was becoming as disgusted with the whites as he was with black Americans. And finally, William Pierce's refusal to pay even part of his fine for uttering a racist slur was, as Tom now concedes, a major disappointment.

The case of Thomas Martinez is a suggestive and exceedingly valuable one that makes a major contribution to a more theoretically rich and useful theory of which personal factors help to produce a political terrorist. In the preceding, and present, case studies, each individual 1) had been actively recruited by a political terrorist group, 2) had participated in certain preterrorist activities, and 3) had faced a lack of other, satisfying options. It may, perhaps, be true that those individuals who opt in favor of permanent careers as political terrorists must also 4) lack strong personal inhibitions against violence, and 5) not become disillusioned with their political terrorist group's most fundamental ideological tenets. The case of Tom Martinez, therefore, is as instructive as it is fascinating. To recall the title of a recent motion picture about the evils of racism, Tom Martinez is a man who really did "do the right thing."

Notes

1. The single best study of Thomas Martinez's life, and of The Order, is Thomas Martinez, *Brotherhood of Murder* (New York: McGraw-Hill, 1988). Another excellent account of his involvement with the American ultraracist movement is by Murray Dubin, "Fugitive from Hate," *Philadelphia Inquirer Magazine* (December 18, 1988). Given the rise of American right-wing terrorist groups in recent years, an increasing body of literature on organizations such as The Order also has emerged. These include somewhat factually less-exacting works such as James Coates, *Armed and Dangerous* (New York: Hill and Wang, 1987); Stephen Singular, *Talked to Death* (New York: Berkley, 1989); and Kevin Flynn and Gary Gerhardt, *The Silent Brotherhood* (New York: Free Press, 1989). See also Raphael S. Ezekiel, "Discussions with Members of the Klan, Nazis, and Aryan Nations Groups," paper presented to the Eleventh Annual Scientific Meeting of the International Society of Political Psychology, July 1–5, 1988, at Secaucus, New Jersey. The Order, once the most conspicuous, active, and violent of these groups, has received extensive attention from the news media. See, for example, "US Says White-Power Group Has Links to Prison Gangs," *Boston Globe*, December 26, 1984; "Closing in on the Brotherhood," *Time* (February 11, 1985); "Vast Dragnet Hunts Neo-Nazis," *Denver Post*, February 17, 1985; Robert T. Zintl, "Dream of a Bigot's Revolution," *Time* (February 18, 1985); "Former Neo-Nazi Hangs Himself," *Boston Globe*, February 24, 1985; "Reputed Leader of Racist Group Held in 4 Counts," ibid., March 28, 1985; Peter Lake, "An Exegesis of the Radical Right," *California Magazine* (April 1985); "Murder Suspect Arrested," *Boston Globe*, April 1, 1985; "Tracking Down the

Brotherhood," *Time* (April 8, 1985); "23, Linked to Neo-Nazis, Are Indicted in Seattle," *Boston Globe*, April 16, 1985; "5 Named by U.S. in Berg Case," *Rocky Mountain News*, April 16, 1985; "Neo-Nazi Suspect Arrested in Pa.," *Boston Globe*, April 18, 1985; "Police Surround Armed Camp of White Extremists," ibid., April 20, 1985; "Police Capture Man in Trooper's Killing," ibid., April 21, 1985; "The F. B. I.'s War against a 'Brotherhood' of Haters," *New York Times*, April 21, 1985; "The Order: A Humbled Supremacy," *Rocky Mountain News*, April 22, 1985; "Paramilitary Camp Searched," *Boston Globe*, April 24, 1985; "A Counterattack on Neo-Nazis," *Time* (April 29, 1985); Mark Starr and George Raine, "The Law Attacks The Order," *Newsweek* (April 29, 1985); "Meese Backs Death Penalty," *Boston Globe*, May 6, 1985; "7 Men Linked to Neo-Nazis Are Indicted," ibid., May 17, 1985; L. J. Davis, "Ballad of an American Terrorist," *Harper's* (July 1985); "FCC Probes Supremist Broadcasts," *Boston Globe*, July 28, 1985; "Study: Radical Right Getting Farm Support," ibid., September 22, 1985; Frank Trippett, "Order in Court," *Time* (September 23, 1985); "The Order in the Court," *Newsweek* (September 23, 1985); "10 Convicted of Conspiracy in Slaying of Talk-Show Host," *Boston Globe*, December 31, 1985; "5 in Neo-Nazi Group Get Maximum Terms," ibid., February 7, 1986; "5 Neo-Nazis Given 40-Year Sentences," ibid., February 8, 1986; "White Supremacists Hold Idaho Meeting," ibid., July 12, 1986; "White Supremacists, Rights Advocates Meet 10 Miles Apart," ibid., July 13, 1986; "White Supremacist Speaker Vows to Keep out Mexicans," ibid., July 14, 1986; Richard N. Ostling, "A Sinister Search for 'Identity,' " *Time* (October 20, 1986); "Idaho Group Standing Firm against Neo-Nazis," *Boston Globe*, October 27, 1986; "Jury Indicts 15 'Supremacists' in Plot on US," ibid., April 25, 1987; and "2 from Neo-Nazi Group Convicted in Killing of Denver Talk Show Host," ibid., November 18, 1987.

2. Although it might be heuristically useful to categorize American right-wing political organizations as ultraracist, neo-Nazi, antitax, Identity Christian, or survivalist, it is extremely important to recognize that the ideologies of these groups typically tend to embody various combinations of these ideological strains. An excellent example is the Covenant, Sword, and the Arm of the Lord, a group that has adhered to the tenets of survivalism, ultraracism, and the Identity Christian movement.

3. For example, the neo-Nazi National Alliance, which at one time counted Thomas Martinez and Order leader Robert Mathews among its leading members, served as a social association of like-minded individuals that never actually undertook organizationally sponsored acts of violence. Nor, despite the violent actions of certain of its members, such as Gordon Kahl and Arthur Kirk, does the Sheriff's Posse Comitatus qualify as a political terrorist group. Nor does the Identity Christian movement, which attempts to provide theological justification for its ultraracist ideology by identifying Anglo-Saxons as the true Ten Lost Tribes of Israel, appear to function as much more than a philosophical breeding ground for right-wing violence. On the other hand, a legitimate argument might be made that the Covenant, Sword, and the Arm of the Lord, which has served as a massive armory, individual training ground, and personnel bureau for the right-wing underground, qualifies as a valuable adjunct to American right-wing terrorist groups.

4. The group known best as The Order has at various times termed itself the Bruder Schweigen (Silent Brotherhood) and the White American Bastion. On this point see, for example, "The F. B. I.'s War."

5. Martinez, *Brotherhood of Murder*, 10.

6. Ibid., 11.

7. Ibid.

8. Ibid.

9. Ibid., 12.

10. Ibid.

11. Quoted in Dubin, "Fugitive from Hate."

12. Martinez, *Brotherhood of Murder*, 13.

13. Ibid., 13–14.

14. Ibid., 14. As Tom indicated during our interview, his desire was to become, like Lee, a military policeman. After he failed to receive high enough examination scores to do so, however, he attempted unsuccessfully to become an army baker. He now wishes that he had remained in the army.

15. Ibid., 19.

16. And, indeed, Tom revealed to me that he received a good deal of community support for his ultraracist views, with virtually no opposition.

17. Ibid., 20–21.

18. Ibid., 24.

19. Ibid., 31, 45, 46.

20. Ibid., 48. Pierce is a former physics professor at Oregon State University.

21. Ibid., 50.

22. Ibid., 52.

23. Ibid., 31, 60, 64.

24. Tom recalls that his father's stern coldness helped instill a sense of inferiority in him as well.

25. Ibid., 60.

26. Ibid., 98–99.

27. Dubin, "Fugitive from Hate." See also Martinez, *Brotherhood of Murder*, 100.

28. See ibid., 133–35.

29. See ibid., 148–83.

30. Ibid., 146, 189.

CHAPTER NINE

"The Famous Carlos": Ilich Ramírez Sanchez

If there is such an unfortunate phenomenon as the superstar or world-class political terrorist, then Ilich Ramírez Sanchez—popularly known by his nom de guerre, "Carlos the Jackal"—must be regarded as a superb illustration. No individual political terrorist has invited the sheer volume, breadth, and diversity of scholarly, journalistic, literary, and news media attention as "Carlos." And, given Carlos's continuing refuge from prosecution, conviction, and certain imprisonment, that ignominious status is just as this most ruthless of political terrorists would gladly have it.[1]

In several respects Ilich Ramírez Sanchez represents a rather different kettle of fish than most of the other case studies considered in this volume. First, like Victor Gerena, Carlos has managed successfully to evade the two major archenemies of the political terrorist: the agencies of the law, and death itself. Thus, he is a true survivor among fellow political terrorists. Second, and again like Gerena, Carlos's social and cultural roots lie in a Third World nation, Venezuela, rather than in North America or Western Europe. And finally, although he clearly decided to embark upon a career as a political terrorist and derived great psychodynamic rewards from that career, Carlos fails to fit the typical psychobiographical profile of the political terrorist.

Beyond such surface biographical particulars is a more problematic and pivotal concern: the question of why a young Latin American playboy, of dubious political beliefs, decided to embark upon the well-worn path of political terrorism. Unlike Susan Stern or Diana Oughton, whose route was determined at least partially by a shared, psychopolitical need to oppose publicly the core values of their wealthy, conservative parents, Carlos neither spurned his affluence nor received any such conservative parental exhortations. What, then, is known about his personal and psychobiographical background?

Ilich Ramírez Sanchez was born on October 12, 1949, in Caracas in a crazy-quilt milieu of enormous wealth and rabid Marxism. The oldest of the three sons of Dr. José Altagracia Ramírez Navas and Elba Maria Sanchez, Ilich, like his younger brothers, Lenin and Vladimir, was named after Vladimir Ilich Lenin. Although a rigid Stalinist—his revolutionary Marxism was far to the left of either Moscow or the then outlawed Venezuelan Communist party—Dr. Ramírez amassed a large fortune in real estate holdings and other properties.[2] Not long after Vladimir's birth, Ilich's parents separated. Dr. Ramírez continued to support his wife and three sons lavishly, and the four of them spent most of the next few years touring the Caribbean. The four eventually returned to their native Venezuela.[3]

The future Carlos, who would boast to his captive, Saudi Arabian Oil Minister Zaki Yamani, that he first had embarked upon a terrorist career at the age of fourteen, may have been mixing fact and fantasy. Caracas in 1963 was undergoing those political strains common to contemporary Latin America, including student unrest and political terrorist attacks upon the army and security forces. And, indeed, the young Ilich, who began his formal education at the Colegio Fermin Toro, Caracas's largest public school, did receive a political education of the first order during the period immediately following the ouster of dictator Marcos Pérez Jiménez by liberal President Rómulo Betancourt. A large number of students at the school, including Ilich himself, engaged in stone-throwing and street demonstrations in support of the Communists, who had been banned due to their support of anti-Betancourt guerrillas in the Venezuelan countryside.[4]

Ilich's adolescent views of this street violence were a harbinger of Carlos's own perspectives. "Bullets are the only thing that makes sense," Ilich would insist to his friends with great bravado. It is suggestive to point out that Ilich, whom his father remembers as a shy, quiet child with much less self-assurance than his brothers, was driven by an adolescent need for attention. That juvenile desire for attention evidently was channeled through his precocious participation in conspicuous acts of violence.[5]

As an adolescent, Ilich began to become distressed by what would be a lifelong problem with his weight. As Christopher Dobson and Ronald Payne point out, the fourteen-year-old Ilich was "even then tending to put on weight and his thinner, sharper brothers teased him about it. Someone gave him the nickname Muchacho Gordo, the Little Fat One, although some of the local Venezuelan papers have taken to calling him, with some pride, El Gran Carlos. He retaliated to the teasing by promising that one day the world would take notice of him."[6] Colin Smith paints a companion portrait of him as "a plump boy, not much good at sports and nicknamed 'El Gordo'—'the fat one'—by the family."[7]

Ilich left the Colegio Fermin Toro at the age of sixteen. Dr. Ramírez then dispatched him overseas to commence his formal political education. Ilich traveled to the Caribbean, Mexico, and to Camp Mantanzas, one of Cuban President Fidel Castro's Havana training camps for young guerrillas. Ilich's first insurgent actions, the landing of small parties of guerrillas on the Venezuelan coast and the attempted provocation of students at the University of Caracas, were humiliating fiascoes.[8] At this point, Dr. Ramírez decided to send Ilich to London, where Mrs. Ramírez and the younger boys were living. This more-or-less permanent move served to finalize the physical separation of Ilich's parents, whose marriage had disintegrated. According to Smith, Dr. Ramírez bitterly regretted his inability to live with Elba, a Catholic who refused to divorce him. As always, he continued to provide generously for his wife, and she quickly became a fixture in Latin American diplomatic society in London.[9]

It was during Ilich's early residence in London that the political terrorist-in-training began to display another and ostensibly contradictory dimension of his complex personality: a serious taste for the playboy life-style. Indeed, his playboy ways were the most conspicuous characteristic of his nearly ten years of residence in Western Europe. Yet, one aspect of that life-style, his taste for women, could not always be satisfied during his months in London. As Claire Sterling reports, "The fastidious

Anglo-Saxons who went to Cheltenham were put off by his fleshy lips, tightly waved dark hair, and stoutish figure." Nonetheless, Ilich was popular with Latin women, and he frequently dated three or four at one time. And, in retrospect, the swinging life-style that he was pursuing became a perfect cover for the budding political terrorist, for he appeared as nothing more than a superficial bon vivant.[10]

After his wife and children had been living in London for about a year, Dr. Ramírez went there in order to make college arrangements for Ilich and Lenin. Settling upon the idea of sending his sons to Patrice Lumumba Friendship University in Moscow, he soon dispatched them to the Soviet capital. The true nature of Ilich's enrollment is an issue of some dispute. Some observers, such as Sterling, Dobson and Payne, and Ovid Demaris, argue that the university served as a KGB training center for promising young Third World recruits. On the other hand, others, such as Smith and Edgar O'Ballance, concur that it is impossible to verify the possibility that Ilich was Lumumba's most successful student.[11]

What is known about the young Ramírezes' two years in Moscow? Both Ilich and Lenin were overwhelmed by the university workload, for their preparation in the Russian language had been inadequate. And, judging solely by the outward manifestations of Ilich's behavior, it seems difficult to believe that he ever might have been considered a worthy candidate for training by Soviet intelligence. As Sterling comments, Ilich was a public disgrace during his second and final year at Lumumba. From all apparent indications, this "rich boy in Moscow," as Smith calls him, was hardly resigned to forsake his growing penchant, whetted by a generous allowance, for the hedonistic life-style of a Western playboy. Tales of public drunkenness and womanizing dot the standard accounts of his Lumumba years. Together with his scorn for anything so "dreary" as the Communist party, Ilich publicly was antagonizing his Soviet hosts.[12]

Perhaps in a spirit of compromise, the miscreant established himself with the Arab, and particularly Palestinian, students at Lumumba. The true purpose behind Ilich's early association with the university's Palestinian faction—an affiliation that would extend to Carlos's central labors as a political terrorist in the hire of the most radical Palestinian groups, such as the Popular Front for the Liberation of Palestine (PFLP)—may never be known. However, it was during this same period that Ilich first met Mohammed Boudia, a former Algerian rebel who had worked for the KGB prior to becoming head of the PFLP's European cell in 1969. Ilich's contact with Boudia and other Palestinian leaders led to his visits to the PFLP's training camps and to his formal recruitment into the political terrorist group. During a visit to Beirut, Ilich was introduced to George Habash, head of the PFLP, and Wadi Haddad, the director of the group's training camps.[13]

Ilich reappeared at the university in February 1970. He quickly resumed his drinking and womanizing and assumed an even more casual attitude toward his studies. Then, in June, with much ceremony and ado, he and Lenin, whose behavior at Lumumba generally had been above reproach, were expelled. If his expulsion was merely a cover for his true activities, then Ilich said nothing to Lenin about this fact, nor did he inform his younger brother that he had accepted an offer to spend the summer at a PFLP training camp,[14] the last such camp to be located in Jordan.

In September, Jordan's King Hussein expelled the Palestine Liberation Organization (PLO) after a bloody civil war that resulted in the massacre of a large number of Palestinian guerrillas. "Black September" soon became the label for a fanatical faction of the PLO, whose avowed aim was to overcome Palestinian demoralization and reject a more moderate Arab overture toward Israel. Black September's major tactical successes included both the 1971 assassination of Jordanian Prime Minister Wasfi Tal and the 1972 massacre of eleven Israeli athletes and coaches at the Munich Olympics. The most enduring consequence of Black September, however, has been the Europeanization of the Arab-Israeli conflict, a development that has featured political terrorist attacks upon civilian targets in Western Europe. And it is as a highly conspicuous figure in the Europeanization of the Palestinian cause that Ilich Ramírez Sanchez began and pursued his career as Carlos, the political terrorist.

In spite of his dramatic dismissal from Lumumba University, Ilich came to the PFLP training camp highly recommended by Haddad's associate in Moscow, Mohammed Boudia. While in Jordan, Ilich undertook the usual guerrilla training and displayed an intense dislike of living conditions in the capital of Amman.

Smith comments, for example, that Ilich, who hated his living quarters, "found the food and the squalor of Amman almost intolerable." He also showed a contemptuous condescension toward those Palestinians in whose name he ostensibly would be fighting. Ilich's rude behavior toward his hosts was no more unnoticed in Amman than it had been in Moscow, and Haddad was forced to criticize him for his behavior.[15] As the expected confrontation between King Hussein and the PLO approached, Haddad decided to send his foreign apprentices, Ilich included, to a comparatively safer Beirut. There the city's cosmopolitan nightlife proved more to his liking than Amman. It was also in Beirut that Ilich met with Leila Khaled, the recently released skyjacker of an El Al airliner.[16]

By November 1970, Ilich had returned to London, where he was reunited with his mother and brothers. By this time, Haddad and Boudia were already organizing a Palestinian network of political terrorists with cells in London, Paris, and elsewhere in Europe. Arrangements also were under way for Ilich to receive further training, chiefly in political terrorist tactics more suitable to urban, European conditions.[17]

For the next three years, from November 1970 to December 1973, Ilich pursued a pleasant double life as a playboy on the one hand, and as a political terrorist-in-training on the other. To appear to be "doing something," Ilich also accepted a part-time position as an instructor of Spanish at a local secretarial college. But Ilich was doing something during his residence in Europe; indeed, the congenial facade that he had established for himself served merely to conceal his true vocation. And, as he gradually nurtured that segment of his identity known as Carlos, he not only was doing something but also was putting into action the paternal, rabidly Marxist teachings of which Dr. Ramírez merely had spoken.[18]

During the early part of 1971, Ilich began to set up safe houses in London and Paris for his political terrorist cell. Pending his future performance, he took temporary command of the Paris cell, the Boudia Commando. He also received additional advanced training at a PFLP camp in southern Lebanon. Thus, the Ilich Ramírez Sanchez who emerged from that PFLP camp departed as a fully trained political terrorist eager for his first serious action.[19]

Ilich soon proved to be as ebullient toward the execution of his craft as he was proficient in it. He became an enthusiastic expert in the creation and assumption of false identities: Adolfo José Muller, a Chilean engineer; Charles Clarke, a New Yorker; or Glenn H. Gebhard, another New Yorker. As Smith points out, however,

> the person [whom Ilich] felt most comfortable being was Carlos Andres Martinez-Torres, a Peruvian economist born 4 May 1947. This was a young man who, in keeping with the Zeitgeist, was certainly *of* the Left although just a little too fond of the good life to be taken very seriously. The photograph on the Peruvian passport is the one the world has come to know him by: a thick-lipped, unsmiling, almost baby face half hidden behind an enormous pair of sunglasses.[20]

Ilich also established additional safe houses in the London and Paris apartments of at least four unwitting girlfriends. He used these locations to conceal an astonishing array of weapons, explosives, and false papers. Although these women, without exception, were kept ignorant of their lover's actual vocation, most of them ultimately would serve abbreviated prison sentences as his unknowing, yet de facto, accessories.[21]

One of these four mistress-pawns, Maria Angeles (Angela) Otaola, a Basque waitress living in West London, also had begun a relationship with Barry Woodhams, a local biochemist. With a small armory of automatic pistols and ammunition clips, a gas gun, grenades, plastic explosives, and rubber truncheons safely hidden away, Ilich and the unknowing Woodhams frequently would converse about weapons, political terrorism, crime, sex, and money. Although never actually divulging his true profession to Woodhams, Ilich aroused his suspicions. As Smith points out, "The conversations with Woodhams are revealing because they show that Carlos was far from always being the cool professional. His main problem was ego. He could hardly bear to keep a secret, even when his liberty and perhaps his life were at risk."[22]

Smith cites several examples of the good-natured and illuminating banter between the two men:

> Once, for instance, they were talking about the best way to fire a certain type of game rifle. [Woodhams] crouched in the sitting room to show how he had used the weapon while stalking deer

in the Zambian bush. "Not like that," snorted Carlos. "If you do it like that you'll make a profile and people will shoot back." Obviously it was not the way they had taught him to use a Dragunov sniper's rifle at the camp in Lebanon. Woodhams ignored it and put it down to Carlos's desire to impress.[23]

On another occasion, Woodhams informed Ilich that he could score nineteen out of twenty on a firing range with a .22 rifle. Ilich retorted that he could achieve the same score with a handgun.[24]

Woodhams also recalled Ilich's rather flippant, yet revealing, stance toward airport security:

> One night we got going on security systems at airports. I told him about seeing a television program on how they had increased security precautions at airports, but he just shrugged it off: "They're a waste of time because they won't work for someone who knows what he's doing." Then he went on to tell me about Charles de Gaulle Airport in Paris. He explained about the all-glass tunnels with the moving walks that took people to their planes. There were two security guards at the head of the tunnel and one up on top looking down. "If you have three or four people who are well organized," Carlos said, "and who are absolutely determined, all you have to do is shoot the two guards on the gate and run like hell down the tunnel. You can forget about the guard on top. The tunnel is crowded with people and with the distortion in the glass, we'll be on the plane before he gets a shot off. We might lose one man, but no more than that." He wasn't giving it as a hypothetical situation. He was saying, "I've been there lots and lots of times and I know what can be done." When I mentioned the new devices that check your luggage and sniff for explosives, his answer was the same: "It's easy if you're absolutely determined. You can get anything through."[25]

As Woodhams would later put it, "It was a wonder [Ilich] did not wear a T-shirt with 'I am a terrorist' stencilled on the front."[26]

Ilich also boasted of his membership in Churchill's, an ultraexclusive after-theater dining club where he drank "nothing but Napoleon brandy." Woodhams reflected:

> His main interest seemed to be sex and money. "I love all girls," he used to say. On money matters his fantasies really ran wild. One moment he saw himself as a big-time gambler making a fortune at the turn of a single card; the next he was some master criminal, Jack Hawkins in *The League of Gentlemen*, coolly planning some billion-dollar heist. [Woodhams] remembers

Carlos exulting over a headline in the *Evening Standard* about an armed raid on the American Express office in Kensington. "God, I wish I'd been with them," he said.[27]

By the time Ilich had moved his London safe house base from Angela's apartment to that of another of his many mistresses, he already had been involved in the bulk of his operations as a political terrorist. Under his leadership of the PFLP's European cell, an extensive inventory of political terrorist attacks launched either by him or by the Boudia Commando may be reliably confirmed. These assaults included: 1) the taking of hostages at Austria's Schonau transit camp for Soviet Jewish émigrés (September 1973), 2) Ilich's mistaken shooting of British insurance broker Alan Quartermaine (November 1973), 3) his shooting of prominent British Zionist J. Edward Sieff (December 1973), 4) his bombing of the Israeli Bank of Hapoalin in London (January 1974), 5) the car bombing of several French newspapers and broadcasting offices and the United Jewish Social Fund headquarters in Paris (August 1974), 6) a raid on the French embassy in The Hague (September 1974), 7) Ilich's tossing of a fragmentation grenade into the Paris café Le Drugstore (September 1974), 8) rocket attacks and the taking of hostages at Orly Airport in Paris (January 1975), and 9) the infamous taking of hostages at an Organization of Petroleum Exporting Countries (OPEC) conference in Vienna (December 1975). Given the enlightening nature of Carlos's behavior during the last of these events, the OPEC operation, I shall focus upon this final act of Ilich Ramírez Sanchez's political terrorist career.

By the time of the OPEC operation, the world already had learned a great deal about Carlos. Some months after his group had launched rocket attacks and taken hostages at Orly Airport, he narrowly escaped arrest by French security agents. Firing five shots from his 7.65-mm Russian automatic pistol, he killed two agents and critically wounded a third. Then, some six months later, in December 1975, he struck at OPEC.[28]

Extremely careful and thorough groundwork already had been laid when, on the morning of December 21, 1975, six political terrorists—Ilich Ramírez Sanchez, Hans-Joachim Klein, Gabriele Krocher-Tiedemann, and three Palestinian underlings—burst into a regular quarterly meeting of OPEC in Vienna. Three security guards were killed during the initial takeover of the

OPEC conference area, and Klein was injured when a stray bullet lodged in his stomach.[29] After securing the reception area and offices, the political terrorists turned their attention to the main conference room and its occupants. Inside were eleven oil ministers and their respective staffs, representing Algeria, Ecuador, Gabon, Indonesia, Iran, Iraq, Kuwait, Libya, Nigeria, Saudi Arabia, and Venezuela. Some seventy hostages were taken. Within minutes, the building was cordoned off by police, and Ilich began to issue his political demands. Referring to his group as the Arm of the Arab Revolution, he added: "I am from Venezuela, and my name is Carlos. They all know me. I am the famous Carlos."[30]

He then began twenty hours of negotiations with the quivering Austrian government. His ultimatum stipulated his terms: a six-page, radically rejectionist statement to be broadcast over the Austrian radio network every two hours, a specially equipped bus to transport the political terrorists and their hostages to the Vienna airport, and a DC-9 jetliner. The government was left to deal with the situation at hand. Demaris recounts a meeting held between the anxious Austrian chancellor, Bruno Kreisky, and the ambassadors of each of the OPEC nations: " 'This Carlos is very dangerous,' Kreisky said, looking around the table at the ambassadors nervously awaiting his decision. 'We have heard much about him and his ruthless methods. In my opinion, we have to go along with him.' The ambassadors were so relieved that they applauded."[31]

Kreisky agreed to accede to Ilich's ultimatum on the condition that the political terrorists free those Austrians and foreigners who were not members of the OPEC delegation. To this, Ilich sneered, "I am the commander here, I command Kreisky and everybody else. Nobody can tell me what to do. I shall decide who I take with me and who I leave behind. . . . I don't want anybody telling me what I can and cannot do. This is my operation."[32] The chancellor then assented to each of the demands.

From all accounts, Ilich appeared to be positively rhapsodic about the success of his operation. As Smith observes, "There can be no doubt that Carlos enjoyed being Carlos, and that once inside the OPEC building he shed his anonymity like an old coat. . . . [Throughout the operation] he acted like a young man at the top of his profession, who knew he had won first prize."[33] For example, shortly after his demand was met that a sumptuous buffet luncheon be prepared for his hostages, Ilich crowed: "Look, I treat them very well. They feel like they are in a party at the Hilton."[34]

He and other members of the Arm of the Arab Revolution also could content themselves by monitoring news coverage of the OPEC operation. As Smith points out, Ilich was satisfied with the massive media attention that his operation received. As Demaris reports, he was "visibly relaxed, almost euphoric, as he strolled around . . . answering all questions, a small smile playing at the corners of his mouth."[35]

In his communications with the Arab governments, Kreisky determined that Algeria, a destination acceptable to Ilich as a "revolutionary country," would accept the political terrorists upon the immediate release of all hostages. An Austrian Airways DC-9 jetliner was fully ready by the next morning, and the wounded terrorist, Klein, was transported to the airport by ambulance. Waving to observers of these proceedings, Ilich seemed to be satisfied with the apparent success of his operation.[36]

He certainly had a very pleasant flight to Algiers, signing autographs and, according to Valentin Hernandez Acosta, the Venezuelan oil minister, generally acting like a movie star. He even demonstrated that he was a devoted son. Ilich leisurely sought out the company of Hernandez and asked him to transfer a handwritten letter to his mother, then in Caracas. Although the French police later asked to see the letter, the minister refused, protesting that its contents were personal. Hernandez, however, did permit the French security agents to Xerox the handwriting on the envelope, which positively established its author as the world's most-wanted political terrorist: Ilich Ramírez Sanchez.[37]

After touchdown in Algiers, Ilich requested an on-board audience with Algerian Foreign Minister Abdelaziz Bouteflika. After their conference, Ilich began releasing all non-Arab oil ministers and their staffs. Fifteen captives, including Oil Ministers Jamshid Amouzegar of Iran and Sheik Yamani of Saudi Arabia, were forced to remain on board the aircraft. Both Kreisky and Algerian President Houari Boumedienne believed that Ilich had lied about his true plans, which were to parade the OPEC ministers around the radical capitals of the Middle East.[38]

Insisting that Libyan leader Moammar Qaddafi be present to meet the arriving jetliner, Ilich then ordered the DC-9 on to

Tripoli. During the flight, Ilich spoke to Sheik Yamani, whom he had threatened to execute at some point while in Vienna. According to Yamani, Ilich "spoke happily of putting pressure on the Austrian government" and "boasted of his power and of his sexual exploits." Upon arrival in the Libyan capital, Ilich ordered the plane's pilot to taxi to Qaddafi's own landing area. However, the Tripoli control tower, much to Ilich's anger, refused permission.[39]

The hostage drama finally ended when a frustrated Ilich decided to order the jetliner to fly back to Algiers. As part of the arrangements made between Algeria and the political terrorists, all participating members of the Arm of the Arab Revolution were guaranteed absolute political asylum by Algeria. In fact, no government seemed anxious to seek Ilich's extradition, the consequences of which may have posed more of a peril than his continued freedom. In addition, he received an indeterminate amount of ransom money, estimated at between $2 million to $50 million.[40]

On December 24 the five uninjured political terrorists made their way to neighboring Libya, where, according to O'Ballance, they were personally welcomed by Qaddafi. Some sources claim that Ilich Ramírez Sanchez remains an honored guest in Libya, while others have suggested that he has, or had, taken up residence in Moscow, Aden, Beirut, Baghdad, London, or Bonn. In the meantime, Ilich could content himself with his father's *London Observer* interview, in which the elder Ramírez proclaimed, "My son has turned out to be a general," and that he was in total philosophical agreement with him.[41]

The issue of whether Carlos the Jackal, if he remains alive, will continue to live either on past misdeeds or sporadic rumors regarding his return is problematic at best. Will he ever reappear on the world's satellite-transmitted stage? In this case, as in so many others, only time itself will tell.

Unlike most political terrorists, neither narcissistic injury nor narcissistic disappointment appears to have played any significant role in Ilich Ramírez Sanchez's assumed psychological predisposition toward a career as a political terrorist. Nevertheless, various factors might be cited, however spuriously, as potential instances of either narcissistic injury or narcissistic disappointment: 1) Ilich's perceived role status, 2) his possibly acute sense of personal failure owing to his actions and behavior in Venezuela and Moscow, 3) his enforced isolation from his father, 4) his disillusionment with his father, or 5) his own disappointment in himself. Since none of these factors appears to have made any difference whatsoever in Ilich's decision to become a political terrorist, let us briefly consider their relative psychological insignificance.

First, Ilich's perceived role status as an overweight Latin American playboy living abroad never seems to have been of major concern to him. Thus, despite some indications of sensitivity over his chronic weight problem, his perceived role status does not appear to constitute any significant source of narcissistic injury.

Second, Ilich never expressed any recorded sense of personal failure owing either to his futile actions as a young Cuban-trained Venezuelan insurgent or to his behavior as a foreign student at Lumumba University in Moscow. In fact, his disruptive and dilettantish behavior may well have been intended as a clever means of dispelling future notions of any Soviet connection to Carlos.

Third, there is no evidence to indicate that his parents' chronic separation caused him to experience any sense of narcissistic injury. Moreover, there is no evidence to suggest that that separation transposed into Dr. Ramírez's actual chronic isolation, enforced or otherwise, from his itinerant sons.

Fourth, there is no evidence at all that Ilich experienced a sense of narcissistic disappointment in his revolutionary Marxist, millionaire father. Ilich not only accepted but also embraced his father's seemingly hypocritical, and certainly contradictory, standards and beliefs. This near-identity of views was illustrated best in Dr. Ramírez's 1975 *London Observer* interview.

And fifth, despite his ostensible behavior in Moscow, Ilich did not experience any sense of narcissistic disappointment in himself. Again, it may be assumed that his behavior and his eventual expulsion from the university were merely intended to camouflage the true nature of Carlos's Soviet connections.

Although neither narcissistic injury nor narcissistic disappointment apparently played any significant role in Ilich's psychological predisposition toward political terrorism, the fact is that he did decide to become a political terrorist. It appears that his case is that of an individual whose thirst for the psychodynamic rewards of political terrorism alone served as the psychological factor that may have contributed to his decision. Therefore, I must postulate that, although the psychodynamic rewards of political terrorism might prove especially attractive to victims of narcissistic injury and narcissistic disappointment, such narcissistic personality disturbances do not serve as psychological prerequisites to the individual decision to become a political terrorist.

The political terrorist's psychic sense of omnipotence is powerfully illustrated in the case of Ilich Ramírez Sanchez. For example, manifestations of his psychic sense of omnipotence dominate his revealing conversations with Barry Woodhams. Yet, perhaps the most notable manifestations of Ilich's sense of omnipotence may be evidenced through his behavior and verbal statements during the OPEC hostage-taking operation.

Ilich's role status as a political terrorist in large part was predicated upon the establishment, assumption, and maintenance of a designated pseudoidentity as Carlos the Jackal or, simply, Carlos. And, as Woodhams later would remark, Ilich's enthusiasm for his new, as-if other pseudoidentity occasionally verged on the foolhardy. As Smith points out, for Ilich "there was never the spy's secret satisfaction in being different to what he seemed"; he wanted everybody to know what he was. And finally, Ilich's firm intentions to maintain this as-if other pseudoidentity are borne out by his flamboyant behavior and inflated self-characterizations during his last hurrah as a political terrorist, the OPEC operation of 1975.[42]

Notes

1. It is commonly believed that Ilich Ramírez Sanchez chose the code name "Carlos" as a tribute to Carlos Marighella, the author of the "Minimanual of the Urban Guerrilla" and *For the Liberation of Brazil*. "The Jackal" is taken from Frederick Forsythe's novel, *The Day of the Jackal*, about the attempted assassination of French President Charles de Gaulle. Carlos is himself the subject of several novels, including: Uri Dan and Peter Mann, *Carlos Must Die* (New York: W. W. Norton, 1978); Denis Eisenberg and Eli Landau, *Carlos: Terror International* (London: Corgi, 1976); and David Atlee Phillips, *The Carlos Con-*

tract: A Novel of International Terrorism (New York: Macmillan, 1978). Nonfiction sources on Ilich Ramírez Sanchez include, for example, Ovid Demaris, "Carlos," in *Brothers in Blood* (New York: Scribner's, 1977), 1–64; Christopher Dobson and Ronald Payne, *The Carlos Complex: A Study in Terror* (New York: G. P. Putnam's, 1977); Ron Laytner, "An Interview with the Jackal Leads to a Life of Constant Fear," *Boston Globe*, July 8, 1982; Edgar O'Ballance, "Carlos the Jackal," in *The Language of Violence* (San Rafael, CA: Presidio, 1979), 205–20; Colin Smith, *Carlos: Portrait of a Terrorist* (New York: Holt, Rinehart, 1976); idem, "Portrait of a Terrorist: The World's Most Wanted Criminal," *Present Tense* 4 (1977): 52–57; Claire Sterling, "Carlos," in *Terror Network*, 129–46; Nydia Tobon, *Carlos: Terrorist or Guerrilla?* (Barcelona: Ediciones Grijalbo, 1978); and "Trading in Terror, Carlos Becomes the World's Most Wanted Criminal," *People Weekly* (October 11, 1976): 24–27.

2. See Dobson and Payne, *Carlos Complex*, 32; Christopher Dobson and Ronald Payne, *The Terrorists* (New York: Facts on File, 1979), 40; Smith, *Carlos*, 25, 28; and Demaris, "Carlos," 23.

3. See Dobson and Payne, *Carlos Complex*, 32; Demaris, "Carlos," 23; and Smith, *Carlos*, 28.

4. See Dobson and Payne, *Carlos Complex*, 32–33; Smith, *Carlos*, 28–29; and Demaris, "Carlos," 23.

5. See Smith, *Carlos*, 29; and Dobson and Payne, *Carlos Complex*, 32.

6. Ibid.

7. Smith, *Carlos*, 29.

8. See Demaris, "Carlos," 23; and Dobson and Payne, *Carlos Complex*, 33–35.

9. See Smith, *Carlos*, 29; Dobson and Payne, *Carlos Complex*, 35; and Demaris, "Carlos," 24.

10. See Sterling, *Terror Network*, 130–31.

11. See Sterling, *Terror Network*, 131–34; Dobson and Payne, *Carlos Complex*, 35, 38; Demaris, "Carlos," 23–24; Smith, *Carlos*, 30–34; and O'Ballance, "Carlos the Jackal," 207.

12. See Sterling, *Terror Network*, 134; Smith, *Carlos*, 25–46; Demaris, "Carlos," 24; and O'Ballance, "Carlos the Jackal," 207.

13. Smith, *Carlos*, 35, 40–41; O'Ballance, "Carlos the Jackal," 206–7; Dobson and Payne, *Carlos Complex*, 38; idem, *The Terrorists*, 40; Demaris, "Carlos," 25; and Sterling, *Terror Network*, 134–35.

14. See Smith, *Carlos*, 44–46.

15. See ibid., 78–82; and O'Ballance, "Carlos the Jackal," 207.

16. Smith, *Carlos*, 82–83.

17. See ibid., 84.

18. See Demaris, "Carlos," 24; Smith, *Carlos*, 84–86, 88; and Dobson and Payne, *Carlos Complex*, 38–39.

19. See Demaris, "Carlos," 23, 25; Dobson and Payne, *Carlos Complex*, 39; O'Ballance, "Carlos the Jackal," 207; and Smith, *Carlos*, 92–93.

20. Ibid., 99–100 (emphasis in original). For a further discussion of Ilich's false identities see, for example, Dobson and Payne, *Carlos Complex*, 43; and Demaris, "Carlos," 26.

21. See especially ibid., 23, 47–48, 58, 60–61; Smith, *Carlos*, 149, 160–61, 163–65; Dobson and Payne, *Carlos Complex*, 43; and O'Ballance, "Carlos the Jackal," 214.

22. Smith, *Carlos*, 154. See also ibid., 151–53, 215; Demaris, "Carlos," 42–45, 59–60; Dobson and Payne, *Carlos Complex*, 43; and O'Ballance, "Carlos the Jackal," 214.

23. Smith, *Carlos*, 154.

24. See Demaris, "Carlos," 44.

25. Quoted in ibid., 45.

26. Quoted in Smith, *Carlos*, 208.

27. Ibid., 156.

28. See Smith, *Carlos*, 199–212, 216–17; O'Ballance, "Carlos the Jackal," 213–14; Demaris, "Carlos," 49–55, 61–62; Sterling, *Terror Network*, 129–30, 140; Dobson and Payne, *Carlos Complex*, 7.

29. See Smith, *Carlos*, 174–75, 245, 262; Demaris, "Carlos," 4, 7–9; Sterling, *Terror Network*, 79–91, 137–38, 140, 142–45, 155, 230, 235, 246, 282, 287; and O'Ballance, "Carlos the Jackal," 215, 217.

30. Quoted in ibid., 216. See also Demaris, "Carlos," 6–7; Smith, *Carlos*, 244–45; and Dobson and Payne, *Carlos Complex*, 89.

31. Demaris, "Carlos," 11. For the use of the term "quivering," used to characterize the Kreisky government during this episode, see Dobson and Payne, *Carlos Complex*, 89. See also Demaris, "Carlos," 8; O'Ballance, "Carlos the Jackal," 216–17; and Smith, *Carlos*, 246.

32. Quoted in Demaris, "Carlos," 12. See also Smith, *Carlos*, 262; and O'Ballance, "Carlos the Jackal," 217.

33. Smith, *Carlos*, 154.

34. Quoted in Demaris, "Carlos," 12–13. See also Smith, *Carlos*, 262.

35. Smith, *Carlos*, 265; and Demaris, "Carlos," 14.

36. See ibid., 16; O'Ballance, "Carlos the Jackal," 217; and Smith, *Carlos*, 270.

37. See ibid., 276; O'Ballance, "Carlos the Jackal," 205, 218; and Demaris, "Carlos," 16–17.

38. Ibid., 17; Smith, *Carlos*, 278; O'Ballance, "Carlos the Jackal," 218; and Dobson and Payne, *Carlos Complex*, 96–97.

39. On Yamani's recollections see Dobson and Payne, *The Terrorists*, 41. See also Demaris, "Carlos," 17–18; O'Ballance, "Carlos the Jackal," 218; and Dobson and Payne, *Carlos Complex*, 94–95.

40. See Demaris, "Carlos," 18–20; Dobson and Payne, *Carlos Complex*, 98–101, 125; O'Ballance, "Carlos the Jackal," 218–20; Smith, *Carlos*, 283–84, 292; and Sterling, *Terror Network*, 143–44.

41. For Dr. Ramírez's 1975 comments in the *London Observer* see Demaris, "Carlos," 22. See also O'Ballance, "Carlos the Jackal," 219; Dobson and Payne, *Carlos Complex*, 124; Sterling, *Terror Network*, 143–45; Smith, *Carlos*, 297; and Laytner, "Interview with the Jackal."

42. Smith, *Carlos*, 208.

CHAPTER TEN

Better Red than Misled: Ulrike Meinhof and Renato Curcio

No study of the political terrorist may be considered reasonably complete without some reference to the charter figures of West Germany's Red Army Faction (RAF), also known as the Baader-Meinhof Gang, and Italy's Red Brigades. These two political terrorist groups generally have been regarded as among the most conspicuous and active such organizations in Western Europe. Moreover, subsequent generations of both the RAF and its Italian counterpart have reemerged, in Hydra-like fashion, on numerous occasions since the early 1970s. The purpose of this chapter will be to examine psychopolitical case studies of Ulrike Meinhof of the Red Army Faction and Renato Curcio of the Red Brigades.

Typically portrayed as the ideological high priestess of the RAF, Ulrike Meinhof is one of the most fascinating of all political terrorists. As biographer Melvin Lasky puts it, this gifted journalist became a political terrorist "by some process which has defied analysis by police psychologists." Another of her biographers, Ovid Demaris, characterizes her as the most famous woman in postwar Germany. Who was she, and what psychological factors might have motivated her to become a political terrorist?[1]

Ulrike Marie Meinhof, the second child of an art museum director and an art historian, was born on October 7, 1934, in

Oldenburg, an industrial town just west of Bremen, Germany. Ulrike's father, notes Jillian Becker, hailed from a long line of theologians and minor public officials, while her mother was the product of a recently successful and Socialist-leaning petit bourgeois family. As Demaris notes, Ulrike Meinhof, the only member of the Red Army Faction able to recall the early years of the Third Reich, had a strong sense of social conscience that derived from both her father's theological background and her mother's Socialist tendencies. Indeed, Mrs. Meinhof's family repeatedly provided sanctuary to Communist German Resistance fighters throughout the Third Reich years.[2]

Ulrike's father died of cancer when she was six years old. Demaris, Stefan Possony and Francis Bouchey, and others have noted that Dr. Meinhof's death had come on the heels of acute depression brought on by his wife's short-lived infidelity. The significance of this sequence of events also has been addressed by Frederick Hacker, who states that "there may have been a connection in the mind of the child between her mother's marital indiscretions and her father's death."[3]

Shortly after Dr. Meinhof's death, his financially strapped widow rented a room to Renate Riemeck, a Socialist historian with whom Mrs. Meinhof had become acquainted. Ulrike and Renate became extremely close, and, when Mrs. Meinhof also died of cancer in 1949, Renate assumed responsibility for the two children's upbringing. The Meinhof children were extremely fortunate in this regard, for none of their relatives had evinced the slightest interest in their fate. As Becker notes, this family rejection undoubtedly reinforced the "insecurity and abnormality of being left an orphan" that Ulrike experienced after her mother's death.[4]

Despite Renate's solicitude, Ulrike "needed, and was to seek in the years to come, 'family' groups to which she could belong and be central." This obsession for belonging, attention, and approval is central to Becker's personality portrait of the young Ulrike Meinhof. According to Demaris, Renate Riemeck, the first woman to attain the rank of university professor in West Germany, also exerted a decisive influence upon Ulrike's emerging sense of social conscience. Ulrike first became politically involved in the 1950s when she, like Renate, led an activist group opposed to nuclear weapons.[5]

Ulrike's participation in the nascent antinuclear movement directly led to her career as a famous journalist as well as to her unhappy marriage to Klaus Reiner Rohl, publisher of the leftist magazine, *Konkret*. Ulrike's brilliant intellect and polemical and debating skills made her a glamorous "Gloria Steinem of the German media," as Demaris characterizes her. Ulrike and her new mentor, Rohl, embarked upon a highly successful professional relationship in Hamburg, and Rohl, who had become intensely attracted to his soon-to-be editor in chief, married her in 1961. Twin daughters were born the following year.[6]

Despite her lofty professional achievements and lavish lifestyle, Ulrike's marriage and career proved to be sources of profound narcissistic injury and disappointment to her. The star columnist was unprepared for all that her meteoric celebrity apparently entailed. As Possony and Bouchey point out, Ulrike quickly learned that her husband had been, and would remain, chronically unfaithful. Perhaps in light of her parents' own marital travails, Ulrike ultimately found this situation to be intolerable.[7]

She also became strongly disillusioned with *Konkret*'s increasing preoccupation with the seamier side of West German society. Pointing out that *Konkret*'s style was more *Playboy* than *Pravda*, Demaris also acknowledges that

> exactly when she became disenchanted with her life is impossible to pinpoint. As more nudes, pornography, and crime stories began to fill the pages of *Konkret* to revive its faltering circulation, she gradually turned her attention to the misery of social groups on the periphery—the real victims of the capitalistic system. "She knew she was living a lie," says Renate Riemeck, "cavorting with the rich and yearning to liberate the poor." . . . [Noted the Hamburg weekly, *Die Zeit*,] "Her honesty, also against herself, spoke from every line she wrote."[8]

Further afflicting Ulrike were medical problems that dated from emergency brain surgery shortly after her twins were born. Although the chronic headaches she experienced during her pregnancy proved to be due to a hematoma, or swollen blood vessel, rather than to the brain tumor that her parents' medical history had caused her to suspect and fear, the procedure led to great pain and anxiety. The five-hour operation included the drilling of a small hole in Ulrike's skull, a portion of which had to be removed. After the operation, morphine was withheld from her in order to determine the possible presence of nerve damage. Hence, as Possony and Bouchey indicate, the operation and its aftermath, coming at the time that it did, "resulted in an inordinate amount of pain and psychological anguish which abated only gradually." Ulrike also was left with a permanent souvenir from the experience—a silver clamp inserted into her brain in order to relieve further pressure. This therapeutic measure, however, apparently served only to precipitate severe pain and headaches. Emotionally fragile and insecure, she was unable to return home for three months after the operation.

The next several years were increasingly difficult ones for Ulrike. *Konkret's* contents were becoming more and more decadently bizarre. Moreover, her husband's extramarital affairs and flippant attitude about their life-style and work continued to hurt and annoy her. At some point during the late 1960s she decided that she had had enough—enough of her *haut bourgeois* life-style, enough of her miserable marriage, and enough of *Konkret*. According to Demaris, "the disgust she felt for her way of life became unbearable. Her first step was to sue Rohl for divorce in February 1968. She gained custody of her daughters, while her husband retained their posh house and publishing firm. She also received a generous cash settlement. Yet, in addition to the upheaval caused by her divorce, Ulrike's "actions and words began to express an increasing bitterness and anger—not, she would insist, over hurt pride, remorse, and regret, a sense of having been a victim of unfairness, injustice, of having been exploited and misprized, held too lightly in esteem, humiliated; not over Rohl as faithless husband; but over Rohl as misdirector of *Konkret*."⁹

Nevertheless, she continued her writing for *Konkret* on a regular basis. Now living in politically charged West Berlin, she feverishly attempted to bring some positive meaning to her fractured existence. Her literary humanitarianism gave way to the more strident rhetoric of open rebellion. In a sense, Ulrike seems to have projected her own emotional confusion onto the West German government and other pro-Western interests. As Becker puts it, Ulrike's writings on resistance, struggle, and counterviolence suggested "the same noble motives as she [had], with which to fuse her own cause." She also decided to form an authors' collective—Konkret Berlin[10]—with some of West Berlin's leading student radicals, such as Rudi Dutschke and Bahman Nirumand. The years from 1968 to 1970 saw a tremendous growth of student radical activity in West Germany not unlike that in the United States and elsewhere in the West. The Frankfurt arson and the Springer blockade, student actions directed against the American prosecution of the Vietnam War, profoundly affected Ulrike Meinhof. Thus, she used her column to justify and champion the West German student Left. As she herself, in response to the shooting of Dutschke, wrote:

> The boundary between verbal protest and physical resistance has been transgressed in the protests against the attack on Dutschke these Easter holidays for the first time in a massive way, by many, not just individuals, over days, not just once, at many places, not only in Berlin, in actual fact, not only symbolically. . . . Resistance was practiced. Was that all sense-less, unrestrained, terroristic, apolitical, powerless violence?[11]

She expressed similar sentiments about the firebombing of two Frankfurt warehouses when she declared that "the progressive aspect of warehouse arson consists not in the destruction but in the criminality of the deed, in the legal violation." As a result of her writings, she was invited to visit the four captured arsonists by their attorney, Horst Mahler. The visit was a critical one for Ulrike, who, indicates Demaris, was "deeply impressed by these young people who had taken the final step in divorcing themselves from society."[12]

The stage, therefore, would soon be set for the formation of the Red Army Faction when two of the arsonists—Gudrun Ensslin and Andreas Baader—escaped from prison in the spring of 1970. Baader was soon recaptured but escaped again when he and his visitor, Ulrike Meinhof, leaped out of a library window at the Institute of Social Studies in Dahlem. Together with three other companions, Baader and Meinhof fled in a waiting car. As Demaris notes, Ulrike's next move would be to ravage Rohl's home: "Accompanied by her new comrades, she revisited her old Blankenese villa with the intent of devastating the 'once happy home.' . . . Behaving like vandals, they completely destroyed the furnishings, defaced the walls, and painted a phallus on the front door. In a final act of contempt, they collectively urinated on the old double bed in the master bedroom."[13]

Mahler soon named the new political terrorist group the Red Army Faction. After a brief period underground, Ulrike, Mahler, Baader, Ensslin, and others spent six weeks engaged in urban guerrilla training in Jordan. Upon their return to West Germany, the RAF allegedly assisted in the planning of the Black September attack at the 1972 Munich Olympics. The group also participated in several bank "expropriations" and bombings at the U.S. Army Officers' Club in Frankfurt, the Augsburg and Munich police headquarters, the Springer press building in Hamburg, and the computer center at U.S. Army Headquarters in Heidelberg.[14]

Ulrike and her terrorist companions were arrested in Hannover only one month after their RAF activities commenced. She was sentenced to an eight-year prison term for the Baader escape and was tried for her subsequent deeds at Stammheim Prison. Continuing her writings, she outlined fully her political philosophy. After a lengthy hunger strike and forced feedings by authorities, she committed suicide by hanging herself on May 9, 1976. Her funeral was attended by over four thousand people, hundreds of whom wore masks. One fellow writer present at the funeral praised Ulrike Meinhof as "the most important German woman since Rosa Luxemburg."[15]

Jillian Becker, in her consideration of Ulrike's decision to become a political terrorist, is drawn irresistibly to her symbolic leap out of the library window with Baader. In an altogether appropriate summation, both on Ulrike Meinhof in particular and on the individual political terrorist in general, she asserts that

> [her leap from the window] was an act as irreversible as suicide; and for a while at least it did very well instead. To leap out of an old unsatisfactory life into a new, of excitement and urgent purpose, romantically at pitch and in peril, and with a new name, was virtually—so she must have hoped—to lose the old identity and to leave the old melancholy separateness behind; for the new identity was that of the group. So now too there would be the close companionship she had always craved, this time welded by mutual dependence, shared danger, and common aims to be pursued with total dedication, of extreme personal risk, and without scruple. For once one had broken the law, one was surely freed from all constraint: if there was

no going back, there was also no limit ahead, other than the limit of the outlaws' own capabilities. An illusory sense of power and a certainty of victory would make them feel their capabilities to be great. Each could seek personal relief through acts of violence and blood and terror, and always with a grandiose moral justification. They could call a lust for revenge "a thirst for justice," and terrorism a righteous fury that "society" was a euphemism (which she could not recognize, her insight into her own motives not having matured with her years) for her own failings, and for Klaus Reiner Rohl. And her committing of herself to a life outside the law was a venture to overcome not governments, not systems, but private despair.[16]

Clearly, Ulrike Meinhof was psychologically afflicted both by narcissistic injury and narcissistic disappointment. Her narcissistic injuries appear to have derived from 1) the nature of her object relations with significant others, and 2) her serious physical illness. Her narcissistic injury-engendering object relations seem to have centered upon the early death of her parents and upon her perceived rejection by her remaining family and, later, by her husband. As Becker notes, none of her surviving relatives demonstrated the least concern for the orphaned Meinhof children following their mother's death. Ulrike's lifelong obsession for belonging, attention, and approval may have been one result of that family rejection. Given his frequent and brazen infidelities, Ulrike's marriage to Klaus Rohl appears to have been an even more profound source of narcissistic injury. And one last source seems to lie in the medical complications ensuing from Ulrike's emergency brain surgery.

Her fervent embrace of political terrorism appears to have been most strongly influenced by her direct, narcissistic disappointment in herself. That narcissistic disappointment, which resulted from Ulrike's perceived, and actual, inability to adhere to those positive and desirable standards of behavior put forth in her own ego ideal, seems to have been caused by several factors. Viewed as a whole, it is apparent that she was extremely vulnerable to ego ideal-induced narcissistic disappointment; she thus proved unable to carry out the tyrannical dictates of an overly grandiose ego ideal. The development of that ego ideal may be clearly traced both to Ulrike's own parents and to the intense relationship that she shared with her guardian-savior, Renate Riemeck. Riemeck's highly idealistic standards and beliefs became the major component in what emerged as a tyrannical ego ideal. Hence, when Ulrike's increasing disgust and disillusionment with her *haut bourgeois* life-style and work at *Konkret* came to a head, she did, indeed, suffer a severe narcissistic disappointment in herself. Given her other psychobiographical experiences, from that point on Ulrike Meinhof was a prime candidate for recruitment into the RAF.

Like Ulrike Meinhof, Renato Curcio is widely recognized as the central ideological leader of a major, first-generation West European political terrorist group. Also like Meinhof, Curcio was the product of a fundamentally middle-class upbringing complicated by difficult family circumstances. And, like his West German counterpart, Curcio immersed himself in relatively legitimate activities that ultimately served as sources of profound, narcissistic disappointment for him. Now, as the long-imprisoned leader of Italy's Red Brigades, Curcio has not received the enormous academic, literary, and journalistic notice rendered to political terrorists such as Ulrike Meinhof or Ilich Ramírez Sanchez. His comparatively obscure psychopolitical path toward a career of political terrorism, however, has been exceedingly well documented in Alessandro Silj's superb study, *Never Again without a Rifle.*[17]

Renato Curcio, the product of an extramarital affair between Renato Zampa and Yolanda Curcio, was born in a maternity home near Rome on September 23, 1941. Then stationed at the Russian front, Zampa instructed Yolanda, a Waldensian, to have the infant baptized in a Catholic church. Luigi Zampa and his wife served as godparents at the baptism, looked after the baby, and helped find a family to take in Yolanda.[18] Silj's portrait of Renato's early years indicates that this was a trying period for both mother and child. Moving around from one family, and one job, to another, Yolanda finally settled in the Waldensian community of Torre Pellice. Leaving Renato in his aunt's care in Torre Pellice, Yolanda again moved and accepted a series of menial positions.[19]

Renato's dim memories of these wartime years, 1943 to 1945, center upon the brief moments he spent with his beloved maternal uncle, Armando, who had returned from Yugoslavia following the disbandment of the Italian army forces stationed there. In

April 1945, Armando and several of his fellow partisans were massacred in a Fascist ambush. Renato's hazy memories of Armando, claims Silj, ultimately would "assume precise contours, no longer only those of an affectionate uncle." Moreover, his perceptions of Armando played a major psychopolitical role in his ultimate decision to become a political terrorist. Later, during his initial prison confinement, Renato would write the following letter to his mother:

> Yolanda dearest, mother mine, years have passed since the day on which I set out to encounter life and left you alone to deal with life. I have worked, I have studied, I have fought. . . . Distant memories stirred. Uncle Armando who carried me astride his shoulders. His limpid and ever smiling eyes that peered far into the distance towards a society of free and equal men. And I loved him like a father. And I picked up the rifle that only death, arriving through the murderous hand of the nazi-fascists, had wrested from him. . . . My enemies are the enemies of humanity and of intelligence, those who have built and build their accursed fortunes on the material and intellectual misery of the people. Theirs is the hand that has banged shut the door of my cell. And I cannot be but proud. But I am not merely an "idealist" and it is not enough for me to have, as is said, "a good conscience." For this reason I will continue to fight for communism even from the depths of a prison.[20]

In the course of his childhood and adolescent years in Torre Pellice, Renato completed school and awaited the return of his long-itinerant mother. Up until this point, the boy's father had never even met him. Zampa suddenly appeared in Torre Pellice to discuss his son's education. Acceding to his father's wishes, Renato was enrolled in high school and became the guest of a family in Imperia, where Zampa and his American wife were living. Renato failed three subjects during his first year, and, after repeating the entire year, he again received failing grades. A highly exercised Zampa recommended that Renato enroll instead in a hotel-management program. Both Renato and his mother refused to take Zampa up on this suggestion. Resuming his studies in Imperia, Renato easily passed the three vocational training classes that he had previously failed.[21]

Yolanda, who had moved to Milan, took Renato to live with her. The teenager got a job as an elevator operator in a luxury hotel run by a friend of Zampa's. Then, rather than enter the hotel-management business, Renato decided to enroll in the Ferrini Institute at Albenga. He and his mother moved to the area, where he quickly became a model student.[22] Zampa made occasional, token visits to his son, but these gestures proved awkward and difficult for both of them. According to Zampa, his son appeared to be a reserved, introverted boy; hence, "there wasn't much of a dialogue with him." Yet, by way of contrast, Renato was remembered by his teachers and fellow students at the Ferrini Institute as an outgoing and occasionally jocular young man who had an extremely active social life.[23]

Then came a watershed event in the life of Renato Curcio: Zampa offered to give him his surname. After some thought, the son refused the father's offer. As Silj comments, Renato had "decided that the name Curcio suited him well, [and] that there was no point in changing it after so many years."[24]

Renato completed his degree in 1962 and won a scholarship to study at the new Institute of Sociology at Trento University, where the relatively young discipline of sociology was being taught. The Trentine "experiment" was perceived as a clean break from Italian society, both by young Italians, in general, and by Renato Curcio, in particular. Indeed, in one of his many letters to Yolanda, Renato reminded his mother that she had taught him not to be afraid of the new. And, as Silj surmises, "In Trento, Curcio sought a new identity."[25]

The Trentine experiment proved to be a bitter disappointment to its students, however, for their optimistic expectations that the new university would break ground for a new society were dashed both by logic and events. (Here, the case of Patricia Soltysik and of Berkeley's People's Park may be recalled.) Violent conflicts with residents of the town, the university administration, and the local police dampened the hopes of the more politically aware students, who became cynical, disillusioned, and increasingly radical in their views. These students, whose ranks included Renato, eventually came to believe that a new Italian society had to emerge before the university's own problems might be addressed.[26]

Throughout the mid-1960s Renato's acceptance of radical politics came slowly. His eventual embrace of Marxism came by way of his interest in existentialism and the self. As Silj learned, "The fact of [Renato's] not having a father often cropped up in his conversation, and once he said, seriously, 'God is my father!' " By the late 1960s he had become a committed revolutionary and Marxian theoretician. Silj catalogs three political events that helped to transform him into a radical man of action and, ultimately, a political terrorist: two fairly bloody demonstrations at Trento and the Avola massacre of 1968, in which police, firing on protesting farm laborers, killed two and wounded numerous others. Renato also had been involved in two Marxist university groups since 1967: the Movement for a Negative University and the review *Lavoro Politico* (Political Work). During this period of violent confrontation, *Lavoro Politico* became an increasingly polarized editorial collective that split between a radical Red line and a more moderate Black line. By December 1968, Renato and his allies had sided firmly with the Red faction.[27]

Then, in August 1969, the Reds themselves expelled Renato and his supporters for "political adventurism" and "organized factionalism." This denunciation and expulsion was a bitter pill for him to swallow. It also marked his decision to leave Trento behind, for, although he already had passed his final examinations, he chose not to take his degree. The erstwhile Red then decided to transfer his base of activities to Milan.[28]

Prior to the move, Renato married his longtime lover, Margherita Cagol, a Trentine sociology major and fellow radical. Their relationship, as Silj and Robert Katz note, was an extremely intense personal bond further reinforced by the pair's shared political fanaticism. This is revealed in their correspondence with Yolanda Curcio. As Renato, in a typical letter, put it, "Margherita is magnificent. Every day I discover all the more how important and beautiful it is to have her at my side."[29]

It was in Milan that Renato Curcio became a full-fledged political terrorist. The actual birth of the Red Brigades came during the latter part of 1970, when two collectives, Renato's Proletarian Left and Alberto Franceschini's Workers' and Students' Political Collective, merged under the common designation of the Proletarian Left. By early 1971, Renato and Margherita had come to the conclusion that events compelled them to effect a complete move underground. In February the Curcios were arrested by police following their occupation of houses in the Oggidaro quarter of Milan. Margherita, then pregnant, suffered a miscarriage as a direct result of her part in the scuffle. This came as a real blow to the couple, who had decided in favor of a child despite the fact that they also had decided to go underground. After these arrests the Curcios, Franceschini, and the most militant members of the Proletarian Left went completely underground. What followed was the organization of a new group, the Red Brigades, into "columns" directed by a central committee.[30]

This political terrorist group spent the next three years, from 1972 to 1975, engaging in a series of bombings and kidnappings of prominent figures. Most noteworthy was the month-long people's trial of kidnapped Genoa prosecutor Mario Sossi. Equally dramatic was Margherita's successful raid to free her husband from Casale Monferrato Prison some five months after he and Franceschini had been apprehended. Then, only three weeks later, Margherita herself was killed in a shootout with the *carabinieri*; she had been among those members of the Red Brigades holding kidnapped distiller Vittorio Vallarino Gancia. In January 1976, Renato was again apprehended. He was tried and convicted, and he is still serving a thirty-one-year prison sentence for "forming an armed band to subvert the state," and for other offenses.[31]

What psychological factors might have helped lead Renato Curcio toward a career, however short-lived, as a political terrorist? Like so many political terrorists, he appears to have been subject to a psychobiographical battery of severe narcissistic injury, and narcissistic disappointment in significant others, similar to that manifested in the case of Ulrike Meinhof.

Renato's most fundamental narcissistic injuries seem to have resulted from two factors: 1) his overall role status, and 2) his actual, and perceived, object relations with significant others. His actual role status as an illegitimate child need not have led to any sense of narcissistic injury. The manner in which Renato's father dealt with this sensitive issue, however, contributed to his narcissistic injury-engendering, perceived role status. It thus comes as no surprise that Renato refused to accept Zampa's surname.

Another source of narcissistic injury lay in the nature of Renato's object relations with significant others. To a large extent, these relations were governed by his overall role status as Zampa's illegitimate offspring. Such narcissistic injury-engendering object relations included Renato's 1) sense of rejection, first by Zampa and then by the *Lavoro Politico* Reds; 2) enforced isolation from his mother; and 3) actual loss of his uncle Armando and, later, of his expected first child.

I already have noted Renato's perception of, and negative reaction to, his father's long-term rejection. The latter had no personal contact with Renato until well into his adolescent years. From that point on, Zampa's pitiful attentions must have been viewed by Renato as condescending, to say the least. It is also interesting to note that Renato's apparent academic failures were made to appear as sources of Zampa's own rejection of him. And finally, as in the case of Susan Stern's ejection from the Weathermen and the Sundance Collective, Renato's denunciation and expulsion by the Reds of *Lavoro Politico* caused him to suffer an acute sense of rejection by significant others.

Given Renato's rejection by Zampa and his enforced isolation from his mother, the tragic loss of his beloved uncle was a clear source of narcissistic injury. Renato himself was able to perceive a psychopolitical relationship between this narcissistic injury and his ultimate decision to become a political terrorist. Moreover, later in his life, Renato would sustain a profound narcissistic injury occasioned by Margherita's miscarriage.

Renato's psychological predisposition toward political terrorism also appears to have been determined by narcissistic disappointment in significant others. That disappointment seems to have derived from the behavior of 1) the administrators of the once-promising Trentine "experiment," and 2) the *Lavoro Politico* Reds. This deep sense of disappointment is detailed in Silj's *Never Again without a Rifle*.

Renato Curcio's own awareness of his many narcissistic injuries and disappointments is plainly manifested in an early letter to his mother written from prison: "While seeking my road, I found exploitation, injustice, oppression. And people who suffered them. I was among these latter. And these people were in the great majority. Thus I understood that my personal history was their personal history, that my future was their future."[32]

Notes

1. Melvin J. Lasky, "Ulrike Meinhof and the Baader-Meinhof Gang," *Encounter* (June 1975): 10; and Demaris, *Brothers in Blood*, 217. The literature on Ulrike Meinhof and the RAF is vast. See especially Jillian Becker, *Hitler's Children* (Philadelphia: Lippincott, 1977). See also Jillian Becker, "Case Study 1: Federal Germany," in David Carlton and Carlo Schaerf, eds., *Contemporary Terror* (New York: St. Martin's, 1981), 122–38; Gunther Wagenlehner, "Motivation for Political Terrorism in West Germany," in Marius Livingston, ed., *International Terrorism in the Contemporary World* (Westport, CT: Greenwood, 1978), 195–203; Stefan Possony and L. Francis Bouchey, *International Terrorism* (Washington: ACWF, 1978); Hans Josef Horchem, "West Germany's Red Army Anarchists," *Conflict Studies* 46 (1974); idem, "European Terrorism: A German Perspective," *Terrorism* 6 (1982): 27–51; Jane Kramer, "A Reporter in Europe," *The New Yorker* (March 20, 1978): 44; David Binder, "Anarchist Leaders Seized in Frankfurt," *New York Times*, June 2, 1972; Paul Bookbinder, "Ulrike Meinhof and Andreas Baader: The Idealist and the Adventurer," *TVI Journal* 2 (1981): 9–13; Henry Brandon, "The German Terrorists Have a Bond: It's Hatred," *New York Times*, October 30, 1977; Ralf Dahrendorf, "Baader-Meinhof—How Come? What's Next?" ibid., October 20, 1977; George Eckstein, "Germany: Democracy in Trouble," *Dissent* (Winter 1978): 82–83; John D. Elliott, "Action and Reaction: West Germany and the Baader-Meinhof Guerrillas," *Strategic Review* 4 (1976): 60–67; Paul Kemezis, "West Germany's Leftist Guerrillas Reawaken Sensitive Political Issues," *New York Times*, March 4, 1975; Melvin J. Lasky, "Ulrike and Andreas," *New York Times Magazine* (May 11, 1975); Horst Mahler, "Terrorism in West Germany," *Socialist Review* 39 (1978): 118–23; Bowman H. Miller and Charles A. Russell, "The Evolution of Revolutionary Warfare: From Mao to Marighella and Meinhof," in Robert H. Kupperman and Darrell M. Trent, eds., *Terrorism* (Stanford, CA: Hoover Institution Press, 1979), 185–99; Clarence W. Pate, "The Psychology of the Left-Wing Radical Terror in Post-World War II Germany: The Baader-Meinhof Group," paper presented to the Conference on Terrorism in the Contemporary World, April 26–28, 1976, at Glassboro State College, Glassboro, New Jersey; Sterling, *Terror Network*, 93–110; A. Stumper, "Remarks on the Baader-Meinhof Affair," *Revue de Droit pénal et de criminologie* (October 1973): 33–44; "Terrorist Leader Seized in Germany," *New York Times*, June 17, 1972; "Ulrike Meinhof, An Anarchist Leader in Germany, Is Found Hanged in Cell," ibid., May 10, 1976; Frederick Weibgen, "Compensating for a Childhood in Germany," ibid., January 17, 1978; Otto Billig, "The Lawyer Terrorist and His Comrades," *Political Psychology* 6 (1985): 29–46; Klaus Wasmund, "The Political Socialization of West German Terrorists," in Peter H. Merkl, ed., *Political Violence and Terror* (Berkeley: University of California Press, 1986), 191–228; David Th. Schiller, "Coping with Terrorism: West Germany in the 1970s and 1980s," in Anat Kurz, ed., *Contemporary Trends in World Terrorism* (New York: Praeger, 1987), 132–39; and Hans-Georg Janze, "Terrorism: Germany, Ulrike Marie Meinhof, and the RAF" (unpublished manuscript).

2. See Demaris, *Brothers in Blood*, 218; and Becker, *Hitler's Children*, 110.

3. Quoted in Demaris, *Brothers in Blood*, 218. See also Possony and Bouchey, *International Terrorism*, 134.

4. Becker, *Hitler's Children*, 111–12. See also Demaris, *Brothers in Blood*, 218; and Possony and Bouchey, *International Terrorism*, 134–35.

5. See Becker, *Hitler's Children*, 116–17; Demaris, *Brothers in Blood*, 218; and Possony and Bouchey, *International Terrorism*, 134–35.

6. See Demaris, *Brothers in Blood*, 218–19; Possony and Bouchey, *International Terrorism*, 137; and Becker, *Hitler's Children*, 129–42.

7. Demaris, *Brothers in Blood*, 219; and Possony and Bouchey, *International Terrorism*, 136–37.

8. Demaris, *Brothers in Blood*, 219.

9. Becker, *Hitler's Children*, 159. See also Demaris, *Brothers in Blood*, 220.

10. Becker, *Hitler's Children*, 159.

11. Quoted in ibid., 161.

12. Quoted in Demaris, *Brothers in Blood*, 222.

13. Ibid., 226. See also Becker, "Case Study 1," 130.

14. See Possony and Bouchey, *International Terrorism*, 145; Becker, *Hitler's Children*, 300; and Elliott, "Action and Reaction," 62.

15. Quoted in Possony and Bouchey, *International Terrorism*, 148. See also Becker, *Hitler's Children*, 300. For a further consideration of the RAF's political philosophy see, for example, Possony and Bouchey, *International Terrorism*, 114–27; Wagenlehner, "Motivation for Political Terrorism," 195–97; Horchem, "European Terrorism," 28; and Janze, "Terrorism," 6. On the capture of Ulrike Meinhof and other RAF members see "Anarchist Leaders Seized in Frankfurt" and "Terrorist Leader Seized." On the suicide of Ulrike Meinhof see "Ulrike Meinhof."

16. Becker, *Hitler's Children*, 176.

17. See Alessandro Silj, *Never Again without a Rifle* (New York: Karz, 1979). Other sources on Renato Curcio include, for example, Robert Katz, *Days of Wrath* (Garden City, NY: Doubleday, 1980), 157–60; Alessandro Silj, "Case Study II: Italy," in Carlton and Schaerf, eds., *Contemporary Terror*, 143–45; Albert Ronchey, "Terror in Italy between Red and Black," *Dissent* 25 (1978): 153–54; idem, "Guns and Gray Matter," *Foreign Affairs* 57 (1979): 928n–29n; Michael Ledeen, "Inside the Red Brigades," *New York* (May 1, 1978); Sterling, *Terror Network*, 289, 317n; and Richard Drake, "The Red and the Black," *International Political Science Review* 5 (1984). Additional sources on the Red Brigades include Robin Erica Wagner-Pacifica, *The Moro Morality Play* (Chicago: University of Chicago Press, 1986); Yonah Alexander, *Terrorism in Italy* (New York: Crane, Russak, 1979); Ciro Elliott Zoppo, " 'Never Again without a Rifle,' by Alessandro Silj: A Review of a Book and a Situation," *Terrorism* 2 (1979): 271–81; Sue Ellen Moran, "The Case of Terrorist Patrizio Peci," *TVI Journal* 5 (1985): 34–36; Leonard Weinberg and William Lee Eubank, *The Rise and Fall of Italian Terrorism* (Boulder, CO: Westview, 1987); idem, "Italian Women Terrorists," *Terrorism* 9 (1987): 241–62; Percy Allum, "Political Terrorism in Italy," *Contemporary Review* (August 1978): 75–84; J. Bowyer Bell, "The Italian Experience," in *A Time of Terror* (New York: Basic Books, 1978); Ernesto Fiorillo, "Terrorism in Italy," *Terrorism* 2 (1979): 261–70; Paul Furlong, "Political Terrorism in Italy," in Juliet Lodge, ed., *Terrorism: A Challenge to the State* (New York: St. Martin's, 1981), 57–90; "Phenomenological and Dynamic Aspects of Terrorism in Italy," *Terrorism* 2 (1979): 159–70; Vittorfranco S. Pisano, "A Survey of Terrorism of the Left in Italy," *Terrorism* 2 (1979): 171–211; idem, "Who's Fighting Italian Terrorism?" *TVI Journal* 1 (1979): 18–20; idem, *The Red Brigades* (London: Institute for the Study

of Conflict, 1980); Possony, "Kaleidoscopic Views on Terrorism," 96–104; Theodor Weiser, "Italy: The Terrorist War on the State," *Swiss Review of World Affairs* (December 1978): 11–13; Lawrence L. Whetten, "Italian Terrorism," *Terrorism* 1 (1978): 377–96; A. Aglietta, *Diary of a Jury Member at the Red Brigades Trial* (Milan: Libiri Edizioni, 1979); Giorgio Bocca, *Moro: An Italian Tragedy* (Rome: Tascabili Bompani, 1978); John Caserta, *The Red Brigades* (New York: Manor, 1978); Sari Gilbert, "Italian Terrorism on Display at Moro Trial," *Boston Globe*, December 16, 1982; Albert Ronchey, "Terror in Italy after Moro's Murder," *Dissent* 25 (1978): 383–85; and Gustavo Selva and E. Marucci, *The Martyrdom of Aldo Moro* (Bologna: Capelli, 1978).

18. See Silj, *Never Again*, 71–72.
19. See ibid., 72.
20. Quoted in ibid., 72–73.
21. See Ibid., 73.
22. See ibid., 74.
23. See ibid., 74–75.
24. Ibid.
25. Ibid., 42, 76, 77.
26. Ibid., 48. Silj, too, refers to the "disappointments" that the Trentine experiment generated among these students.
27. See ibid., 48–49, 52–70, 77–80, 81, 207.
28. See ibid., 69–71, 88–89.
29. Ibid., 82. See also Katz, *Days of Wrath*, 58.
30. Silj, *Never Again*, 90–91. See also Katz, *Days of Wrath*, 58.
31. See Katz, *Days of Wrath*, 59–60; Silj, *Never Again*, 11, 91–95; Silj, "Case Study II," 145; Ronchey, "Terror in Italy between Red and Black," 153; Ronchey, "Guns and Gray Matter," 929; and Ledeen, "Inside the Red Brigades," 38.
32. Quoted in Silj, *Never Again*, 72–73.

CHAPTER ELEVEN

Conclusion

The underlying purpose of this book has been to examine the individual psychological determinants of political terrorism. More specifically, this study has attempted to analyze the psychological backgrounds and motivations of a demographically disparate sample of political terrorists. My ultimate aim, as previously stated, has not been to construct a theory that might be applicable to every individual case of political terrorism, nor is this book intended as a comprehensive analysis of those causative factors underlying either political terrorism in toto or the specific decision to become a political terrorist.[1]

However, I have pursued a far more realistic and modest course, implicitly guided by several basic concerns: What is the psychological and psychopolitical background and development of the individual political terrorist like? What psychoanalytic factors, if any, might help motivate an individual to become a political terrorist? And finally, despite the clear absence of any such monolithic abstraction as a "terrorist personality," what is the nature and meaning of whatever psychological and psychopolitical generalizations, or commonalities, that might emerge from a reasonably diverse sample of nine political terrorists? In responding to these questions, I have endeavored to illustrate, identify, and analyze the existence of an individual psychological predisposition or propensity toward the psychodynamic rewards of political terrorism.

One suspects that political terrorism is such a peculiar and intense way of life that it must be determined in part by some combination of psychological and other personal factors. Indeed, the very term "terrorism" is itself an allusion to a psychological fait accompli: "terror." Decoding the past, however, is not an easy task. Fyodor Dostoevsky's sagacious caveat that, "while nothing is easier than to denounce the evildoer, nothing is more difficult than to understand him," underlines this point. Although a move to the first or original causes of evil behavior is fraught with intellectual peril, a more specific and circumscribed issue may be addressed: those psychological determinants underlying the individual decision to become a political terrorist. Now that that issue has been examined, I must draw attention again to an extremely useful psychoanalytic concept: narcissism, or the psychology of the self.

Suggestions of an interrelationship between the psychology of narcissism and the practice of political terrorism have been raised by a growing number of observers. Despite the presence of a rather well-defined body of literature on the relation between narcissism and aggression, broadly construed, no systematic investigation into the interrelationship between narcissism and political terrorism has ever been made a part of the public record. This study has attempted to delineate the most fundamental aspects of that critical, complex, and fascinating interrelationship.

The evidence upon which this study has been based is a reasonably diverse and representative sample of nine individuals who were faced with the opportunity to become a political terrorist and who, with one exception, opted in favor of such a career: Susan Stern, Diana Oughton, Donald DeFreeze, Patricia Soltysik, Victor Gerena, Thomas Martinez, Ilich Ramírez Sanchez, Ulrike Meinhof, and Renato Curcio. In attempting to determine which specific psychoanalytic factors, if any, might help account for why these otherwise heterogeneous individuals made their decision, I have attempted to explore, and apply, the fundamental concept of narcissism.

In general, I have defined narcissism as a range of psycho-analytic orientations, impulses, or behavioral patterns either wholly or overwhelmingly subject to ego concern, as opposed to object concern. More specifically, narcissism has been defined as the mode or manner in which an individual relates to the object world either solely or predominantly upon the latter's potential capacity to provide that individual with ego reinforcement, compensation, or satisfaction. Hence, narcissism itself has been defined in terms of object relations; that is to say, narcissistic object relations. One such manifestation of narcissistic object relations is narcissistic object manipulation.

Based upon the case study evidence, the external psychological determinants or sources of political terrorism appear to lie in what are termed narcissistic injury and narcissistic disappointment. For the purposes of this study, the term "narcissistic injury" has been defined as profound and lasting damage or harm to an individual's self-image or sense of self-esteem. The term "narcissistic disappointment" has been defined on two levels of analysis: 1) as profound disappointment in the self prompted by an individual's pronounced inability to measure up to what he perceives as positive and desirable standards of conduct, or 2) as harsh disillusionment with individuals or groups who represent or advocate those standards of conduct, with a resultant disappointment in the self for ever having embraced those standards. In no fewer than seven of the nine case studies featured in this book, narcissistic injury or narcissistic disappointment played key psychobiographical roles in the individual decision to become a political terrorist.

Why might the practice of political terrorism itself be psychologically attractive to victims of narcissistic injury or narcissistic disappointment? In responding to this query, it is useful to recall that theoretical definition of narcissism employed in this study. Hence, narcissism has been specifically defined as the mode or manner in which an individual—for whatever reasons—relates to the object world either solely or predominantly upon the latter's potential capacity to provide that individual with ego reinforcement, compensation, or satisfaction. Narcissism, therefore, has been construed in terms of narcissistic object relations. And political terrorism might be interpreted as an excellent example of narcissistic object manipulation.

Friedrich Nietzsche once observed that "nothing on earth consumes a man more quickly than the passion of resentment." Indeed, the apparent ease and spontaneity with which the victim of narcissistic injury or disappointment qua terrorist defends himself from such psychic harm merely serves to reflect that psychological journey typically taken by such individuals. I refer here both to 1) an overall regression to secondary narcissism, and

2) the direct, and indirect, aftermath of narcissistic injury and disappointment: narcissistic rage, some manner of narcissistic defense, and, all too typically, some form of narcissistic aggression. Taken as a whole, these manifestations of secondary narcissism may be termed the "narcissistic rage-defense-aggression nexus." And again, political terrorism may be regarded as an outstanding example of narcissistic aggression.

Finally, political terrorism offers to its practitioners certain distinct psychic benefits or rewards. These psychodynamic rewards may be classified into two distinct categories. The first is the syndrome of political terrorism as autocompensatory violence, itself an interrelated cluster of psychological and psychopolitical factors. These include what have been termed 1) the psychic sense of omnipotence; 2) the establishment, assumption, and maintenance of a new, as-if other pseudoidentity; and 3) the unquestioned psychological utility of political terrorist group membership. The other class of psychodynamic rewards, which springs from the contextual justification of political terrorism, actually enables the political terrorist to assume the mask of omnipotence, yet eschew the mask of villainy—that is to say, the role of political terrorist as a negative identity. These indirect psychodynamic rewards may be realized through the contemporary sanctification of political terrorism as a mode of personal liberation, and through the brutally egoistic rationalization of contemporary political terrorism.

What is the utility, and what are the operational consequences, of this study? More specifically, why, beyond pure intellectual curiosity about the psychological motivations of the political terrorist, is the interrelationship between narcissism and political terrorism significant?[2]

It is widely recognized that there is a demonstrable need for basic research into the underlying motivations, particularly the psychological motivations, and behavior of political terrorists. Indeed, the absence of such basic research will continue to hamper those analysts, managers, and other specialists under whose purview falls the critical issue of political terrorism. The theoretical concept of narcissism, as delineated and applied in this study, offers an indispensable linkage between 1) the intrapsychic sources, or external psychological determinants, and 2) the interpersonal behavioral dynamics, or internal psychological determinants, of political terrorism. The theoretical concept of narcissism, therefore, lays the basis for a unified and logically consistent pattern of behavior. In sum, the psychoanalytic concept of narcissism is the most complete and thus most intellectually satisfying theory regarding the personal logic of political terrorism.

We must recognize, however, that beyond every solution lie even greater problems—particularly for such complex, intractable, and seemingly insoluble issues as political terrorism. In contemplating the overall question of the ultimate utility, operational consequences, and applicability of this study's findings, one must consider three of the most bewildering issues of contemporary political terrorism: 1) the delicate matter of hostage negotiations and other bargaining exercises, 2) the news media's role in the delivery of certain of those psychodynamic rewards inherent in political terrorism, and 3) the possibility of predicting the tactical nature of future political terrorist attacks.

First, it is frequently necessary to negotiate with political terrorists. This is particularly true when the lives and well-being of innocent hostages are at stake. In fact, the now-routine expectation that such bargaining exercises will take place has led major law-enforcement and other officials periodically to enact simulated or mock hostage incidents.

Given the necessity to interact with political terrorists, we might well recall that apt Pentagon dictum, "know thine enemy." A foreknowledge of what Robert Jervis has termed "those presumably uncontrolled aspects of personal behavior that are indices to an adversary's goals, estimate of the situation, and resolve" is an invaluable resource. Hence, if a hostage negotiator is in any way able to anticipate or, ideally, confirm that he indeed is bargaining with a specific personality type—such as a victim of narcissistic personality disturbances—then that negotiator could and should act accordingly.[3]

Martin Reiser and Martin Sloane concur, stating that the hostage negotiator "needs to consider the type and personality characteristic of the hostage taker with whom he is communicating." Their main point, however, is that through suggestion, which "conveys ideas or thoughts by means of implication, hinting, intimidation or insinuation," a negotiator evokes and utilizes potentials and life experiences already present in [hostage takers] but beyond their usual control mechanism. . . . Like others, hostage takers are connected to persons, places, experiences, or ideas that consciously or subconsciously influence their behavior. With proper motivation, positive rapport, and pertinent cues, the [hostage taker] likely will follow suggestions that are relevant subconsciously.[4]

The first such suggestibility technique, "fixation of attention," enables the hostage negotiator to focus the hostage taker's attention by persuading the latter to talk about himself with the negotiator. What is relevant here is that such an interpersonal technique actually might enable a skillful negotiator to ascertain "the type and personality characteristic of the hostage taker with whom he or she is negotiating." In particular, this suggestibility technique may help to indicate to the negotiator that he is dealing with a victim of narcissistic personality disturbances. Should this prove to be the case, a skillful negotiator then could provide whatever verbal cues that might help sway a hostage taker to "follow suggestions that are relevant subconsciously." (Conversely, that negotiator also would avoid verbal cues that might yield defiant or otherwise unfavorable responses.) For example, it may be possible to suggest a feigned "appreciation" of what the hostage taker qua victim of narcissistic personality disturbances is doing without yielding unnecessary, concrete rewards.[5]

A second relevant suggestibility technique, "encouraging a new frame of reference," might further assist the hostage negotiator who already has attempted verbal cueing. As Reiser and Sloane rightly indicate, hostage takers—like all individuals—possess a "hierarchy of needs." For example, "some hostage takers may develop a preoccupation with . . . ego (acceptance, recognition, worth) needs. By concentrating skillfully on these needs, the negotiator can subtly influence the [hostage taker's] response. The concept of buying time during a prolonged negotiation process implies an ongoing deprivation of [such] needs and an increasing focus on their satisfaction."[6]

Given the apparent prevalence of hostage takers with such ego needs, it might be beneficial to employ verbal cues that subtly allude to the autocompensatory, psychodynamic rewards of political terrorism. Reiser and Sloane thus recognize:

For ego needs (acceptance, affiliation, recognition, worth), these indirect cue themes are suggested:
"I'm wondering how you feel about the prospect of talking to the reporter when you come out."
"I'm very curious about when you first decided. . ."
"And you fully realize so well. . ."
"You can continue to feel the satisfaction of. . ."
"It takes a courageous kind of person to come out and work out the problem."[7]

Most significantly, this subtle allusion to the inherent psychodynamic rewards of political terrorism actually may enable a skillful hostage negotiator to deflect attention away from the less expeditiously granted, concrete political rewards of political terrorism.

Second, this study's findings also might be applied to the news media's role in the delivery of certain of the psychodynamic rewards of political terrorism. What recent news media coverage of specific political terrorist events accomplishes is threefold in nature: 1) The massive and uniquely intense coverage of political terrorism serves to recertify the political terrorist's clearly manifested, psychic sense of omnipotence. Moreover, the visual and verbal content of political terrorism news coverage frequently conveys an explicit aura of omnipotence to the news audience. That audience includes, of course, both present and would-be political terrorists. 2) Recent news reports of political terrorist activity have served to recertify and perhaps even actualize the political terrorist's attempt to maintain a new, as-if other pseudoidentity. Hence, the news media actually have helped the political terrorist, who has donned a mask of omnipotence, to display that mask! And 3) recent news media coverage has provided the political terrorist with an ideal forum for the contextual justification of his acts. Thus, the news media, in part, have enabled the political terrorist to assume the mask of omnipotence rather than the mask of villainy.[8]

The verbal and visual content of media coverage frequently suggests an explicit aura of omnipotence to its news audience. This observation may be applied to both the electronic and print news media. As Robert Picard and Paul Adams note in their recent study of the elite print media, reported government characterizations of political terrorist acts and perpetrators tend to be judgmental, inflammatory, and sensationalistic. Hence, political terrorist incidents may be characterized as "brutal acts," and terrorist perpetrators may be described by government officials as "evil" or "criminal." And, as Picard and Adams note, print media personnel and witnesses "tend to use terms that are generally more neutral than those used by government officials." Allow me, then, to pose the question: How often have other elite and nonelite print and electronic media personnel also utilized such descriptive characterizations of terrorist acts as "spectacular" and the like? And, to load the equation even further, to what extent might such sensationalistic and obliquely laudatory characterizations serve as direct psychodynamic rewards delivered to the victim of narcissistic personality disturbances qua political terrorist?[9]

Recent coverage of political terrorist activity also has served to recertify and perhaps even actualize the perpetrator's attempt to maintain a new, as-if other pseudoidentity. One practical means through which the electronic and print news media have enabled the political terrorist to wear the mask of omnipotence is in their usage of political terrorist pseudonyms. In fact, these pseudonyms—such as "General Field Marshal Cinque" or "Carlos the Jackal"—also might be conceptualized as the political terrorist's own characterization of his new, as-if other, omnipotent pseudoidentity. We know that news media personnel frequently share, in Picard's words, "uncertainty of the perpetrator's identity" during unfolding terrorist incidents. In a number of instances, however, these personnel indeed are aware of a political terrorist's old or true identity. If so, the news media should reveal and continue to report the true identity of a political terrorist. If not, then they might well utilize more neutral designations and refrain from rendering another valuable psychodynamic reward to the political terrorist.[10]

Recent news media interviews of political terrorists also provide the subjects with an extraordinary forum for their political views. As Picard points out,

> ... the publicity provided through interviews has the effect of putting the terrorists on an equal footing with government officials. . . . This type of legitimization is another desire of those engaged in such violence. . . . [Moreover,] interviews and the publication of statements and demands often provide

terrorists unedited access to the media that makes the media handmaidens to propaganda efforts. Other groups operating within the normal constraints of society do not enjoy the opportunity of unfettered access to the public via the media. Unedited access to the media is rarely given by the media under normal circumstances (except for live interviews with major government figures).[11]

By thus placing a political terrorist on an equal footing with major government officials and providing him with unedited access to their own channels, the news media have helped to 1) enable the political terrorist to assume the mask of omnipotence, and 2) provide him with an unrivaled medium through which a contextual justification or legitimization of his acts might proceed. This process provides the political terrorist with political, tactical, ideological, and psychodynamic rewards. Therefore, it would be exceedingly useful for the news media to alter their common practice of providing political terrorists with extraordinary access. Another issue to be pondered is the manipulative process whereby political terrorist groups are allowed contextually to justify and legitimize their own actions. The political terrorist must be forced to assume the mask of villainy and the negative identity that he so richly deserves.

Third, my findings also might be applied to the critical problem of predicting future attacks. Concerns for superterrorist scenarios, involving the use of nuclear, chemical, or biological weapons, have been raised on numerous occasions. Backpack or suitcase nuclear devices, nerve gas, and ultradeadly botulinal toxins constitute only a miniscule sample of the devastating arsenal available to political terrorists. In addition, the impending danger that increasingly vulnerable, sensitive, and high-profile targets—such as water, power, energy, transportation, communications, space, and computer networks, or top-level government officials or facilities—might fall prey to such superterrorist scenarios must be squarely faced. The possibilities clearly are unlimited.

As Robert Kupperman and other terrorism specialists already have averred, however, resorting to superterrorist acts such as nuclear terrorism almost certainly would prove to be counterproductive to the political cause of the superterrorist. The public rage and outcry engendered by such monstrous misdeeds would be so massive and unconditional as to preclude whatever marginal political rewards might be offered by far lower intensity political terrorist incidents. Hence, aside from the effect of demonstrating the utter inability of a target state to protect its mass citizenry from superterrorist attack, or virtually compelling a democratically constituted government to take the drastic step of suspending civil liberties, thereby repressively stripping away its democratic facades, acts of superterrorism probably would offer few concrete political rewards.

Although ultimately counterproductive from a political standpoint, nuclear, chemical, or biological terrorism might be extraordinarily satisfying from a psychological perspective. As David Ronfeldt and William Sater point out, given the "mystical, magical powers" of even the least powerful nuclear weapons, the nuclear terrorist of the future might well (psychologically) resemble the "dynamite-prone terrorists" of the late nineteenth century: "What make the analogy meaningful, and potentially instructive . . . are the psychopolitical attributes. The dynamite-prone terrorists believed that dynamite endowed them with extraordinary power to accomplish grandiose purposes—much as we suspect might be the case with nuclear terrorists."[12]

Whatever manifestations of superterrorism any blend of political disincentives and psychodynamic rewards might yield, it is difficult to deny that chemical, biological, and nuclear terrorism would provide its practitioners with the most profound psychic sense of omnipotence and contribute mightily to the concomitant establishment, assumption, and maintenance of a new, as-if other, omnipotent pseudoidentity. Moreover, given the contemporary sanctification of political violence as a mode of personal liberation and the brutally egoistic rationalization of contemporary political terrorism, the practice of superterrorism might readily lend itself, like its more conventional counterpart, to an analogous contextual justification. As a result, the victim of narcissistic personality disturbances qua superterrorist very well might eschew an even more severely negative identity—the "mask of supervillainy." In sum, the potentially enormous psychodynamic rewards of superterrorism might overwhelm any obvious political disincentives posed by nuclear, chemical, or biological terrorism. Based upon the findings of this study, therefore, it might become less difficult to perceive superterrorism as something more than the fevered imaginings of science fiction.[13]

This study must be considered only a beginning, and not a conclusion, to the complex and formidable issue of the individual psychodynamics underlying political terrorism. Particularly for seemingly intractable problems such as political terrorism, beyond every solution lie other questions. Given the conclusions yielded by this study, those questions might provide excellent bases for further research.

I might cite, for example, the potential relevance of those other sociopolitical factors alluded to earlier. It already has been noted that the victim of narcissistic personality disturbances qua political terrorist also has been molded psychologically by 1) certain preterrorist activities, 2) a lack of other satisfying options, 3) the presence of some form of political terrorist recruitment effort, 4) a lack of inhibitions against violence, and 5) a lack of disillusionment with the most fundamental tenets of that political terrorist group which he has joined or is considering joining. The probability that these factors exert a rather direct and straightforward influence upon those individuals who become political terrorists is obviously great. Questions of how, why, and when the above factors interact with the individual psychological determinants of political terrorism, therefore, might be explored. For example, might these sociopolitical factors themselves act as potential, or actual, psychological reinforcements upon those who become political terrorists? Precisely which preterrorist activities—membership in nonviolent reformist, radical, or antiwar groups, or common criminal activities, or incarceration—are most influential in the gradual psychopolitical evolution of political terrorists?

Another conceivably fruitful area of research involves the issue of the likely psychovictimological reinforcements of political terrorism. Already well understood, for example, is the role of the Stockholm syndrome—whereby hostages actually begin to sympathize or otherwise identify with their captors—upon the *victim* of political terrorism. Indeed, the existence of such general behavioral patterns has been noted in several of the case studies considered in this book. Given, then, the reality of the Stockholm syndrome, how, why, and when might such victimological dynamics serve as psychodynamic rewards or reinforcements for the *victimizer*—that is to say, the political terrorist himself? What effect might such events as the conversion, and conviction, of Patricia Hearst have upon political terrorists? How are they psychologically affected when, at a press conference, the first question posed to a former Red Brigades hostage—in this case, U.S. Brigadier General James L. Dozier—is, "General, in what respect might you fault *yourself* for your having been kidnapped?" Given, then, the potential, albeit oblique, psychodynamic rewards inherent in blaming the victim and praising the victimizer, this issue, too, deserves further attention.[14]

Notes

1. For a consideration of these factors see Chapter 1.
2. My point about intellectual curiosity is illustrated in Virgil's adage, "happy is he who knows the causes of things," and in Cicero's perspective that "the causes of events are infinitely more interesting than the events themselves."
3. Robert Jervis, *The Logic of Images in International Relations* (Princeton, NJ: Princeton University Press, 1970), 33.
4. Martin Reiser and Martin Sloane, "The Use of Suggestibility Techniques in Hostage Negotiation," in Freedman and Alexander, eds., *Perspectives on Terrorism*, 213–14, 223.
5. Ibid., 213, 218, 223.
6. Ibid., 220.
7. Ibid., 221.
8. For a more detailed discussion of these points see Richard M. Pearlstein, "Tuned-in Narcissus: The Gleam in the Camera's Eye," in Yonah Alexander and Robert G. Picard, eds., *Mediated Portrayals of Terrorism* (Washington, DC: Pergamon-Brassey's International Defense, 1990). The political terrorist's manifest taste for news media attention may be most clearly shown in this book's case studies of Patricia Soltysik, Victor Gerena, and Ilich Ramírez Sanchez.
9. Robert G. Picard and Paul D. Adams, "Characterizations of Acts and Perpetrators of Political Violence in Three Elite U.S. Daily Newspapers," *Political Communication and Persuasion* 4 (1987): 5–7.
10. Robert G. Picard, "The Conundrum of News Coverage of Terrorism," *University of Toledo Law Review* 18 (1986): 146.
11. Ibid., 148–49.
12. David Ronfeldt and William Sater, "The Mindsets of High-Technology Terrorists: Future Implication from an Historical Analog," in Yonah Alexander and Charles K. Ebinger, eds., *Political Terrorism and Energy: The Threat and the Response* (New York: Praeger, 1982), 17.
13. For more on the general issue of superterrorism see, for example, Yonah Alexander, "Super-Terrorism," in Alexander and Gleason, eds., *Behavioral and*

Quantitative Perspectives, 343–61; Neil C. Livingstone, "The Impact of Technological Innovation," in Uri Ra'anan et al., eds., *Hydra of Carnage* (Lexington, MA: Lexington, 1986), 137–53; and Robert K. Mullen, "Mass Destruction and Terrorism," *Journal of International Affairs* 32 (1978): 63–89. On the more specific issue of nuclear terrorism see, for example, Paul Leventhal and Yonah Alexander, eds., *Nuclear Terrorism: Defining the Threat* (Washington, DC: Pergamon-Brassey's, 1986); idem, eds., *Preventing Nuclear Terrorism*; Augustus R. Norton and Martin H. Greenberg, eds., *Studies in Nuclear Terrorism* (Boston: G. K. Hall, 1979); Louis René Beres, *Terrorism and Global Security: The Nuclear Threat* (Boulder, CO: Westview, 1979); Bruce Hoffman and Peter deLeon, *A Reassessment of Potential Adversaries to U.S. Nuclear Programs* (Santa Monica, CA: Rand Corporation, 1986); Bruce Hoffman, *Terrorism in the United States and the Potential Threat to Nuclear Facilities* (Santa Monica, CA: Rand Corporation, 1986); R. William Mengel, "The Impact of Nuclear Terrorism on the Military's Role in Society," in Marius Livingston, ed., *International Terrorism in the Contemporary World* (Westport, CT: Greenwood, 1978), 402–14; and Jeremiah Denton, "International Terrorism—The Nuclear Dimension," *Terrorism* 9 (1987): 113–23. For more on the specific issue of the psychodynamic rewards of nuclear terrorism see Post, "Prospects."

14. The question posed to General Dozier referred to whether he had exercised proper security precautions prior to his kidnapping. For more on the general subject of victimology see especially Ezzat A. Fattah, "The Use of the Victim as an Agent of Self-Legitimization: Toward a Dynamic Explanation of Criminal Behavior," *Victimology* 1 (1976): 29–53. For more on the general victimological dynamics of political terrorism see especially H. H. A. Cooper, "The Terrorist and His Victim," *Victimology* 1 (1976): 229–39; Ronald D. Crelinsten, ed., *Dimensions of Victimization in the Context of Terrorist Acts* (Montreal: International Center for Comparative Criminology, 1977); Ezzat A. Fattah, "Some Reflections on the Victimology of Terrorism," *Terrorism* 3 (1979): 81–108; and Hacker, *Crusaders, Criminals, Crazies*, 103–78. For more on the issue of the Stockholm syndrome see especially Thomas Strentz, "The Stockholm Syndrome: Law Enforcement Policy and Ego Defenses of the Hostage," *Annals of the New York Academy of Sciences* (June 20, 1980): 137–50; and idem, "The Stockholm Syndrome: Law Enforcement Policy and Hostage Behavior," in Frank M. Ochberg and David A. Soskis, eds., *Victims of Terrorism* (Boulder, CO: Westview Special Studies in National and International Terrorism, 1982). For the origins of the term, "blaming the victim," see William Ryan's classic study, *Blaming the Victim* (New York: Vintage, 1976).

Bibliography

Abenheimer, Karl M. "On Narcissism—Including an Analysis of Shakespeare's 'King Lear.' " *British Journal of Medical Psychology* 20 (1945): 322–29.

Abrahamsen, David. *The Murdering Mind.* New York: Harper Colophon, 1973.

Adam, F. C. "Saints or Sinners: A Selective and Political Study of Certain Nonstate Terrorists." Ph.D. diss., University of Alberta, 1979.

Adams, James. *The Financing of Terror: How the Groups that Are Terrorizing the World Get the Money to Do It.* New York: Simon and Schuster, 1986.

Adler, Alfred. *Study of Organ Inferiority and Its Psychical Compensation.* New York: Nervous and Mental Diseases Publishing Company, 1917.

Aeschylus. *The Orestes Plays.* New York: Mentor, 1962.

Aglietta, A. *Diary of a Jury Member at the Red Brigades Trial.* Milan: Libri Edizioni, 1979.

Alexander, Shana. *Anyone's Daughter: The Times and Trials of Patty Hearst.* New York: Viking, 1979.

Alexander, Yonah. "Communications Aspects of International Terrorism." *International Problems* 16 (1977): 55–60.

————. "Contemporary Terrorism: Perspectives." Paper presented to the Conference on Psychopathology and Political Violence, November 16–17, 1979, at the University of Chicago, Chicago, Illinois.

————. "Some Perspectives on International Terrorism." *International Problems* 14 (1975): 24–29.

_____. "Super-Terrorism." In *Behavioral and Quantitative Perspectives on Terrorism*. Edited by Yonah Alexander and John M. Gleason. New York: Pergamon, 1981.

_____. *Terrorism in Italy*. New York: Crane, Russak, 1979.

Alexander, Yonah, and Katwan, Jakov. "Editor's Note." *Terrorism* 3 (1980): vii–viii.

Alexander, Yonah, et al. *Terrorism: What Should Be Our Response?* Washington, DC: American Enterprise Institute for Public Policy Research, 1982.

Alexander, Yonah, ed. *International Terrorism: National, Regional, and Global Perspectives*. New York: AMS, 1976.

_____. *Terrorism: Moral Aspects*. Boulder, CO: Westview, 1980.

Alexander, Yonah, and Myers, Kenneth A., eds. *Terrorism in Europe*. London: Croom Helm, 1982.

Alford, C. Fred. *Narcissism: Socrates, the Frankfurt School, and Psychoanalytic Theory*. New Haven, CT: Yale University Press, 1988.

Allum, Percy. "Political Terrorism in Italy." *Contemporary Review* (August 1978): 75–84.

Alpert, Jane. *Growing Up Underground*. New York: Morrow, 1981.

_____. "Profile of Sam Melville." In *Letters from Attica*. By Sam Melville. New York: Morrow, 1972.

Amon, Moshe. "The Devil's Righteousness: A Romantic Model of Secular Gnosticism." Paper presented to the Conference on the Moral Implications of Terrorism, March 14–16, 1979, at the University of California at Los Angeles, Los Angeles, California.

_____. "Terrorism: Problems of Good and Evil." Paper presented to the Conference on Psychopathology and Political Violence, November 16–17, 1979, at the University of Chicago, Chicago, Illinois.

Anable, David. "Terrorism: Violence as Theater." *The Inter-Dependent* 3 (1976): 1.

Anderson, Quentin. *The Imperial Self: An Essay in American Literary and Cultural History*. New York: Knopf, 1971.

Anderson-Sherman, Arnold. "The Social Construction of 'Terrorism.' " In *Rethinking Criminology*. Edited by Harold E. Pepinsky. Beverly Hills, CA: Sage, 1982.

Arblaster, Anthony. "Terrorism: Myths, Meanings, and Morals." *Political Studies* 25 (1977): 413–24.

Arendt, Hannah. *Crises of the Republic*. New York: Harcourt Brace Jovanovich, 1972.

_____. *Eichmann in Jerusalem: A Report on the Banality of Evil*. New York: Viking, 1964.

_____. *The Human Condition: A Study of the Central Dilemmas Facing Modern Man*. Garden City, NY: Doubleday, 1958.

_____. *The Origins of Totalitarianism*. New York: Meridian, 1958.

_____. *On Revolution*. New York: Viking, 1965.

_____. "On Violence." In *Crises of the Republic*. New York: Harcourt Brace Jovanovich, 1972.

Aristotle. *The Politics*. London: Oxford University Press, 1977.

Ashley, Karen, et al. "You Don't Need a Weatherman to Know Which Way the Wind Blows." In *Debate within SDS: RYM II vs. Weatherman*. Detroit, MI: Radical Education Project, 1970.

Augustine, Saint. "The 'Just' War." In *The Political Writings of St. Augustine*. Edited by Henry Paolucci. Chicago: Henry Regnery, 1962.

Bailey, Dennis. "Underground." *Boston Globe Magazine* (March 26, 1989): 28.

Baker, Marilyn, and Brompton, Sally. *Exclusive! The Inside Story of Patricia Hearst and the SLA*. New York: Macmillan, 1974.

Balint, M. "Primary Narcissism and Primary Love." *Psychoanalytic Quarterly* 29 (1960): 6–43.

Ball-Rokeach, Sandra J. "The Legitimation of Violence." In *Collective Violence*. Edited by James F. Short, Jr., and Marvin E. Wolfgang. Chicago: Aldine, 1972.

Bandura, Albert. *Aggression: A Social Learning Analysis*. Englewood Cliffs, NJ: Prentice Hall, 1973.

Barber, James David. *The Presidential Character: Predicting Performance in the White House*. Englewood Cliffs, NJ: Prentice Hall, 1972.

Barker, Ralph. *Not Here, But in Another Place*. New York: St. Martin's, 1981.

Barnsley, John H. *The Social Relativity of Ethics*. London: Routledge and Kegan Paul, 1972.

Baumann, Bommi. *How It All Began*. Vancouver: Pulp, 1975.

Baumann, Michael. *Terror or Love? Bommi Baumann's Own Story of His Life as a West German Urban Guerrilla*. New York: Grove Press, 1977.

Becker, Ernest. *Angel in Armor*. New York: Braziller, 1969.

Becker, Jillian. "Case Study 1: Federal Germany." In *Contemporary Terror: Studies in Sub-State Violence*. Edited by David Carlton and Carlo Schaerf. New York: St. Martin's, 1981.

_____. *Hitler's Children: The Story of the Baader-Meinhof Gang*. Philadelphia: Lippincott, 1977.

_____. "Introduction." *Terrorism* 3 (1980): 191–200.

"Behavioral Science: Its Potential in the War against Terrorism." *TVI Journal* 2 (1981): 6–10.

Belcher, Jerry, and West, Don. *Patty/Tania*. New York, 1976.

Bell, J. Bowyer. "The Case of the Croatians." In *A Time of Terror: How Democratic Societies Respond to Revolutionary Violence*. New York: Basic Books, 1978.

_____. "The Italian Experience: Democracy and Armed Dissent, 1946–1977." In *A Time of Terror: How Democratic Societies Respond to Revolutionary Violence*. New York: Basic Books, 1978.

_____. *The Profile of a Terrorist.* New York: Columbia Institute of War and Peace Studies, n.d.

_____. "Psychology of Leaders of Terrorist Groups." *International Journal of Group Tensions* 12 (1982): 84–104.

_____. *The Secret Army: The IRA, 1916–1979.* Cambridge, MA: MIT Press, 1983.

_____. *A Time of Terror: How Democratic Societies Respond to Revolutionary Violence.* New York: Basic Books, 1978.

_____. *Transnational Terror.* Washington, DC: American Enterprise Institute for Public Policy Research, 1975.

Belz, Mary, et al. "Is There a Treatment for Terror?" *Psychology Today* (October 1977): 54.

Benedek, E. P. *The Psychiatric Aspects of Terrorism.* Washington, DC: American Psychiatric Association, 1980.

Bensman, Joseph, and Lilienfeld, Robert. *Between Public and Private: The Lost Boundaries of the Self.* New York: Free Press, 1979.

Benson, Mike; Evans, Mariah; and Simon, Rita. "Women as Political Terrorists." *Research in Law, Deviance, and Social Control* 4 (1982): 121–30.

Beres, Louis René. *Terrorism and Global Security: The Nuclear Threat.* Boulder, CO: Westview, 1979.

Bergman, J. *Vera Zasulich: A Biography.* Stanford, CA: Stanford University Press, 1983.

Berkman, Alexander. *Prison Memoirs of an Anarchist.* Pittsburgh, PA: Frontier, 1970.

Berkowitz, Leonard. *Aggression: A Social Psychological Analysis.* New York: McGraw-Hill, 1962.

_____. "Catharsis." In *Aggression: A Social Psychological Analysis.* New York: McGraw-Hill, 1962.

_____. "The Frustration-Aggression Hypothesis Revisited." In *The Roots of Aggression: A Reexamination of the Frustration-Aggression Hypothesis.* Edited by Leonard Berkowitz. New York: Atherton, 1969.

Berkowitz, Leonard, and Cottingham, D. H. "The Interest Value and Relevance of Fear-Arousing Communications." *Journal of Abnormal and Social Psychology* 60 (1960): 37–43.

Berman, Marshall. *The Politics of Authenticity: Radical Individualism and the Emergence of Modern Society.* New York: Atheneum, 1970.

Billig, Otto. "The Case History of a German Terrorist." *Terrorism* 7 (1984): 1–10.

_____. "The Lawyer Terrorist and His Comrades." *Political Psychology* 6 (1985): 29–46.

Binder, David. "Anarchist Leaders Seized in Frankfurt." *New York Times,* June 2, 1972.

Bing, James F., and Marburg, Rudolf. "Panel Report: Narcissism." *Journal of the American Psychoanalytic Association* 10 (1962): 593–605.

Bing, James F.; McLaughlin, Francis; and Marburg, Rudolf. "The Metapsychology of Narcissism." *Psychoanalytic Study of the Child* 14 (1959): 9–28.

Binion, Rudolph. "Doing Psychohistory." *Journal of Psychohistory* 5 (1978): 313–23.

Blei, Herman. "Terrorism, Domestic and International: The West German Experience." In *Report of the Task Force on Disorders and Terrorism*. Washington, DC: National Advisory Committee on Criminal Justice Standards and Goals, 1976.

Blumler, Jay G., and Katz, Elihu, eds. *The Uses of Mass Communication: Current Perspectives on Gratifications Research*. Beverly Hills, CA: Sage, 1974.

Bocca, Giorgio. *Moro: An Italian Tragedy: Letters, Documents, Polemics.* Rome: Tascabili Bompiani, 1978.

Bollinger, L. "Terrorist Conduct as a Result of a Psychological Process." In *Psychiatry: The State of the Art*, vol. 6. New York: Plenum, 1985.

Bolz, Frank A., Jr. "Hostage Confrontation and Rescue." In *Terrorism: Threat, Reality, Response.* Edited by Robert H. Kupperman and Darrell M. Trent. Stanford, CA: Hoover Institution Press, 1979.

Bonanate, Luigi. "Some Unanticipated Consequences of Terrorism." *Journal of Peace Research* 16 (1979): 197-212.

Bookbinder, Paul. "Ulrike Meinhof and Andreas Baader: The Idealist and the Adventurer." *TVI Journal* 2 (1981): 9-13.

Boulton, David. *The Making of Tania Hearst.* London: New English Library, 1975.

Bouthoul, Gaston. "Definitions of Terror." In *International Terrorism and World Security.* Edited by David Carlton and Carlo Schaerf. London: Croom Helm, 1975.

Bradshaw, Jon. "A Dream of Terror." *Esquire Fortnightly* (July 18, 1978): 24–50.

Branden, Nathaniel. *The Psychology of Self-Esteem: A New Concept of Man's Psychological Nature.* New York: Bantam, 1981.

Brandon, Henry. "The German Terrorists Have a Bond: It's Hatred." *New York Times*, October 30, 1977.

Braungart, Margaret M., and Braungart, Richard G. "The Life-Course Development of Left- and Right-Wing Youth Activist Leaders from the 1960s." Paper presented to the Eleventh Annual Scientific Meeting of the International Society of Political Psychology, July 1–5, 1988, at Secaucus, New Jersey.

Brockman, R. "Notes While Being Hijacked: Croatian Terrorists." *Atlantic* (December 1976): 68–75.

Brodey, Warren M. "Image, Object, and Narcissistic Relationships." *American Journal of Orthopsychiatry* 31 (1961): 67–73.

_____. "On the Dynamics of Narcissism: Externalization and Early Ego Development." *Psychoanalytic Study of the Child* 20 (1965): 165–93.

Brown, Norman O. *Life against Death: The Psychoanalytical Meaning of History.* Middletown, CT: Wesleyan University Press, 1959.

Bryan, John. *This Soldier Still at War.* New York: Harcourt Brace Jovanovich, 1975.

Burnham, James. "Roots of Terrorism." *National Review* 26 (1974): 311.

Burns, Carol. *The Narcissist.* London: Calder and Boyars, 1967.

Burton, Anthony M. "Post-Communist Revolutionaries—The New Left." In *Urban Terrorism: Theory, Practice and Response.* London: Leo Cooper, 1975.

_____. *Revolutionary Violence: The Theories.* New York: Crane, Russak, 1978.

Buss, Arnold H. "Aggression Pays." In *The Control of Aggression and Violence.* Edited by Jerome L. Singer. New York: Academic Press, 1971.

Camus, Albert. *The Rebel: An Essay on Man in Revolt.* New York: Vintage, 1956.

_____. *Resistance, Rebellion, and Death.* New York: Vintage, 1960.

Carmichael, D. J. C. "Of Beasts, Gods, and Civilized Men: The Justification of Terrorism and of Counterterrorist Measures." *Terrorism* 6 (1982): 1–26.

_____. "Terrorism: Some Ethical Issues." *Chitty's Law Journal* 24 (1976): 233–39.

Carroll, John, ed. *Max Stirner: The Ego and His Own.* New York: Harper and Row, 1971.

Caserta, John. *The Red Brigades: Italy's Agony.* New York: Manor, 1978.

Chanteur, Janine. "Violence in Plato's Work." In *Violence and Aggression in the History of Ideas.* Edited by Philip P. Wiener and John Fisher. New Brunswick, NJ: Rutgers University Press, 1974.

Chapman, Robert D. *The Crimson Web of Terror.* Boulder, CO: Paladin, 1980.

Chessick, Richard D. *Intensive Psychotherapy of the Borderline Patient.* New York: Aronson, 1977.

Citizens Research and Investigation Committee and Tackwood, Louis E. *The Glass House Tapes: The Story of an Agent-Provocateur and the New Police Intelligence Complex.* New York: Avon, 1973.

Clark, Robert P. "Patterns in the Lives of ETA Members." *Terrorism* 6 (1983): 423–54.

Clutterbuck, Richard. *Protest and the Urban Guerrilla.* New York: Abelard Schuman, 1974.

Coates, James. *Armed and Dangerous: The Rise of the Survivalist Right.* New York: Hill and Wang, 1987.

Cohen, G. *Women of Violence: Memoirs of a Young Terrorist*. Stanford, CA: Stanford University Press, 1966.

Coleman, L. S. "Perspectives on the Medical Study of Violence." *American Journal of Orthopsychiatry* 44 (1974): 675–87.

Collins, John M. "Definitional Aspects." In *Political Terrorism and Energy: The Threat and the Response*. Edited by Yonah Alexander and Charles K. Ebinger. New York: Praeger, 1982.

Comay, M. "Political Terrorism." *Mental Health and Society* 3 (1976): 249–61.

Combs, James E., and Mansfield, Michael, eds. *Drama in Life: The Uses of Communication in Society*. New York: Hastings House, 1976.

"The Concept of the Urban Guerrilla." In *The Terrorism Reader: A Historical Anthology*. Edited by Walter Laqueur. New York: Meridian, 1978.

Cooper, H. H. A. "Psychopath as Terrorist." *Legal Medical Quarterly* 2 (1978): 253–62.

————. "Terrorism: The Problem of a Problem of Definition." *Chitty's Law Journal* 26 (1979): 105.

————. "The Terrorist and His Victim." *Victimology* 1 (1976): 229–39.

————. "What Is a Terrorist: A Psychological Perspective." *Legal Medical Quarterly* 1 (1977): 16–32.

Copley, Gregory. "A Sociological Profile of Terrorism." *Defense and Foreign Affairs Digest* 4 (1978): 38–39.

Cordes, Bonnie, et al. *A Conceptual Framework for Analyzing Terrorist Groups*. Santa Monica, CA: Rand Corporation, 1985.

Corning, Peter A., and Corning, C. H. "Toward a General Theory of Violent Aggression." *Social Science Information* 11 (1972): 7.

Corrado, Raymond R. "A Critique of the Mental Disorder Perspective of Political Terrorism." *International Journal of Law and Psychiatry* 4 (1981): 293–309.

————. "Ethnic and Student Terrorism in Western Europe." In *The Politics of Terrorism*. Edited by Michael Stohl. New York: Marcel Dekker, 1979.

Cranston, Maurice William. *The New Left: Six Critical Essays on Che Guevara, Jean-Paul Sartre, Herbert Marcuse, Frantz Fanon, Black Power, R. D. Laing*. New York: Library Press, 1971.

Crawford, Thomas J., and Naditch, Murray. "Relative Deprivation, Powerlessness, and Militancy: The Psychology of Social Protest." *Psychiatry* 33 (1970): 208–23.

Crayton, John W. "Terrorism and the Psychology of the Self." In *Perspectives on Terrorism*. Edited by Lawrence Zelic Freedman and Yonah Alexander. Wilmington, DE: Scholarly Resources, 1983.

Crelinsten, Ronald D. "The Root Causes of Terrorism." Paper presented to the Second Annual Meeting of the International Society of Political Psychology, May 24–26, 1979, at Washington, DC.

Crelinsten, Ronald D., ed. *Dimensions of Victimization in the Context of Terrorist Acts*. Montreal: International Center for Comparative Criminology, 1977.

Crenshaw, Martha. "The Psychology of Political Terrorism." In *Handbook of Political Psychology*. Edited by Margaret Hermann. San Francisco: Jossey-Bass, 1985.

_____. "The Subjective Reality of the Terrorist: Ideological and Psychological Factors in Terrorism." In *Current Perspectives on International Terrorism*. Edited by Robert O. Slater and Michael Stohl. London: Macmillan, 1987.

Crenshaw, Martha, ed. *Terrorism, Legitimacy, and Power: The Consequences of Political Violence*. Middletown, CT: Wesleyan University Press, 1983.

Dahrendorf, Ralf. "Baader-Meinhof—How Come? What's Next?" *New York Times*, October 20, 1977.

Daly, L. N. "Terrorism: What Can the Psychiatrist Do?" *Journal of Forensic Sciences* 26 (1981): 116–22.

Dan, Uri, and Mann, Peter. *Carlos Must Die*. New York: W. W. Norton, 1978.

Dane, Leila F. "The Iran Hostage Wives: Long-Term Coping." Ph.D. diss., Florida Institute of Technology, 1984.

Daniels, Stuart. "The Weathermen." *Government and Opposition* 9 (1974): 430–59.

Davidson, William D., and Montville, Joseph V. "Foreign Policy According to Freud." *Foreign Policy* 45 (1982): 145–57.

Davies, James R. *Terrorists: Youth, Biker, and Prison Violence*. San Diego, CA: Grossmount, 1978.

Davis, L. J. "Ballad of an American Terrorist." *Harper's* (July 1985).

De Gramont, S. "How a Pleasant, Scholarly Young Man from Brazil Became a Kidnapping, Gun-Toting, Bombing Revolutionary." *New York Times Magazine* (November 15, 1970).

Demaris, Ovid. *Brothers in Blood: The International Terrorist Network*. New York: Scribner's, 1977.

_____. "Carlos." In *Brothers in Blood: The International Terrorist Network*. New York: Scribner's, 1977.

_____. "The People's War of Ulrike Meinhof." In *Brothers in Blood: The International Terrorist Network*. New York: Scribner's, 1977.

Demause, Lloyd. *Foundations of Psychohistory*. New York: Creative Roots, 1982.

Denton, Jeremiah. "International Terrorism—The Nuclear Dimension." *Terrorism* 9 (1987): 113–23.

Dervin, Daniel. "Steve and Adam and Ted and Dr. Lasch: The New Culture and the Culture of Narcissism." *Journal of Psychohistory* 9 (1982): 355–73.

DiRenzo, Gordon J., ed. *Personality and Politics*. Garden City, NY: Doubleday, 1974.

Dispot, L. *The Machine of Terror: Genealogy of Terrorism*. Venice: Marsiolio, 1978.

Dobson, Christopher, and Payne, Ronald. *The Carlos Complex: A Study in Terror*. New York: G. P. Putnam's, 1977.

_____. "The Reasons Why." In *The Carlos Complex: A Study in Terror*. New York: G. P. Putnam's, 1977.

_____. "Terrorism: The Reasons Why." In *The Terrorists: Their Weapons, Leaders, and Tactics*. New York: Facts on File, 1979.

_____. "Terrorists: Behind the Mask." In *The Terrorists: Their Weapons, Leaders, and Tactics*. New York: Facts on File, 1979.

_____. *The Terrorists: Their Weapons, Leaders, and Tactics*. New York: Facts on File, 1979.

Dollard, John, et al. *Frustration and Aggression*. New Haven, CT: Yale University Press, 1939.

Doob, A. N. "Catharsis and Aggression: The Effect of Hurting One's Enemy." *Journal of Experimental Research in Psychology* 4 (1970): 491–96.

Dostoevsky, Fyodor. *Notes from Underground*. New York: Bantam, 1981.

_____. *The Possessed*. New York: Signet, 1962.

Douglass, Joseph D., Jr., and Livingstone, Neil C. *America the Vulnerable: The Threat of Chemical and Biological Warfare*. Lexington, MA: Lexington, 1987.

Dowling, Joseph A. "A Prolegomena to a Psychohistorical Study of Terrorism." In *International Terrorism in the Contemporary World*. Edited by Marius Livingston. Westwood, CT: Greenwood, 1978.

Drake, Richard. "The Red and the Black: Terrorism in Contemporary Italy." *International Political Science Review* 5 (1984).

_____. "The Red Brigades and the Italian Political Tradition." In *Terrorism in Europe*. Edited by Yonah Alexander and Kenneth A. Myers. New York: St. Martin's, 1982.

Dubin, Murray. "Fugitive from Hate." *Philadelphia Inquirer Magazine* (December 18, 1988): 26–35.

Dugard, John. "International Terrorism and the Just War." *Stanford Journal of International Studies* (Spring 1977): 21–38.

Eckstein, George. "Germany: Democracy in Trouble. Coping with Trouble." *Dissent* (Winter 1978): 82–83.

Edelhertz, Herbert, and Walsh, Marilyn. *The White-Collar Challenge to Nuclear Safeguards*. Lexington, MA: Lexington, 1978.

Edelman, Murray. "Political Symbols, Myths, and Language as Factors in Terrorism." Paper presented to the Conference on Terrorism in the Contemporary World, April 26–28, 1976, at Glassboro State College, Glassboro, New Jersey.

_____. *The Symbolic Uses of Politics.* Urbana, IL: University of Illinois Press, 1964.

Eichelman, Burr; Soskis, David A.; and Reid, William H., eds. *Terrorism: Interdisciplinary Perspectives.* Washington, DC: American Psychiatric Association, 1983.

Eidelberg, Ludwig. "A Second Contribution to the Study of Narcissistic Mortification." *Psychiatric Quarterly* 33 (1959): 634–46.

_____. "The Concept of Narcissistic Mortification." *International Journal of Psychoanalysis* 40 (1959): 163–68.

Eisenberg, Denis, and Landau, Eli. *Carlos: Terror International.* London: Corgi, 1976.

Eisnitz, A. J. "Narcissistic Object Choice, Self Representation." *International Journal of Psychoanalysis* 50 (1969): 15–25.

Elkisch, P. "The Psychological Significance of the Mirror." *Journal of the American Psychoanalytic Association* 5 (1957): 15–25.

Elliott, John D. "Action and Reaction: West Germany and the Baader-Meinhof Guerrillas." *Strategic Review* 4 (1976): 60–67.

_____. "Terrorism in West Germany." Unpublished manuscript.

Ellis, Havelock. "The Concept of Narcissism." *Psychoanalytic Review* 14 (1927): 129–53.

Ephron, Lawrence R. "Narcissism and the Sense of Self." *Psychoanalytic Review* 54 (1967): 499–509.

Erikson, Erik H. *Childhood and Society.* New York: W. W. Norton, 1963.

_____. *Gandhi's Truth: On the Origins of Militant Nonviolence.* New York: W. W. Norton, 1968.

_____. *Identity: Youth and Crisis.* New York: W. W. Norton, 1968.

Ermlich, Fred. "Ethical Implications of Terrorism." Paper presented to the Eighteenth Annual Convention of the International Studies Association, March 16–20, 1977, at St. Louis, Missouri.

Evans, Ernest. "The Causes of Terrorism." In *Calling a Truce to Terror: The American Response to International Terrorism.* Westport, CT: Greenwood, 1979.

Ezekiel, Raphael S. "Discussions with Members of the Klan, Nazis, and Aryan Nations Groups." Paper presented to the Eleventh Annual Scientific Meeting of the International Society of Political Psychology, July 1–5, 1988, at Secaucus, New Jersey.

Falk, Richard. "The Terrorist Mind-Set: The Moral Universe of Revolutionaries and Functionaries." In *Revolutionaries and Functionaries: The Dual Face of Terrorism.* New York: E. P. Dutton, 1988.

Fanon, Frantz. *Black Skin, White Masks.* New York: Grove Press, 1967.

_____. *The Wretched of the Earth.* New York: Grove Press, 1963.

Farrell, William Regis. "Terrorism Is . . . ?" In *The U.S. Government Response to Terrorism: In Search of an Effective Strategy.* Boulder, CO: Westview, 1982.

Fattah, Ezzat A. "Some Reflections on the Victimology of Terrorism." *Terrorism* 3 (1979): 81–108.

_____. "Terrorist Activities and Terrorist Targets: A Tentative Typology." In *Behavioral and Quantitative Perspectives on Terrorism.* Edited by Yonah Alexander and John M. Gleason. New York: Pergamon, 1981.

_____. "The Use of the Victim as an Agent of Self-Legitimization: Toward a Dynamic Explanation of Criminal Behavior." *Victimology* 1 (1976): 29–53.

Federn, P. "On the Distinction between Healthy and Pathological Narcissism." In *Ego Psychology and the Psychoses.* Edited by E. Weiss. New York: Basic Books, 1952.

"Female Terrorists—A Growing Phenomenon." *Executive Risk Assessment* 1 (1979): 1–6.

Fernandez, Ronald. *Los Macheteros: The Wells Fargo Robbery and the Violent Struggle for Puerto Rican Independence.* New York: Prentice Hall, 1987.

Ferracuti, Franco. "A Sociopsychiatric Interpretation of Terrorism." *Annals of the American Academy of Political and Social Science* 463 (1982): 129–41.

Ferracuti, Franco, and Bruno, F. "Psychiatric Aspects of Terrorism in Italy." In *The Mad, the Bad, and the Different.* Edited by I. L. Barak-Glantz and U. R. Huff. Lexington, MA: Lexington, 1981.

_____. "A Psychiatric Comparative—Analysis of Left and Right Terrorism in Italy." In *Psychiatry: The State of the Art,* vol. 6. New York: Plenum, 1985.

Ferrarotti, F. *At the Roots of Violence.* Milan: Rizzoli, 1979.

Feshbach, Seymour. "Dynamics and Morality of Violence and Aggression: Some Psychological Considerations." *American Psychologist* 26 (1971): 281–92.

Fields, Rona M. "Psychological Sequelae of Terrorization." In *Behavioral and Quantitative Perspectives on Terrorism.* Edited by Yonah Alexander and John M. Gleason. New York: Pergamon, 1981.

_____. *Society under Siege: A Psychology of Northern Ireland.* Philadelphia: Temple University Press, 1977.

Fink, Steven. *Crisis Management: Planning for the Inevitable.* New York: AMACOM, 1986.

Fiorillo, Ernesto. "Terrorism in Italy: Analysis of a Problem." *Terrorism* 2 (1979): 261–70.

Fisher, Roger, and Ury, William. *Getting to Yes: Negotiating Agreement without Giving In.* New York: Penguin, 1981.

Fleming, Marie. "Propaganda by the Deed: Terrorism and Anarchist Theory in Late Nineteenth-Century Europe." In *Terrorism in Europe.* Edited by Yonah Alexander and Kenneth A. Myers. New York: St. Martin's, 1982.

Flynn, Kevin, and Gerhardt, Gary. *The Silent Brotherhood: Inside America's Racist Underground.* New York: Free Press, 1989.

Foucault, Michel. *Madness and Civilization: A History of Insanity in the Age of Reason.* New York: Vintage, 1965.

Frank, J. D. "Some Psychological Determinants of Violence and Its Control." *Australian and New Zealand Journal of Psychiatry* 6 (1971): 158–64.

Frankfurt, Ellen. *Kathy Boudin and the Dance of Death.* New York: Stein and Day, 1983.

Frazier, S. H. "Mass Media and Psychiatric Disturbance." *Psychiatric Journal of the University of Ottawa* 40 (1976): 171–73.

Freedman, Lawrence Zelic. "Assassination: Psychopathology and Social Pathology." In *Social Structure and Assassination Behavior.* Edited by Doris Y. Wilkinson. Cambridge, MA: Schenkman, 1976.

_____. "Psychopathology of Assassination." In *Assassinations and the Political Order.* Edited by William J. Crotty. New York: Harper and Row, 1971.

_____. "Terrorism: Problems of the Polistaraxic." In *Perspectives on Terrorism.* Edited by Lawrence Zelic Freedman and Yonah Alexander. Wilmington, DE: Scholarly Resources, 1983.

_____. "Terrorism and Change." Paper presented to the Second Annual Meeting of the International Society of Political Psychology, May 24–26, 1979, at Washington, DC.

_____. "Why Does Terrorism Terrorize?" *Terrorism* 6 (1983): 389–401.

Freedman, Lawrence Zelic, and Alexander, Yonah, eds. *Perspectives on Terrorism.* Wilmington, DE: Scholarly Resources, 1983.

Freeman, Thomas. "The Concept of Narcissism in Schizophrenic States." *International Journal of Psychoanalysis* 44 (1963): 293–303.

_____. "Narcissism and Defensive Processes in Schizophrenic States." *International Journal of Psychoanalysis* 43 (1962): 415–25.

_____. "Some Aspects of Pathological Narcissism." *International Journal of Psychoanalysis* 46 (1964): 540–61.

Freud, Anna. *The Ego and the Mechanisms of Defense.* New York: International Universities Press, 1946.

Freud, Sigmund. *Beyond the Pleasure Principle.* New York: W. W. Norton, 1960.

_____. *Civilization and Its Discontents.* New York: W. W. Norton, 1961.

_____. *The Ego and the Id.* New York: W. W. Norton, 1960.

_____. *Group Psychology and the Analysis of the Ego.* New York: W. W. Norton, 1959.

_____. "Mourning and Melancholia." In *Standard Edition,* vol. 14. London: Hogarth, 1957.

_____. *New Introductory Lectures on Psychoanalysis.* New York: W. W. Norton, 1965.

_____. "On Narcissism: An Introduction." In *Essential Papers on Narcissism.* Edited by Andrew P. Morrison. New York: New York University Press, 1986.

_____. *An Outline of Psychoanalysis.* New York: W. W. Norton, 1949.

_____. *Psychopathology of Everyday Life.* New York: Signet, n.d.

_____. *Totem and Taboo.* New York: W. W. Norton, 1950.

Freud, Sigmund, and Bullitt, William C. *Thomas Woodrow Wilson, Twenty-eighth President of the United States: A Psychological Study.* Boston: Houghton Mifflin, 1967.

Fried, Risto. "The Psychology of the Terrorist." In *Terrorism and Beyond: An International Conference on Terrorism and Low-Level Conflict.* Edited by Brian M. Jenkins. Santa Monica, CA: Rand Corporation, 1982.

_____. "Questions on Terrorism." *Terrorism* 3 (1980): 219–38.

Friedland, Nehemia. "Hostage Negotiations: Dilemmas about Policy." In *Perspectives on Terrorism.* Edited by Lawrence Zelic Freedman and Yonah Alexander. Wilmington, DE: Scholarly Resources, 1983.

Friedland, Nehemia, and Merari, Ariel. "The Psychological Impact of Terrorism: A Double-Edged Sword." *Political Psychology* 6 (1985): 591–604.

Friedlander, Robert A. "Psychological Aspects." In *Terror-Violence: Aspects of Social Control.* London: Oceana, 1983.

_____. "The Psychology of Terrorism: Contemporary Views." In *Managing Terrorism: Strategies for the Corporate Executive.* Edited by Patrick J. Montana and George S. Roukis. Westport, CT: Quorum, 1983.

_____. "Terrorism and Political Violence: Do the Ends Justify the Means?" *Chitty's Law Journal* 24 (1976): 240–45.

Fromkin, David. "The Strategy of Terrorism." *Foreign Affairs* 53 (1975): 683–98.

Fromm, Erich. *The Anatomy of Human Destructiveness.* Greenwich, CT: Fawcett, 1973.

_____. *Escape from Freedom.* New York: Avon, 1969.

_____. *The Heart of Man: Its Genius for Good and Evil.* New York: Harper and Row, 1964.

_____. *Man for Himself: An Inquiry into the Psychology of Ethics.* Greenwich, CT: Fawcett, 1947.

Furlong, Paul. "Political Terrorism in Italy: Responses, Reactions, and Immobilism." In *Terrorism: A Challenge to the State.* Edited by Juliet Lodge. New York: St. Martin's, 1981.

Galvin, Deborah M. "The Female Terrorist: A Socio-Psychological Perspective." *Behavioral Sciences and the Law* 1 (1983): 19–32.

Galvin, John R. *Psychological Aspects of Terrorism*. Carlisle Barracks, PA: Army War College, 1983.

Geen, R. G., and Stoner, D. "Context Effects in Observed Violence." *Journal of Personal and Social Psychology* 25 (1973): 145–50.

George, Alexander L. "Power as a Compensatory Value for Political Leaders." *Journal of Social Issues* 24 (1968): 24–49.

George, Alexander L., and George, Juliette L. *Woodrow Wilson and Colonel House: A Personality Study*. New York: John Day, 1964.

Georges-Abeyie, Daniel E. "Women as Terrorists." In *Perspectives on Terrorism*. Edited by Lawrence Zelic Freedman and Yonah Alexander. Wilmington, DE: Scholarly Resources, 1983.

Gerbner, George. *Symbolic Functions of Violence and Terror*. Boston: Terrorism and the News Media Research Project, 1988.

Gilbert, Sari. "Italian Terrorism on Display at Moro Trial." *Boston Globe*, December 16, 1982.

Glass, James M. *Delusion: Internal Dimensions of Political Life*. Chicago: University of Chicago Press, 1985.

_____. "Hobbes and Narcissism: Pathology in the State of Nature." *Political Theory* 8 (1980): 335–63.

Goffman, Erving. *The Presentation of Self in Everyday Life*. New York: Overlook, 1973.

Goldman, Emma. *The Psychology of Political Violence*. New York: Gordon, 1974.

Goldstein, Jeffrey H. *Aggression and Crimes of Violence*. London: Oxford University Press, 1975.

Goode, Stephen. *Affluent Revolutionaries: A Portrait of the New Left*. New York: New Viewpoints, 1974.

Grathwohl, Larry. *Bringing Down America: An FBI Informer with the Weathermen*. New Rochelle, NY: Arlington House, 1976.

Greaves, Douglas. "The Definition and Motivation of Terrorism." *Australian Journal of Forensic Science* 13 (1981): 160–66.

Green, G. *Terrorism: Is It Revolutionary?* New York: Outlook, 1970.

Green, L. C. "The Legalization of Terrorism." In *Terrorism: Theory and Practice*. Edited by Yonah Alexander, David Carlton, and Paul Wilkinson. Boulder, CO: Westview, 1979.

Greenberg, Jay R., and Mitchell, Stephen A. *Object Relations in Psychoanalytic Theory*. Cambridge, MA: Harvard University Press, 1983.

Greening, Thomas. "The Psychological Study of Assassins." In *Assassinations and the Political Order*. Edited by William J. Crotty. New York: Harper and Row, 1971.

Greenstein, Fred I. *Children and Politics*. New Haven, CT: Yale University Press, 1970.

_____. *Personality and Politics: Problems of Evidence, Inference, and Conceptualization*. New York: W. W. Norton, 1969.

Greenstein, Fred I., and Lerner, Michael, eds. *A Source Book for the Study of Personality and Politics*. Chicago: Markham, 1971.

Greth, Roma. *Narcissus*. New York: Smith, 1978.

Gross, Feliks. "Causation of Terror." In *The Terrorism Reader: A Historical Anthology*. Edited by Walter Laqueur. New York: Meridian, 1978.

_____. "Social Causation of Individual Political Violence." Paper presented to the Conference on Terrorism in the Contemporary World, April 26–28, 1976, at Glassboro State College, Glassboro, New Jersey.

"The Growing Psychological Aspects of International Terrorism." *Defence and Foreign Affairs Digest* 6 (1978): 36–37.

Grunberger, Bela. *Narcissism: Psychoanalytic Essays*. New York: International Universities Press, 1982.

Grundy, Kenneth W., and Weinstein, M. A. *Ideologies of Violence*. Columbus: Ohio State University Press, 1975.

Guevara, Ernesto. "Guerrilla Warfare: A Method." In *Che: Selected Writings of Ernesto Guevara*. Edited by Rolando E. Bonachea and Nelson P. Valdes. Cambridge, MA: MIT Press, 1969.

Guiness, Os. *Violence: Crisis or Catharsis?* Downers Grove, IL: Intervarsity, 1974.

Gunn, John. "The Psychiatrist and the Terrorist." In *Terrorism: Interdisciplinary Perspectives*. Edited by B. Eichelman, D. Soskis, and W. Reid. Washington, DC: American Psychiatric Association, 1983.

Gurr, Ted Robert. "Psychological Factors in Civil Violence." *World Politics* 20 (1968): 245–78.

_____. *Why Men Rebel*. Princeton, NJ: Princeton University Press, 1970.

Gutman, David. "Killers and Consumers: The Terrorist and His Audience." *Social Research* (Autumn 1979): 517–26.

Guttmacher, Manfred S. *The Mind of the Murderer*. New York: Farrar, Strauss, and Cudahy, 1960.

Haan, N.; Smith, N. B.; and Black, J. "Moral Reasoning of Young Adults." *Journal of Personality and Social Psychology* 10 (1968): 183–201.

Habermas, Jurgen. *Toward a Rational Society: Student Protest, Science, and Politics*. Boston: Beacon, 1970.

Hachey, Thomas. *Voices of Revolution: Rebels and Rhetoric*. Hinsdale, IL: Dryden, 1973.

Hacker, A. "Dostoevsky's Disciples: Man and Sheep in Political Theory." *Journal of Politics* 18 (1955): 590–612.

Hacker, Frederick J. "Contagion and Attraction of Terror and Terrorism." In *Behavioral and Quantitative Perspectives on Terrorism*. Edited by Yonah Alexander and John M. Gleason. New York: Pergamon, 1981.

_____. *Crusaders, Criminals, Crazies: Terror and Terrorism in Our Time.* New York: W. W. Norton, 1976.

_____. "Devils and Poor Devils (Perpetrators, Victims, and Perpetrator Victims among Terrorists and Cultists)." Paper presented to the Second Annual Meeting of the International Society of Political Psychology, May 24–26, 1979, at Washington, DC.

_____. "Dialectical Interrelationships of Personal and Political Factors in Terrorism." In *Perspectives on Terrorism.* Edited by Lawrence Zelic Freedman and Yonah Alexander. Wilmington, DE: Scholarly Resources, 1983.

_____. "Pathology: Personal and Political." Paper presented to the Conference on Psychopathology and Political Violence, November 16–17, 1979, at the University of Chicago, Chicago, Illinois.

_____. "Psychology of Terror." Address to the Wackenhut Corporation's Seminar on Terrorism, November 21, 1974.

_____. *Terror and Terrorism.* New York: W. W. Norton, 1976.

_____. "Terror and Terrorism: Modern Growth Industry and Mass Entertainment." *Terrorism* 4 (1980): 143–59.

Hamilton, M. P. "Terrorism: Its Ethical Implications for the Future." *Futurist* (December 1977): 351–54.

Hampton-Turner, C. *Radical Man: The Process of Psycho-Social Development.* Cambridge, MA: Schenkman, 1970.

Hannay, William A. "International Terrorism: The Need for a Fresh Perspective." *International Lawyer* 8 (1974): 268–84.

Harris, F. Gentry. "Hypothetical Facets or Ingredients of Terrorism." *Terrorism* 3 (1980): 239–44.

Harris, Jonathan. "The Mind of the Terrorist." In *The New Terrorism: Politics of Violence.* New York: Julian Messner, 1983.

Hart, Henry Harper. "Narcissistic Equilibrium." *International Journal of Psychoanalysis* 28 (1947): 106–14.

Hartmann, Heinz. *Ego Psychology and the Problem of Adaptation.* New York: International Universities Press, 1958.

Hassel, Conrad V. "Interactions of Law Enforcement and Behavioral Science Personnel." In *Victims of Terrorism.* Edited by Frank M. Ochberg and David A. Soskis. Boulder, CO: Westview Special Studies in National and International Terrorism, 1982.

_____. "Political Assassin." *Journal of Police Science and Administration* 2 (1974): 399–403.

_____. "Terror: The Crime of the Privileged—An Examination and Prognosis." *Terrorism* 1 (1977): 1–16.

Haynal, André; Molnar, Miklos; and De Puymege, Gérard. *Fanaticism: A Historical and Psychoanalytical Study.* New York: Schocken, 1983.

Hearst, Patricia Campbell. *Every Secret Thing.* Garden City, NY: Doubleday, 1982.

Herman, Edward S., and O'Sullivan, Gerry. *The "Terrorism" Industry: The Experts and Institutions that Shape Our View of Terror.* New York: Pantheon, 1990.

Heskin, Ken. *Northern Ireland: A Psychological Analysis.* New York: Columbia University Press, 1980.

_____. "The Psychology of Terrorism in Northern Ireland." In *Terrorism in Ireland.* Edited by Yonah Alexander and Alan O'Day. London: Croom Helm, 1984.

Higgins, R. "Can Terrorism Be Justified?" *Listener* 99 (1978): 558–59.

Hirschman, Albert O. *Exit, Voice, and Loyalty: Responses to Decline in Firms, Organizations, and States.* Cambridge, MA: Harvard University Press, 1970.

Hobbes, Thomas. *Leviathan: On the Matter, Form and Power of a Commonwealth Ecclesiastical and Civil.* New York: Collier, 1977.

_____. *Man and Citizen.* Garden City, NY: Doubleday, 1972.

Hodges, Donald C., ed. *Philosophy of the Urban Guerrilla: The Revolutionary Writings of Abraham Guillen.* New York: Morrow, 1973.

Hoffer, Eric. *The True Believer: Thoughts on the Nature of Mass Movements.* New York: Harper and Row, 1951.

Hoffman, Bruce. *Terrorism in the United States and the Potential Threat to Nuclear Facilities.* Santa Monica, CA: Rand Corporation, 1986.

Hoffman, Bruce, and deLeon, Peter. *A Reassessment of Potential Adversaries to U.S. Nuclear Programs.* Santa Monica, CA: Rand Corporation, 1986.

Holden, Constance. "Study of Terrorism Emerging as an International Endeavor." *Science* 203 (1979): 33–35.

Holland, Carolsue. "The More Deadly of the Species: Relevant Scholarship Dealing with Female Terrorists." Paper presented to the Center for Research on Women, February 2, 1989, at Wellesley College, Wellesley, Massachusetts.

Holland, Carolsue, and Brandon-Koster, Janet. "Women on Women Terrorists: A Review Article." Unpublished manuscript.

Homer. *The Iliad.* Garden City, NY: Doubleday, 1974.

_____. *The Odyssey.* Chicago: Henry Regnery, 1950.

Homer, Frederic D. "Terror in the United States: Three Perspectives." In *The Politics of Terrorism.* Edited by Michael Stohl. New York: Marcel Dekker, 1979.

Hook, Sidney. "The Ideology of Violence." *Encounter* (April 1970): 26–38.

Horchem, Hans Josef. "European Terrorism: A German Perspective." *Terrorism* 6 (1982): 27–51.

_____. "Patterns of 'Urban Guerrilla.' " In *The Terrorism Reader: A Historical Anthology.* Edited by Walter Laqueur. New York: Meridian, 1978.

_____. "Urban Guerrilla in West Germany: Origins and Prospects." Paper presented to the Conference on International Terrorism, U.S. Department of State, March 1976, at Washington, DC.

_____. "West Germany's Red Army Anarchists." *Conflict Studies* 46 (1974).

Horowitz, Irving L. *Political Terrorism and Personal Deviance.* Washington, DC: U.S. Department of State, 1973.

Hougan, Jim. *Decadence: Radical Nostalgia, Narcissism, and Decline in the Seventies.* New York: Morrow, 1975.

Howe, Irving. "Maniacs and Murder." *Dissent* 21 (1974): 372–73.

Hubbard, David G. "A Glimmer of Hope: A Psychiatric Perspective." In *International Terrorism and Political Crimes.* Edited by M. Cherif Bassiouni. Springfield, IL: Thomas, 1975.

_____. "A Story of Inadequacy: Hierarchical Authority vs. the Terrorist." In *Political Terrorism and Business: The Threat and the Response.* Edited by Yonah Alexander and Robert A. Kilmarx. New York: Praeger, 1979.

_____. "The Psychodynamics of Terrorism." In *International Violence.* Edited by Yonah Alexander and T. Adeniran. New York: Praeger, 1983.

_____. *The Skyjacker: His Flights of Fantasy.* New York: Macmillan, 1971.

_____. "The Terrorist Mind." *Counterforce* (April 1971): 12–13.

_____. *Winning Back the Sky: A Tactical Analysis of Terrorism.* Dallas, TX: Saybrook, 1986.

Hutchinson, Martha Crenshaw. "The Concept of Revolutionary Terrorism." *Journal of Conflict Resolution* 16 (1971): 383–96.

Hyams, Edward S. *A Dictionary of Modern Revolution.* New York: Taplinger, 1973.

_____. "The Terrorist Ego." In *Terrorists and Terrorism.* New York: St. Martin's, 1974.

Ilfeld, F. W., Jr. "Overview of the Causes and Prevention of Violence." *Archives of General Psychiatry* 20 (1969): 675–89.

Ivianski, Zeev. "The Moral Issue: Some Aspects of Individual Terror." In *The Morality of Terrorism: Religious and Secular Justifications.* Edited by David C. Rapoport and Yonah Alexander. New York: Pergamon, 1982.

Jackson, Geoffrey. "Maruja Echegoyen Interview." In *Surviving the Long Night: An Autobiographical Account of a Political Kidnapping.* New York: Vanguard, 1974.

Jacobs, Harold, ed. *Weatherman.* Palo Alto, CA: Ramparts, 1970.

Jacobson, Edith. *The Self and the Object World.* London: Hogarth, 1965.

Jager, Herbert; Schmidtchen, Gerhard; and Süllwold, Lieselotte, eds. *Analysen zum Terrorismus,* vol. 2. Wiesbaden: Westdeutscher Verlag, 1981.

Janis, Irving L. *Victims of Groupthink: A Psychological Study of Foreign-Policy Decisions and Fiascoes.* Boston: Houghton Mifflin, 1972.

Janke, Peter. *Guerrilla and Terrorist Organizations: A World Directory and Bibliography.* New York: Macmillan, 1983.

Janze, Hans-Georg. "Terrorism: Germany, Ulrike Marie Meinhof, and the RAF." Unpublished manuscript.

Jaquett, J. S. "Women in Revolutionary Movements in Latin America." *Journal of Marriage and the Family* 35 (1973): 344–54.

Jaszi, Oscar, and Lewis, John D. *Against the Tyrant: The Tradition and Theory of Tyrannicide.* Glencoe, IL: Free Press, 1970.

Jenkins, Brian M. "American Terrorism." *TVI Journal* 1 (1980): 2–8.

_____. "Effective Communication in a Hostage Crisis: Some Simple Principles Based on Experience." In *Diplomats and Terrorists: What Works, What Doesn't.* Edited by Martin F. Herz. Washington, DC: Institute for the Study of Diplomacy, 1982.

_____. *International Terrorism: A New Mode of Conflict.* Los Angeles, CA: Crescent, 1975.

_____. *International Terrorism: The Other World War.* Santa Monica, CA: Rand Corporation, 1985.

_____. "Some Observations on the Behavior of the Terrorist Adversary." Paper presented to the Eighth Annual Symposium on the Role of the Behavioral Sciences in Physical Security, June 7–8, 1983, at Springfield, Virginia.

_____. "The Study of Terrorism: Definitional Problems." In *Behavioral and Quantitative Perspectives on Terrorism.* Edited by Yonah Alexander and John M. Gleason. New York: Pergamon, 1981.

_____. "The Terrorist Mindset and Terrorist Decisionmaking: Two Areas of Ignorance." *Terrorism* 3 (1980): 245–48.

_____. "Terrorist Mindsets and Their Implications." In *Terrorism and Beyond: An International Conference on Terrorism and Low-Level Conflict.* Edited by Brian M. Jenkins. Santa Monica, CA: Rand Corporation, 1982.

_____. "The U.S. Response to Terrorism: A Policy Dilemma." *TVI Journal* 6 (1985): 31–36.

Jervis, Robert. *The Logic of Images in International Relations.* Princeton, NJ: Princeton University Press, 1970.

Joffe, W. G., and Sandler, J. "Some Conceptual Problems Involved in the Consideration of Disorders of Narcissism." *Journal of Child Psychotherapy* 2 (1967): 56–66.

Johnson, Chalmers. "Perspectives on Terrorism." In *The Terrorism Reader: A Historical Anthology.* Edited by Walter Laqueur. New York: Meridian, 1978.

Johnson, Paul. "The Seven Deadly Sins of Terrorism." *New Republic* (September 15, 1979): 19–21.

Johnson, Roger. "The Dynamics of Individual and Group Aggression." Paper presented to the Conference on Terrorism in the Contemporary World, April 26–28, 1976, at Glassboro State College, Glassboro, New Jersey.

Johnston, Thomas. *Freud and Political Thought.* New York: Citadel, 1965.

Jonas, Adolphe D. "Introduction." *Terrorism* 3 (1980): 257–64.

Jones, Edward E., and Nisbett, Richard E. "The Actor and the Observer: Divergent Perceptions of the Causes of Behavior." In *Attribution: Perceiving the Causes of Behavior.* Edited by Edward E. Jones et al. Morristown, NJ: General Learning Press, 1972.

Jones, Peter M. "A Psychiatrist Examines the Terrorist Mind." *Scholastic Update* (May 16, 1986): 6.

Kahn, E. J., III. "The Last American Revolutionaries." *Boston Magazine* (February 1987): 181–83.

Kampf, Herbert A. "On the Appeals of Extremism to the Youth of Affluent, Democratic Societies." *Terrorism* 4 (1980): 161–93.

Kanzer, M. "Freud's Use of the Terms 'Autoeroticism' and 'Narcissism.'" *Journal of the American Psychoanalytic Association* 12 (1964): 529–39.

Kaplan, Abraham. "The Psychodynamics of Terrorism." *Terrorism* 1 (1978): 237–54.

Kapp, R. O. "Sensation and Narcissism." *International Journal of Psychoanalysis* 6 (1925): 292–99.

Karagueuzian, Dikran. *Blow It Up!* Boston: Gambit, 1971.

Karanovic, Milivoje. "The Concept of Terrorism." In *International Summaries: A Collection of Selected Translations in Law Enforcement and Criminal Justice.* Washington, DC: U.S. Department of Justice, National Criminal Justice Reference Service, 1979.

Karber, Phillip A. "Some Psychological Effects of Terrorism as Protest." Paper presented to the Annual Convention of the American Psychological Association, August 1973.

Katz, Robert. *Days of Wrath: The Ordeal of Aldo Moro.* Garden City, NY: Doubleday, 1980.

Kellen, Konrad. "The Road to Terrorism: Confessions of a German Terrorist." *TVI Journal* 5 (1985): 36–39.

————. "Terrorists—What Are They Like? How Some Terrorists Describe Their World and Actions." In *Terrorism and Beyond: An International Conference on Terrorism and Low-Level Conflict.* Edited by Brian M. Jenkins. Santa Monica, CA: Rand Corporation, 1982.

Kelly, Aileen. *Mikhail Bakunin: A Study in the Psychology and Politics of Utopianism.* New York: Oxford University Press, 1982.

Kelman, Herbert C. "Violence without Moral Restraint: Reflections on the Dehumanization of Victims and Victimizers." *Journal of Social Issues* 29 (1973): 53–61.

Kemezis, Paul. "West Germany's Leftist Guerrillas Reawaken Sensitive Political Issues." *New York Times*, March 4, 1975.

Keniston, Kenneth. "Student Activism, Moral Development, and Morality." *American Journal of Orthopsychiatry* 40 (1970): 577–92.

_____. *The Uncommitted: Alienated Youth in American Society.* New York: Dell, 1965.

_____. *Young Radicals: Notes on Committed Youth.* New York: Harcourt Brace and World, 1968.

Kent, I., and Nicholls, W. "The Psychodynamics of Terrorism." *Mental Health and Society* 4 (1977): 1–8.

Kernberg, Otto F. *Borderline Conditions and Pathological Narcissism.* New York: Aronson, 1975.

_____. "The Course of the Analysis of a Narcissistic Personality with Hysterical and Compulsive Features." *Journal of the American Psychoanalytic Association* 19 (1971): 451–71.

_____. "Factors in the Psychoanalytic Treatment of Narcissistic Personalities." *Journal of the American Psychoanalytic Association* 18 (1970): 51–85.

_____. "Further Contributions to the Treatment of Narcissistic Personalities." *International Journal of Psychoanalysis* 55 (1974): 215–40.

Khaled, Leila. *My People Shall Live: The Autobiography of a Revolutionary.* London: Hodder and Stoughton, 1973.

Khan, M. M. R. "On Symbiotic Omnipotence." In *The Psychoanalytic Forum.* Edited by John A. Lindon. New York: Aronson, 1969.

Kirkham, James F.; Levy, Sheldon G.; and Crotty, William J. *Assassination and Political Violence: A Report to the National Commission on the Causes and Prevention of Violence.* Washington, DC: U.S. Government Printing Office, 1969.

Kligerman, C. "In Panel: Narcissistic Resistance." *Journal of the American Psychoanalytic Association* 17 (1969): 941–54.

_____. "The Psychology of Herman Melville." *Psychoanalytic Review* 40 (1953): 125–43.

Knutson, Jeanne N. "Personality in the Study of Politics." In *Handbook of Political Psychology.* Edited by Jeanne N. Knutson. San Francisco: Jossey-Bass, 1973.

_____. "The Psychodynamics of the Terrorists' Behavior." Panel held at the Second Annual Convention of the International Society of Political Psychology, May 24–26, 1979, at Washington, DC.

_____. "Social and Psychodynamic Pressures toward a Negative Identity: The Case of an American Revolutionary Terrorist." In *Behavioral and Quantitative Perpectives on Terrorism.* Edited by Yonah Alexander and John M. Gleason. New York: Pergamon, 1981.

_____. "The Terrorists' Dilemmas: Some Implicit Rules of the Game." *Terrorism* 4 (1980): 195–222.

Kohut, Heinz. *The Analysis of the Self.* New York: International Publishers, 1971.

———. "Forms and Transformations of Narcissism." *Journal of the American Psychoanalytic Association* 14 (1966): 243–72.

———. "The Psychoanalytic Treatment of Narcissistic Personality Disorders." *Psychoanalytic Study of the Child* 23 (1968): 86–113.

———. *The Restoration of the Self.* New York: International Universities Press, 1977.

———. *The Search for the Self.* New York: International Universities Press, 1978.

———. "Thoughts on Narcissism and Narcissistic Rage." *Psychoanalytic Study of the Child* 27 (1972): 360–400.

Kovel, Joel. *White Racism: A Psychohistory.* New York: Vintage, 1970.

Kramer, Jane. "A Reporter in Europe." *The New Yorker* (March 20, 1978): 44.

Kupperman, Robert H., and Kamen, Jeff. *Final Warning: Averting Disaster in the New Age of Terrorism.* New York: Doubleday, 1989.

Kupperman, Robert H., and Trent, Darrell M. *Terrorism: Threat, Reality, Response.* Stanford, CA: Hoover Institution Press, 1979.

Kurz, Anat, et al. *InTer 1988: A Review of International Terrorism in 1988.* Boulder, CO: Westview, 1989.

La Chard, J. "The Mind of the Terrorist." *Listener* (June 5, 1975): 722–23.

Laing, R. D. *The Divided Self: An Existential Study in Sanity and Madness.* Baltimore, MD: Penguin, 1969.

———. *The Politics of Experience.* New York: Ballantine, 1967.

———. *Self and Others.* Baltimore, MD: Penguin, 1969.

Laing, R. D., and Esterson, A. *Sanity, Madness, and the Family: Families of Schizophrenics.* Baltimore, MD: Penguin, 1970.

Lake, Peter. "An Exegesis of the Radical Right." *California Magazine* (April 1985).

Laqueur, Walter. "Terrorism—A Balance Sheet." In *The Terrorism Reader: A Historical Anthology.* Edited by Walter Laqueur. New York: Meridian, 1978.

———. *Terrorism: A Study of National and International Political Violence.* Boston: Little, Brown, 1977.

———. "Terrorism Makes a Tremendous Noise." *Across the Board* 15 (1978): 57–67.

Laqueur, Walter, ed. *The Terrorism Reader: A Historical Anthology.* New York: Meridian, 1978.

Larsen, Otto N., and Hill, R. "Mass Media and Interpersonal Communication in the Diffusion of a News Event." *American Sociological Review* 19 (1954): 426–33.

Lasch, Christopher. *The Culture of Narcissism: American Life in an Age of Diminishing Expectations.* New York: W. W. Norton, 1979.

Lasky, Melvin J. "Ulrike and Andreas: The Bonnie and Clyde of West Germany's Radical Subculture May Have Failed to Make a Revolution, But They Have Bruised the Body Politic." *New York Times Magazine* (May 11, 1975): 14.

_____. "Ulrike Meinhof and the Baader-Meinhof Gang." *Encounter* (June 1975): 9–23.

Lasswell, Harold D. *Politics: Who Gets What, When, How.* New York: Meridian, 1958.

_____. *Power and Personality.* New York: W. W. Norton, 1948.

_____. *Psychopathology and Politics.* Chicago: University of Chicago Press, 1977.

_____. "Terrorism and the Political Process." *Terrorism* 1 (1978): 255–63.

Laytner, Ron. "An Interview with the Jackal Leads to a Life of Constant Fear." *Boston Globe*, July 8, 1982.

Le Carre, John. *The Little Drummer Girl.* New York: Bantam, 1983.

Ledeen, Michael. "Inside the Red Brigades: An Exclusive Report." *New York* (May 1, 1978): 36–39.

Leiser, Burton M. "Terrorism, Guerrilla Warfare, and International Morality." *Stanford Journal of International Studies* (Spring 1977): 39–66.

Lenin, V. I. "Left-Wing Communism: An Infantile Disorder." In *Selected Works of V. I. Lenin*, vol. 3. Moscow: Foreign Languages Publishing House, 1961.

Lenzer, Gertrud. "Women and Terrorism." Paper presented to the Conference on Psychopathology and Political Violence, November 16–17, at the University of Chicago, Chicago, Illinois.

Lerner, Melvin J., and Simmons, Carolyn H. "Observer's Reaction to the 'Innocent Victim': Compassion or Rejection?" *Journal of Personality and Social Psychology* 4 (1966): 302–10.

Lessing, Doris. *The Good Terrorist.* New York: Knopf, 1985.

Leventhal, Paul, and Alexander, Yonah, eds. *Nuclear Terrorism: Defining the Threat.* Washington, DC: Pergamon-Brassey's, 1986.

_____. *Preventing Nuclear Terrorism: The Report and Papers of the International Task Force on Prevention of Nuclear Terrorism.* Lexington, MA: Lexington, 1987.

Lichtenstein, H. "The Role of Narcissism in the Emergence and Maintenance of a Primary Identity." *International Journal of Psychoanalysis* 45 (1964): 49–56.

Lichter, S. Robert. "Psychopolitical Models of Student Radicals: A Methodological Critique and West German Case Study." Ph.D. diss., Harvard University, 1977.

_____. "Young Rebels: A Psychological Study of West German Male Radical Students." *Comparative Politics* 12 (1979): 29–48.

Liebert, Robert. *Radical and Militant Youth: A Psychoanalytic Inquiry.* New York: Praeger, 1971.

Lifton, Robert Jay, ed. *Explorations in Psychohistory: The Wellfleet Papers.* New York: Simon and Schuster, 1974.

Lincoln, Alan, and Levinger, George. "Observer's Evaluation of the Victim and the Attacker in an Aggressive Incident." *Journal of Personality and Social Psychology* 22 (1972): 202–10.

Linowitz, Norman S., and Newman, Kenneth M. "The Borderline Personality and the Theatre of the Absurd." *Archives of General Psychiatry* 16 (1967): 268–70.

Lipsitz, Lewis. "Vulture, Mantis and Seal: Proposals for Political Scientists." In *The Post-Behavioral Era.* Edited by George J. Graham and George W. Carey. New York: D. McKay, 1972.

Liston, Robert. *Terrorism.* Nashville, TN: Thomas Nelson, 1977.

Livingstone, Neil C. "The Impact of Technological Innovation." In *Hydra of Carnage: International Linkages of Terrorism: The Witnesses Speak.* Edited by Uri Ra'anan et al. Lexington, MA: Lexington, 1986.

————. "Terrorist Profile: The Secret Lives of Terrorists." In *The War against Terrorism.* Lexington, MA: Lexington, 1982.

Livingstone, Neil C., and Arnold, Terrell E., eds. *Beyond the Iran-Contra Crisis: The Shape of U.S. Anti-Terrorism Policy in the Post-Reagan Era.* Lexington, MA: Lexington, 1988.

————. *Fighting Back: Winning the War against Terrorism.* Lexington, MA: Lexington, 1986.

Loftland, John. *Deviance and Identity.* Englewood Cliffs, NJ: Prentice Hall, 1969.

London, Jack. *The Assassination Bureau, Ltd.* New York: Penguin, 1983.

Lorenz, Konrad. *On Aggression.* New York: Bantam, 1971.

Louch, Alfred. "Terrorism: The Immorality of Belief." In *The Morality of Terrorism: Religious and Secular Justifications.* Edited by David C. Rapoport and Yonah Alexander. New York: Pergamon, 1982.

Lowen, Alexander. *Narcissism: The Denial of the True Self.* New York: Macmillan, 1983.

Lowenstein, Sophie Freud. "Narcissism, Self-Esteem, and the Divided Self." Paper presented on January 19, 1983, at Newton-Wellesley Hospital, Newton, Massachusetts.

Ludwig, Emil. *Kaiser Wilhelm II.* New York: Putnam, 1926.

Lupsha, Peter A. "Explanation of Political Violence: Some Psychological Theories versus Indignation." *Politics and Society* 2 (1971): 88–104.

Lyman, Stanford M., and Scott, Marvin B. *The Drama of Social Reality.* New York: Oxford University Press, 1975.

Lyons, H. A. "Terrorist Bombing and the Psychological Sequelae." *Journal of the British Medical Association* (January 12, 1974): 15–19.

Macdonald, Andrew. *The Turner Diaries*. Washington, DC: National Alliance, 1978.

McGuire, Maria. *To Take Arms: My Years with the IRA Provisionals*. New York: Viking, 1973.

Machiavelli, Niccolò. *The Prince*. Oxford, UK: Clarendon, 1891.

McKnight, Gerald. *The Mind of the Terrorist: Why They Hijack, Bomb and Kill*. London: Michael Joseph, 1974.

McLellan, Vin, and Avery, Paul. *The Voices of Guns*. New York: G. P. Putnam's, 1977.

McLuhan, Marshall. "The Tough as Narcissus." In *The Mechanical Bride: Folklore of Industrial Man*. New York: Vanguard, 1951.

McNeil, Elton D. "Psychology and Aggression." *Journal of Conflict Resolution* 3 (1959): entire issue.

MacStiofain, Sean. *Revolutionary in Ireland*. Farnborough, UK: Gordon Cremonesi, 1975.

McVey, Ronald. "The Terrorist Mind." Paper presented to the Conference on Terror: The Man, the Mind and the Matter, October 15–16, 1976, at the John Jay School of Criminal Justice, New York City.

Madden, Edward H. "Explanation in Psychoanalysis and History." *Philosophy of Science* 33 (1966): 278–86.

Maddi, S. R. *Personality Theories: A Comparative Analysis*. Homewood, IL: Dorsey, 1972.

Mahler, Horst. "Terrorism in West Germany: An Interview with Horst Mahler." *Socialist Review* 39 (1978): 118–23.

Mahler, Margaret S. *On Human Symbiosis and the Vicissitudes of Individuation*. New York: International Universities Press, 1975.

————. "Symbiosis and Individuation." *Psychoanalytic Study of the Child* 29 (1974): 89–106.

Mahler, Margaret S., and Gosliner, Bertram J. "On Symbiotic Child Psychosis." *Psychoanalytic Study of the Child* 10 (1955): 195–212.

Malcolm, Henry. "Violence and Narcissism." In *Generation of Narcissus*. Boston: Little, Brown, 1971.

Mallick, S. H., and McCandless, B. R. "A Study of Catharsis of Aggression." *Journal of Personality and Social Psychology* 4 (1966): 591–96.

Mallin, Jay, ed. *Terror and the Urban Guerrillas: A Study of Tactics and Documents*. Coral Gables, FL: University of Miami Press, 1971.

Malraux, André. *Man's Fate: La Condition Humaine*. New York: Vintage, 1934.

Maple, Terry, and Matheson, Douglas W. *Aggression, Hostility, and Violence: Nature or Nurture?* New York: Holt, Rinehart and Winston, 1973.

Marcus, Anthony M. "Some Psychiatric and Sociological Aspects of Violence." *International Journal of Group Tensions* 4 (1974): 254–68.

Marcuse, Herbert. *An Essay on Liberation*. Boston: Beacon, 1969.

_____. *Eros and Civilization: A Philosophical Inquiry into Freud.* New York: Vintage, 1962.

_____. *One-Dimensional Man: Studies in the Ideology of Advanced Industrial Society.* Boston: Beacon, 1964.

Margolin, Joseph. "Psychological Perspectives in Terrorism." In *Terrorism: Interdisciplinary Perspectives.* Edited by Yonah Alexander and Seymour Maxwell Finger. New York: John Jay, 1977.

Marighella, Carlos. *For the Liberation of Brazil.* London: Penguin, 1971.

_____. "Minimanual of the Urban Guerrilla." *Tricontinental* 16 (1970): 15–56.

Marin, Peter. "The New Narcissism." *Harper's* (October 1975): 45–56.

Martin, David C., and Walcott, John. *Best Laid Plans: The Inside Story of America's War against Terrorism.* New York: Harper and Row, 1988.

Martinez, Thomas. *Brotherhood of Murder: How One Man's Journey through Fear Brought The Order—the Most Dangerous Racist Gang in America—to Justice.* New York: McGraw-Hill, 1988.

Maslow, Abraham H. *Motivation and Personality.* New York: Harper and Row, 1954.

Masterson, James F. *The Narcissistic and Borderline Disorders.* New York: Brunner/Mazel, 1981.

May, Rollo. *Power and Innocence: A Search for the Sources of Violence.* New York: W. W. Norton, 1972.

May, William F. "Terrorism as Strategy and Ecstasy." *Social Research* 41 (1974): 277–98.

Mazlish, Bruce. *In Search of Nixon: A Psychohistorical Inquiry.* Baltimore, MD: Penguin, 1973.

Mazlish, Bruce, ed. *Psychoanalysis and History.* New York: Grosset and Dunlap, 1971.

_____. *The Revolutionary Ascetic: Evolution of a Political Type.* New York: McGraw-Hill, 1976.

Melges, Frederick T., and Harris, Robert F. "Anger and Attack: A Cybernetic Model of Violence." In *Violence and the Struggle for Existence.* Edited by David N. Daniels, Marshall F. Gilula, and Frank M. Ochberg. Boston: Little, Brown, 1970.

Melman, Yossi. *The Master Terrorist: The True Story behind Abu Nidal.* New York: Adama, 1986.

Meltzer, M. *The Terrorists.* New York: Harper and Row, 1983.

Melville, Herman. *Moby Dick; or, The Whale.* New York: Heritage, 1943.

Melville, Samuel. *Letters from Attica.* New York: Morrow, 1972.

Mendel, Arthur P. *Michael Bakunin: Roots of Apocalypse.* New York: Praeger, 1981.

Mengel, R. William. "The Impact of Nuclear Terrorism on the Military's Role in Society." In *International Terrorism in the Contemporary World.* Edited by Marius Livingston. Westport, CT: Greenwood, 1978.

Merari, Ariel. "Problems Related to the Symptomatic Treatment of Terrorism." *Terrorism* 3 (1980): 279–83.

Merari, Ariel, and Friedland, N. "Social Psychological Aspects of Political Terrorism." In *Applied Social Psychology Annual*. Edited by S. Oskamp. Beverly Hills, CA: Sage, 1985.

Merelman, Richard M. "The Development of Policy Thinking in Adolescence." *American Political Science Review* 65 (1971): 1033–47.

Merkl, Peter. "In the Mind of the Terrorist: An Interview with Peter Merkl." *Center Magazine* 19 (1986): 18–24.

Meynel, Viola. *Narcissus*. New York: G. P. Putnam's, 1916.

Middendorf, Wolf. "The Personality of the Terrorist." In *International Summaries: A Collection of Selected Translations in Law Enforcement and Criminal Justice*, vol. 3. Edited by M. Kravitz. Rockville, MD: National Criminal Justice Reference Service, 1979.

Milbank, David L. *International and Transnational Terrorism*. Washington, DC: Central Intelligence Agency, PR 7610030, April 1976.

Miller, Abraham. "Hostage Negotiations and the Concept of Transference." In *Terrorism: Theory and Practice*. Edited by Yonah Alexander, David Carlton, and Paul Wilkinson. Boulder, CO: Westview, 1979.

Miller, Alice. *Prisoners of Childhood*. New York: Basic Books, 1981.

Miller, Bowman H., and Russell, Charles A. "The Evolution of Revolutionary Warfare: From Mao to Marighella and Meinhof." In *Terrorism: Threat, Reality, Response*. Edited by Robert H. Kupperman and Darrell M. Trent. Stanford, CA: Hoover Institution Press, 1979.

Miller, N. E. "Frustration-Aggression Hypothesis." *Psychological Review* 48 (1941): 337–42.

Miller, P. R. "Revolutionists among the Chicago Demonstrators." *American Journal of Psychiatry* 127 (1970): 752–58.

Mills, C. Wright. "Situated Actions and the Vocabulary of Motives." *American Sociological Review* 5 (1940).

————. *The Sociological Imagination*. London: Oxford University Press, 1959.

Milte, Kerry L., et al. "Terrorism: Political and Psychological Considerations." *Australian and New Zealand Journal of Criminology* 9 (1976): 89–94.

Miron, Murray. "Psycholinguistic Analysis of the SLA." *Assets Protection* 1 (1976).

Moore, Burness E. "Toward a Clarification of the Concept of Narcissism." *Psychoanalytic Study of the Child* 30 (1975): 243–76.

Moran, Sue Ellen. "The Case of Terrorist Patrizio Peci: A Character Sketch." *TVI Journal* 5 (1985): 34–36.

Moreno, Francisco J. "Some Psychodynamics of Terrorists in Spain and El Salvador." Paper presented to the Second Annual Meeting of the International Society of Political Psychology, May 24–26, 1979, at Washington, DC.

Morf, Gustave. *Terror in Quebec: Case Studies of the FLQ*. Toronto: Clarke, Irwin, 1970.

Morgan, Robin. *The Demon Lover: On the Sexuality of Terrorism*. New York: W. W. Norton, 1989.

Morgen, A. "Aggressiveness, Aggression, and Terrorism." *Etudes internationales de psycho-sociologie criminelle* 20–23 (1971–72).

Morrison, Andrew P., ed. *Essential Papers on Narcissism*. New York: New York University Press, 1986.

Mosby, J. C. *Prison-Terrorist Link*. Bessemer, AL: Cerberus, 1977.

Moss, Robert. *The War for the Cities*. New York: Coward, McCann and Geoghegan, 1972.

Motley, James B. *U.S. Strategy to Counter Domestic Terrorism*. Washington, DC: National Defense University Press, 1983.

Mueller, M. A. "Revolutionary Terrorist: A Character Analysis." *Military Police Law Enforcement Journal* 3 (1976): 38–43.

Mukerjee, D. *The Terrorist*. New York: Vintage, 1980.

Mulgrew, Ian. *Unholy Terror: The Sikhs and International Terrorism*. Toronto: Key Porter, 1988.

Mullaney, Marie Marmo. "Gender and Revolution: Rosa Luxemburg and the Female Revolutionary Personality." *Journal of Psychohistory* 11 (1984): 463–76.

Mullen, Robert K. "Mass Destruction and Terrorism." *Journal of International Affairs* 32 (1978): 63–89.

Murphy, Lois B. "Pride and Its Relation to Narcissism, Autonomy, and Identity." *Bulletin of the Menninger Clinic* 24 (1960): 136–43.

Murray, John M. "Narcissism and the Ego Ideal." *Journal of the American Psychoanalytic Association* 12 (1964): 477–514.

Nagel, W. H. "Devil's Advocate on the Question of Terrorism." *Etudes internationales de psycho-sociologie criminelle* 20–23 (1971–72).

Nagelburg, Leo, and Spotnitz, Hyman. "Strengthening the Ego through the Release of Frustration-Aggression." *American Journal of Orthopsychiatry* 28 (1958): 794–801.

Nathan, J. A. "Terrorism and the Moral Basis of the International System." Paper presented to the Conference on the Moral Implications of Terrorism, March 14–16, 1979, at the University of California at Los Angeles, Los Angeles, California.

National Advisory Commission on Civil Disorders. *Report*. Washington, DC: U.S. Government Printing Office, 1968.

National Advisory Committee on Criminal Justice Standards and Goals. *Disorders and Terrorism: Report of the Task Force on Disorders and Terrorism*. Washington, DC, 1976.

Nechaev, Sergei. "Cathechism of the Revolutionist." In *Daughter of a Revolutionary*. Edited by M. Confino. London: Alcove Press, n.d.

Nedava, Yosef. "Some Aspects of Individual Terrorism: A Case Study of the Schwartzbard Affair." *Terrorism* 3 (1979): 69–80.

Nelson, Maria Coleman. *The Narcissistic Condition: A Fact of Our Lives and Times.* New York: Human Science Press, 1977.

Nese, Marco. *Terrorism.* Rome: Tipografica, 1978.

Netanyahu, Benjamin, ed. *Terrorism: How the West Can Win.* New York: Farrar, Straus, Giroux, 1986.

Neuberg, A. *Armed Insurrection.* Milan: Feltrinelli, 1970.

Neuhauser, P. "The Mind of a German Terrorist: Interview with M. C. Baumann." *Encounter* (September 1978): 81-88.

New York State Policy Study Group on Terrorism. "Report on the Brinks Incident." *Terrorism* 9 (1987): 169–206.

Nicole, Christopher. *The Self-lovers.* London: Hutchinson, 1968.

Niebuhr, Reinhold. *Moral Man and Immoral Society: A Study in Ethics and Politics.* New York: Scribner's, 1960.

Nieburg, H. L. *Political Violence: The Behavioral Process.* New York: St. Martin's, 1969.

———. "The Uses of Violence." *Journal of Conflict Resolution* 7 (1963): 43–55.

Nietzsche, Friedrich. *Beyond Good and Evil.* New York: Vintage, 1966.

Norton, Augustus R., and Greenberg, Martin H., eds. *Studies in Nuclear Terrorism.* Boston: G. K. Hall, 1979.

O'Ballance, Edgar. "Carlos the Jackal." In *The Language of Violence: The Blood Politics of Terrorism.* San Rafael, CA: Presidio, 1979.

Olmsted, Michael S. *The Small Group.* New York: Random House, 1959.

Oots, Kent Layne, and Wiegele, Thomas C. "Terrorist and Victim: Psychiatric and Physiological Approaches from a Social Science Perspective." *Terrorism* 8 (1985): 1–32.

Orlando, Federico. *P38.* Milan: Editoriale Nuova, 1978.

Ornstein, P. "On Narcissism." *Bulletin of the Philadelphia Association for Psychoanalysis* 23 (1973): 327–29.

———. "On Narcissism: Beyond the Introduction." *Annual of Psychoanalysis* 2 (1974): 127–49.

Ortega y Gasset, José. *The Revolt of the Masses.* New York: W. W. Norton, 1932.

Ostling, Richard N. "A Sinister Search for 'Identity.' " *Time* (October 20, 1986).

Paine, Lauran. *The Terrorists.* London: Robert Hale, 1975.

Parry, Albert. "The Symbionese and Patty Hearst." In *Terrorism: From Robespierre to Arafat.* New York: Vanguard, 1976.

———. "The Weathermen." In *Terrorism: From Robespierre to Arafat.* New York: Vanguard, 1976.

Pascal, John, and Pascal, Francine. *The Strange Case of Patty Hearst.* New York: New American Library, 1974.

Pate, Clarence W. "The Psychology of the Left-Wing Radical Terror in Post-World War II Germany: The Baader-Meinhof Group." Paper presented to the Conference on Terrorism in the Contemporary

World, April 26–28, 1976, at Glassboro State College, Glassboro, New Jersey.

Paterson, R. W. K. *The Nihilist Egoist: Max Stirner.* London: Oxford University Press, 1971.

Paust, Jordan J. "A Definitional Focus." In *Terrorism: Interdisciplinary Perspectives.* Edited by Yonah Alexander and Seymour Maxwell Finger. New York: John Jay, 1977.

―――. "Some Thoughts on 'Preliminary Thoughts' on Terrorism." *American Journal of International Law* 68 (1974): 502–3.

Payne, Leslie, and Findley, Tim. *The Life and Death of the SLA.* New York: Ballantine, 1976.

Pearce, K. I. "Police Negotiations: A New Role for the Community Psychiatrist." *Canadian Psychiatric Association Journal* 22 (1977): 171–75.

Pearlstein, Richard M. "Lives of Disquieting Desperation: An Inquiry into the Mind of the Political Terrorist." Ph.D. diss., University of North Carolina at Chapel Hill, 1986.

―――. "Of Fear, Uncertainty, and Boldness: The Life and Thought of Thomas Hobbes." *Journal of Psychohistory* 13 (1986): 309–24.

―――. "Tuned-in Narcissus: The Gleam in the Camera's Eye." In *Mediated Portrayals of Terrorism.* Edited by Yonah Alexander and Robert G. Picard. Washington, DC: Pergamon-Brassey's International Defense, 1990.

―――. "The Violent Defense of the Self: A Cunning Offense to Democratic Civility." Paper presented to the Eleventh Annual Scientific Meeting of the International Society of Political Psychology, July 1–5, 1988, at Secaucus, New Jersey.

Pearsall, Robert Brainard. *The Symbionese Liberation Army: Documents and Communications.* Amsterdam: Rodopi N. V. Keizergracht, 1974.

Pepitone, Albert. "The Social Psychology of Violence." *International Journal of Group Tensions* 2 (1972): 19–32.

Pepitone, Albert, and Kleiner, R. "The Effects of Threat and Frustration on Group Cohesiveness." *Journal of Abnormal and Social Psychology* 54 (1957): 192–99.

Petzel, T. P., and Michaels, E. J. "Perception of Violence as a Function of Levels of Hostility." *Journal of Consulting Clinical Psychology* 41 (1973): 35–36.

"Phenomenological and Dynamic Aspects of Terrorism in Italy." *Terrorism* 2 (1979): 159–70.

Phillips, David Atlee. *The Carlos Contract: A Novel of International Terrorism.* New York: Macmillan, 1978.

Picard, Robert G. "The Conundrum of News Coverage of Terrorism." *University of Toledo Law Review* 18 (1986): 141–50.

Picard, Robert G., and Adams, Paul D. "Characterizations of Acts and Perpetrators of Political Violence in Three Elite U.S. Daily Newspapers." *Political Communication and Persuasion* 4 (1987): 1–9.

Pieczenik, Steve Richard. "The Analysis of Hostage Negotiation through a Novel." Ph.D. diss., Massachusetts Institute of Technology, 1982.

_____. "The Social Psychological Constraints of the Terrorist Event." Panel held at the Second Annual Convention of the International Society of Political Psychology, May 24–26, 1979, at Washington, DC.

Pierre, Andrew J. "An Overview of the Causes of and Cures for International Terrorism Today." Paper presented to the International Studies Association Convention, February 20, 1975, at Washington, DC.

_____. "The Politics of International Terrorism." *Orbis* 19 (1976): 1251–69.

Pisano, Vittorfranco S. "A Survey of Terrorism of the Left in Italy: 1970–1978." *Terrorism* 2 (1979): 171–212.

_____. *Contemporary Italian Terrorism.* Washington, DC: Library of Congress Law Library, 1979.

_____. *The Red Brigades: A Challenge to Italian Democracy.* London: Institute for the Study of Conflict, 1980.

_____. "Who's Fighting Italian Terrorism?" *TVI Journal* 1 (1979): 18–20.

Plato. *Statesman.* Indianapolis, IN: Bobbs-Merrill, 1977.

Polin, Raymond. "Nietzschean Violence." In *Violence and Aggression in the History of Ideas.* Edited by Philip P. Wiener and John Fisher. New Brunswick, NJ: Rutgers University Press, 1974.

Pollock, G. H. "On Symbiosis and Symbiotic Neurosis." *International Journal of Psychoanalysis* 45 (1964): 1-30.

Porter, C. "Five Women—First to Be Terrorists." *New Society* 35 (1976): 382–84.

"Portrait of a Terrorist." *Science Digest* (June 1974): 70.

Possony, Stefan F. "Giangiacomo Feltrinelli: The Millionaire Dinamitero." *Terrorism* 2 (1979): 213–30.

_____. "Kaleidoscopic Views on Terrorism." *Terrorism* 4 (1980): 89–121.

Possony, Stefan F., and Bouchey, L. Francis. "The Illuminating Case of Ulrike Meinhof." In *International Terrorism: The Communist Connection.* Washington, DC: ACWF, 1978.

Post, Jerrold M. "Group and Organizational Dynamics of Political Terrorism: Implications for Counter-Terrorist Policy." Paper presented to the International Conference on Terrorism Research, April 21–23, 1986, at the University of Aberdeen, Aberdeen, Scotland.

_____. "Individual and Group Dynamics of Terrorist Behavior." In *Psychiatry: The State of the Art*, vol. 6. New York: Plenum, 1985.

_____. "Narcissism and the Charismatic Leader-Follower Relationship." *Political Psychology* 7 (1986): 675–88.

_____. "Notes on a Psychodynamic Theory of Terrorist Behavior." *Terrorism* 7 (1984): 241–56.

_____. "Prospects for Nuclear Terrorism." In *Preventing Nuclear Terrorism*. Edited by Paul Leventhal and Yonah Alexander. Lexington, MA: Lexington, 1987.

_____. "Psychological Insights on Political Terrorism." Paper presented to the Twenty-fourth Annual Convention of the International Studies Association, April 5–9, 1983, at Mexico City, Mexico.

_____. "Rewarding Fire with Fire? Effects of Retaliation on Terrorist Group Dynamics." In *Contemporary Trends in World Terrorism*. Edited by Anat Kurz. New York: Praeger, 1987.

Powers, Thomas. *Diana: The Making of a Terrorist*. Boston: Houghton Mifflin, 1971.

Pridham, Geoffrey. "Terrorism and the State in West Germany during the 1970's: A Threat to Stability or a Case of Political Overreaction?" In *Terrorism: A Challenge to the State*. Edited by Juliet Lodge. New York: St. Martin's, 1981.

"Profile of a Terrorist." *Executive Risk Assessment* 1 (1979): 1–5.

"Psyching Out Terrorists." *Medical World News* (June 27, 1977).

"The Psychology of Terrorism." In *Security Digest*, vol. 18. Washington, DC: Wilson Center Reports, 1987.

"Psycholojournalist Explains 'Emotion behind the Motion.' " *Editor and Publisher* (January 18, 1975): 37.

Pulver, Sydney E. "Narcissism: The Term and the Concept." *Journal of the American Psychoanalytic Association* 18 (1970): 319–41.

Rangell, L. "The Psychology of Poise." *International Journal of Psychoanalysis* 35 (1954): 313–32.

Rapoport, David C. "Fear and Trembling: Terrorism in Three Religious Traditions." *American Political Science Review* 78 (1984): 655–77.

_____. "The Politics of Atrocity." In *Terrorism: Interdisciplinary Perspectives*. Edited by Seymour Maxwell Finger and Yonah Alexander. New York: McGraw-Hill, 1977.

Rapoport, David C., ed. *Inside Terrorist Organizations*. New York: Columbia University Press, 1988.

Rapoport, David C., and Alexander, Yonah, eds. *The Morality of Terrorism: Religious and Secular Justifications*. New York: Pergamon, 1982.

_____. *The Rationalization of Terrorism*. Frederick, MD: University Publications of America, 1981.

Rapoport, Leon, and Pettinelli, J. D. "Social Psychological Studies of the Safeguards Problem." In *Preventing Nuclear Theft—Guidelines for*

Industry and Governments. Edited by R. B. Leachman and P. Althoff. New York: Praeger, 1972.

Rasch, Wilfried. "Individual Career and Group Formation in the German Terrorist Scene." Paper presented to the Second Annual Meeting of the International Society of Political Psychology, May 24–26, 1979, at Washington, DC.

_____. "Psychological Dimensions of Political Terrorism in the FRG." *International Journal of Law and Psychiatry* 2 (1979): 79–85.

Raskin, Jonah, ed. *The Weather Eye: Communications from the Weather Underground.* New York, 1974.

Redlick, Amy Sands. "The Transnational Flow of Information as a Cause of Terrorism." In *Terrorism: Theory and Practice.* Edited by Yonah Alexander, David Carlton, and Paul Wilkinson. Boulder, CO: Westview, 1979.

Reich, Annie. "Early Identification as Archaic Elements in the Superego." *Journal of the American Psychoanalytic Association* 2 (1954): 218–38.

_____. "Narcissistic Object Choice in Women." *Journal of the American Psychoanalytic Association* 1 (1953): 22–44.

_____. "Pathologic Forms of Self-esteem Regulation." *Psychoanalytic Study of the Child* 15 (1960): 215–32.

Reich, Walter, ed. *Origins of Terrorism: Psychologies, Ideologies, Theologies, and States of Mind.* New York: Cambridge University Press, 1990.

Reighard, H. L. "Hijacker Motivations." Paper presented to the Eighteenth International Congress of Aerospace Medicine, September 15, 1969, at Amsterdam, The Netherlands.

Reiser, Martin, and Sloane, Martin. "The Use of Suggestibility Techniques in Hostage Negotiation." In *Perspectives on Terrorism.* Edited by Lawrence Zelic Freedman and Yonah Alexander. Wilmington, DE: Scholarly Resources, 1983.

Renshon, Stanley A. *Psychological Needs and Political Behavior: A Theory of Personality and Political Efficacy.* New York: Free Press, 1974.

Rice, Berkeley. "Between the Lines of Threatening Messages." *Psychology Today* (September 1981): 52–59.

Rivers, Gayle. *The Specialist: Revelations of a Counterterrorist.* New York: Stein and Day, 1985.

_____. *The War against the Terrorist: How to Win It.* New York: Stein and Day, 1986.

Rochlin, Gregory. "The Dread of Abandonment: A Contribution to the Etiology of the Loss Complex and to Depression." *Psychoanalytic Study of the Child* 16 (1961): 451–70.

_____. *Griefs and Discontents.* Boston: Little, Brown, 1965.

_____. "Loss and Restitution." *Psychoanalytic Study of the Child* 8 (1953): 288–309.

_____. "The Loss Complex." *Journal of the American Psychoanalytic Association* 7 (1959): 299–316.

_____. *Man's Aggression: The Defense of the Self*. Boston: Gambit, 1973.

Rogin, Michael Paul. *Fathers and Children: Andrew Jackson and the Subjugation of the American Indian*. New York: Vintage, 1975.

Ronchey, Albert. "Guns and Gray Matter: Terrorism in Italy." *Foreign Affairs* 57 (1979): 921–40.

_____. "Terror in Italy after Moro's Murder." *Dissent* 25 (1978): 383–85.

_____. "Terror in Italy between Red and Black." *Dissent* 25 (1978): 150–56.

Ronfeldt, David, and Sater, William. "The Mindsets of High-Technology Terrorists: Future Implication from an Historical Analog." In *Political Terrorism and Energy: The Threat and the Response*. Edited by Yonah Alexander and Charles K. Ebinger. New York: Praeger, 1982.

Rosenfeld, H. A. "On the Psychopathology of Narcissism." *International Journal of Psychoanalysis* 45 (1964): 333–47.

Roth, Barry H. "Nuclear Arms and Narcissism." Paper presented to the Eleventh Annual Scientific Meeting of the International Society of Political Psychology, July 1–5, 1988, at Secaucus, New Jersey.

Rothstein, Arnold. *The Narcissistic Pursuit of Perfection*. New York: International Universities Press, 1982.

Rothstein, David A. "Presidential Assassination Syndrome: A Psychiatric Study of the Threat, the Deed, and the Message." In *Assassinations and the Political Order*. Edited by William J. Crotty. New York: Harper and Row, 1971.

Roucek, Joseph S. "Sociological Elements of a Theory of Terror and Violence." *American Journal of Economics and Sociology* 21 (1962): 165–72.

Rubin, Jeffrey Z., and Friedland, Nehemia. "Theater of Terror." *Psychology Today* (March 1986): 21.

Rubinstein, Richard E. *Alchemists of Revolution: Terrorism in the Modern World*. New York: Basic Books, 1987.

Rule, Brendan Gail, and Nesdale, Andrew R. "Moral Judgment of Aggressive Behavior." In *Perspectives on Aggression*. Edited by Russell G. Geen and Edgar C. O'Neal. New York: Academic Press, 1976.

Rule, Brendan Gail, et al. "Judgments of Aggression Serving Personal versus Prosocial Purposes." *Social Behavior and Personality* 3 (1975): 55–63.

Rupprecht, Reinhard. "Description of a Research Project to Study the Causes of Terrorism." In *Terrorism and Beyond: An International Conference on Terrorism and Low-Level Conflict*. Edited by Brian M. Jenkins. Santa Monica, CA: Rand Corporation, 1982.

Russell, Charles A., and Miller, Bowman H. "Profile of a Terrorist." *Terrorism* 1 (1977): 17–34.

Ryan, William. *Blaming the Victim*. New York: Vintage, 1976.

Ryter, Stephen L. "Terror: A Psychological Weapon." *The Review* (May–June 1966): 145–50.

Salewski, Wolfgang D. "The Latest Theory Recognized by Sociological Research in Terrorism and Violence." *Terrorism* 3 (1980): 297–301.

Saper, Bernard. "On Learning Terrorism." *Terrorism* 11 (1988): 13–27.

Sartre, Jean-Paul. *Being and Nothingness*. New York: Citadel, 1956.

———. "Preface." In *The Wretched of the Earth*. By Frantz Fanon. New York: Grove Press, 1963.

Saywell, John. *Quebec 70: A Documentary Narrative*. Toronto: University of Toronto Press, 1971.

Schafer, Stephen. *The Political Criminal: The Problem of Morality and Crime*. New York: Free Press, 1974.

Scharff, W. H., and Schlottman, R. S. "The Effect of Verbal Reports of Violence and Aggression." *Journal of Psychology* 84 (1973): 283–90.

Scheff, Thomas J. "Schizophrenia as Ideology." In *Radical Psychology*. Edited by Phil Brown. New York: Harper, 1973.

Schiller, David Th. "Coping with Terrorism: West Germany in the 1970s and 1980s." In *Contemporary Trends in World Terrorism*. Edited by Anat Kurz. New York: Praeger, 1987.

———. "Germany's Other Terrorists." *Terrorism* 9 (1987): 87–99.

Schlagheck, Donna M. *International Terrorism: An Introduction to the Concepts and Actors*. Lexington, MA: Lexington, 1988.

Schlossberg, Harvey. "Developing a Terrorist Profile." Paper presented to the Conference on Terror: The Man, the Mind, and the Matter, October 15–16, 1976, at the John Jay School of Criminal Justice, New York City.

Schlossberg, Harvey, and Freeman, Lucy. *Psychologist with a Gun*. New York: Coward, McCann and Geoghehan, 1974.

Schmid, Alex P., and Jongman, Albert J. *Political Terrorism: A New Guide to Actors, Authors, Concepts, Data Bases, Theories and Literature*. Amsterdam: North-Holland, 1988.

Schreiber, Jan. *The Ultimate Weapon: Terrorists and World Order*. New York: Morrow, 1978.

Segaller, Stephen. "Mind and Motive." In *Invisible Armies: Terrorism into the 1990s*. San Diego, CA: Harcourt Brace Jovanovich, 1987.

Segel, Nathan P. "Narcissistic Resistance." *Journal of the American Psychoanalytic Association* 17 (1969): 941–54.

Seideman, Anthony. "The Alchemy of the Modern Media: Terrorism and the Castration of the Political Act." Unpublished manuscript.

Seigel, J. E. "Violence and Order in Machiavelli." In *Violence and Aggression in the History of Ideas*. New Brunswick, NJ: Rutgers University Press, 1974.

Sellers, Charles Wesley. *The Narcissus Complex.* Detroit, MI: BT Press, 1939.

Selva, Gustavo, and Marucci, E. *The Martyrdom of Aldo Moro.* Bologna: Capelli, 1978.

Selzer, Michael. *Terrorist Chic: An Exploration of Violence in the Seventies.* New York: Howard and Wyndham, 1979.

Sennett, Richard. *The Fall of Public Man.* New York: Knopf, 1977.

Sewell, Alan F. "Political Crime: A Psychologist's Perspective." In *International Terrorism and Political Crimes.* Edited by M. Cherif Bassiouni. Springfield, IL: Thomas, 1975.

Shaw, Eric D. "Political Hostages: Sanction and the Recovery Process." In *Perpectives on Terrorism.* Edited by Lawrence Zelic Freedman and Yonah Alexander. Wilmington, DE: Scholarly Resources, 1983.

_____. "Political Terrorists: Dangers of Diagnosis and an Alternative to the Psychopathology Model." *International Journal of Law and Psychiatry* 8 (1986): 359–68.

Shneidman, Edwin S., ed. *Endeavors in Psychology: Selections from the Personology of Henry A. Murray.* New York: Harper and Row, 1981.

Shoham, S. G., et al. "Interaction in Violence." *Human Relations* 27 (1974).

Siirala, Martti. "Some Theses on Terrorism." *Terrorism* 3 (1980): 311–27.

Silj, Alessandro. "Case Study II: Italy." In *Contemporary Terror: Studies in Sub-State Violence.* Edited by David Carlton and Carlo Schaerf. New York: St. Martin's, 1981.

_____. *Never Again without a Rifle: The Origins of Italian Terrorism.* New York: Karz, 1979.

Silverstein, Martin E. "Hypotheses on Terrorism." *Terrorism* 3 (1980): 329–33.

Simon, Herbert A. "Human Nature in Politics: The Dialogue of Psychology with Political Science." *American Political Science Review* 79 (1985): 293–304.

Singular, Stephen. *Talked to Death: The Murder of Alan Berg and the Rise of the Neo-Nazis.* New York: Berkley, 1989.

Skolnick, Jerome, ed. *The Politics of Protest: A Task Force Report Submitted to the National Commission on the Causes and Prevention of Violence.* New York: Simon and Schuster, n.d.

"S.L.A. Shoots It Out." *The Economist* (May 25, 1974): 64.

Slap, Joseph W. "Freud's Views on Pleasure and Aggression." *Journal of the American Psychoanalytic Association* 15 (1967): 370–75.

Slater, Philip E. "Culture, Sexuality, and Narcissism." Unpublished manuscript.

_____. *The Pursuit of Loneliness: American Culture at the Breaking Point.* Boston: Beacon, 1970.

Sloan, Stephen. *Simulating Terrorism.* Norman: University of Oklahoma Press, 1981.

Slomich, Sidney J., and Kantor, Robert E. "Social Psychopathology of Political Assassination." In *Social Structure and Assassination Behavior: The Sociology of Political Murder.* Edited by Doris Y. Wilkinson. Cambridge, MA: Schenkman, 1976.

Smith, Colin. *Carlos: Portrait of a Terrorist.* New York: Holt, Rinehart, 1976.

————. "Portrait of a Terrorist: The World's Most Wanted Criminal." *Present Tense* 4 (1977): 52–57.

Soltysik, Fred. *In Search of a Sister.* New York: Bantam, 1976.

Sophocles. *Antigone.* Boston: Ginn, 1900.

Sorel, Georges. *Reflections on Violence.* London: Collier, 1969.

Soskis, David A. "Behavioral Scientists and Law Enforcement Personnel: Working Together on the Problem of Terrorism." *Behavioral Sciences and the Law* 1 (1983): 47–58.

————. "Law Enforcement and Psychiatry: Forging the Working Alliance." In *Terrorism: Interdisciplinary Perspectives.* Edited by B. Eichelman, D. A. Soskis, and W. H. Reid. Washington, DC: American Psychiatric Association, 1983.

Spender, Stephen. *The Year of the Young Rebels.* New York: Random House, 1968.

Spotnitz, Hyman. "The Narcissistic Defense in Schizophrenia." *Psychoanalysis and Psychoanalytic Review* 48 (1961): 24–42.

Spotnitz, Hyman, and Meadow, P. *Treatment of Narcissistic Disorders.* New York: Manhattan Center for Advanced Psychoanalytic Studies, n.d.

Stanciu, V. V. "Macrocriminology: Terrorist Psychology." *Revue internationale de criminologie et police technique* 26 (1973): 189–98.

Starr, Mark, and Raine, George. "The Law Attacks The Order." *Newsweek* (April 29, 1985).

Steinhoff, Patricia G. "Portrait of a Terrorist: An Interview with Kozo Okamoto." *Asian Survey* 16 (1976): 830–45.

Sterling, Claire. "Italy: The Feltrinelli Case." *Atlantic Monthly* (July 1972): 10–18.

————. *The Terror Network: The Secret War of International Terrorism.* New York: Berkley, 1982.

Stern, Aaron. *Me: The Narcissistic Americans.* New York: Ballantine, 1979.

Stern, Susan. *With the Weathermen: The Personal Journal of a Revolutionary Woman.* Garden City, NY: Doubleday, 1975.

Stevens, John. "Ideology and Ethics of Terror." In *The Politics of Terror: A Reader in Theory and Practice.* Edited by Michael Stohl. New York: Marcel Dekker, 1977.

Stevernagel, Gertrude A. *Political Philosophy as Therapy: Marcuse Reconsidered.* Westport, CT: Greenwood, 1979.

Stolorow, Robert D. "Toward a Functional Definition of Narcissism." *International Journal of Psychoanalysis* 56 (1975): 179–85.

Storr, Anthony. *Human Aggression.* New York: Atheneum, 1968.

_____. "Sadism and Paranoia." In *International Terrorism in the Contemporary World*. Edited by Marius Livingston. Westport, CT: Greenwood, 1978.

_____. "Violence as Individual Human Response." In *International Terrorism in the Contemporary World*. Edited by Marius Livingston. Westport, CT: Greenwood, 1978.

Strauss, Harlan. "Revolutionary Types." *Journal of Conflict Resolution* 14 (1973).

Strentz, Thomas. "Proxemics and Interview." *Police Chief* 44 (1977): 74–76.

_____. "The Sociopath." Unpublished manuscript.

_____. "The Stockholm Syndrome: Law Enforcement Policy and Ego Defenses of the Hostage." *Annals of the New York Academy of Sciences* 347 (June 20, 1980): 137–50.

_____. "The Stockholm Syndrome: Law Enforcement Policy and Hostage Behavior." In *Victims of Terrorism*. Edited by Frank M. Ochberg and David A. Soskis. Boulder, CO: Westview Special Studies in National and International Terrorism, 1982.

_____. "The Terrorist Organizational Profile: A Psychological Role Model." In *Behavioral and Quantitative Perspectives on Terrorism*. Edited by Yonah Alexander and John M. Gleason. New York: Pergamon, 1981.

Stuart, Grace. *Narcissus: A Psychological Study of Self-Love*. New York: Macmillan, 1955.

Stumper, A. "Remarks on the Baader-Meinhof Affair." *Revue de Droit pénal et de criminologie* (October 1973): 33–44.

Sugerman, Shirley. *Sin and Madness: Studies in Narcissism*. Philadelphia: Westminster, 1976.

Sullwold, L. "Biographical Features of Terrorists." In *Psychiatry: The State of the Art*, vol. 6. New York: Plenum, 1985.

"The Symbionese Liberation Army in Los Angeles: A Report by the Police Commission to Mayor Tom Bradley." Los Angeles, CA: Los Angeles Police Department, 1974.

Taber, Robert. *The War of the Flea*. New York: Lyle Stuart, 1965.

Taylor, Maxwell. *The Terrorist*. London: Brassey's Defense, 1988.

Taylor, Michael. *Anarchy and Cooperation*. New York: John Wiley, 1976.

Teevan, Richard C., and Birney, Robert C., eds. *Theories of Motivation in Personality and Social Psychology*. Princeton, NJ: Van Nostrand, n.d.

"Terrorism: Psyche or Psychos?" *TVI Journal* 3 (1982): 3–11.

Terrorist Group Profiles. Washington, DC: U.S. Government Printing Office, n.d.

Thomas, Tom. "The Second Battle of Chicago." In *Weatherman*. Edited by Harold Jacobs. Palo Alto, CA: Ramparts Press, 1970.

Thomas Aquinas, Saint. "The Summa Theologica." In *The Political Ideas of St. Thomas Aquinas*. Edited by Dino Bigongiari. New York: Hafner, 1953.

Thornton, Thomas Perry. "Terror as a Weapon of Political Agitation." In *Internal War*. Edited by Harry Eckstein. New York: Free Press, 1964.

Thucydides. *The Peloponnesian War*. New York: Modern Library, 1951.

"Thwarting Terrorists: Can Psychiatry Help?" *Science News* (May 17, 1980): 308.

Tiger, Lionel, and Fox, Robin. *The Imperial Animal*. New York: Dell, 1971.

Tobon, Nydia. *Carlos: Terrorist or Guerrilla?* Barcelona: Ediciones Grijalbo, 1978.

Toch, Hans. *The Social Psychology of Social Movements*. Indianapolis, IN: Bobbs-Merrill, 1965.

_____. *Violent Men: An Inquiry into the Psychology of Violence*. Chicago: Aldine, 1969.

Toynbee, Arnold. "Aspects of Psycho-History." *Main Currents in Modern Thought* 29 (1972): 44–46.

"Trading in Terror, Carlos Becomes the World's Most Wanted Criminal." *People Weekly* (October 11, 1976): 24–27.

Trautman, Frederic. *The Voice of Terrorism: A Biography of Johann Most*. Westport, CT: Greenwood, 1980.

Trippett, Frank. "Order in Court." *Time* (September 23, 1985).

Trotsky, Leon. "Terrorism in War and Revolution." In *The Age of Permanent Revolution: A Trotsky Anthology*. Edited by Isaac Deutscher. New York: Dell, 1964.

Truby, J. David. "Women as Terrorists." In *Clandestine Tactics and Technology*, vol. 2. Gaithersburg, MD: International Association of Chiefs of Police, 1976.

Tucker, Gerald D. "Machiavelli and Fanon: Ethics, Violence, and Action." *Journal of Modern African Studies* 16 (1978): 397–415.

Tugwell, Maurice A. J. "Guilt Transfer." In *The Morality of Terrorism: Religious and Secular Justifications*. Edited by David C. Rapoport and Yonah Alexander. New York: Pergamon, 1982.

Turk, Austin T. *Political Criminality: The Defiance and Defense of Authority*. Beverly Hills, CA: Sage, 1982.

Turner, James. "A Systematic Conceptualization Concerning Acts of Terror." Paper presented to the Second Annual Meeting of the International Society of Political Psychology, May 24–26, 1979, at Washington, DC.

Uekert, Brenda K. "National Development, Life Chances, and Terrorism." Paper presented at the Eleventh Annual Scientific Meeting of the International Society of Political Psychology, July 1–5, 1988, at Secaucus, New Jersey.

U.S. Congress. House. Committee on Internal Security. *The Symbionese Liberation Army: A Study.* 93d Cong., 2d sess., 1974.

U.S. Congress. Senate. Committee on the Judiciary. Subcommittee to Investigate the Administration of the Internal Security Act and Other Internal Security Laws. *Hearings: State Department Bombing by Weathermen Underground.* 93d Cong., 1st sess., 1974.

_____. *Terrorist Activity: Inside the Weather Movement, Hearings.* 93d Cong., 1st sess., 1974.

_____. *The Weather Underground: Report.* 94th Cong., 1st sess., 1975.

Valk, Thomas H. "Psychological Dimensions of Terrorism." Unpublished manuscript.

Vallières, Pierre. *White Niggers of America: The Precocious Autobiography of a Quebec "Terrorist."* New York: Monthly Review Press, 1971.

Van Dalen, Robert. "Terrorism and Human Nature." *Military Police Law Enforcement Journal* (Summer 1979): 9–14.

Van der Waals, H. G. "Problems of Narcissism." *Bulletin of the Menninger Clinic* 29 (1965): 293–311.

Van Voris, W. H. *Violence in Ulster: An Oral Documentary.* Amherst: University of Massachusetts Press, 1975.

Vernisy, Jacques. "The New International Terrorism." *World Press Review* (November 1980): 23–25.

Vinge, Louise. *The Narcissus Theme in Western European Literature Up to the Early Nineteenth Century.* Gleerups, 1967.

Von der Mehden, Fred R. "The Justification and Rhetoric of Violence." In *Comparative Political Violence.* Englewood Cliffs, NJ: Prentice Hall, 1973.

Wagenlehner, Gunther. "Motivation for Political Terrorism in West Germany." In *International Terrorism in the Contemporary World.* Edited by Marius Livingston. Westport, CT: Greenwood, 1978.

Wagner-Pacifica, Robin Erica. *The Moro Morality Play: Terrorism as Social Drama.* Chicago: University of Chicago Press, 1986.

Walzer, Michael. *Obligations: Essays on Disobedience, War, and Citizenship.* New York: Simon and Schuster, 1970.

_____. *The Revolution of the Saints: A Study in the Origins of Radical Politics.* New York: Atheneum, 1974.

_____. "Terrorism." In *Just and Unjust Wars.* New York: Basic Books, 1977.

Wardlaw, Grant. "The Problem of Defining Terrorism." In *Political Terrorism: Theory, Tactics, and Countermeasures.* Cambridge, UK: Cambridge University Press, 1982.

_____. "Psychology and the Resolution of Terrorist Incidents." *Australian Psychologist* 18 (1983): 179–90.

Wasmund, Klaus. "The Political Socialization of West German Terrorists." In *Political Violence and Terror: Motifs and Motivations.* Edited by Peter H. Merkl. Berkeley: University of California Press, 1986.

Watson, Francis M. *Political Terrorism: The Threat and the Response.* Washington, DC: R. B. Luce, 1976.

Watson, P., and Moynahan, B. "The Mind of the Terrorist." *Sunday Times-Spectrum* (August 19, 1973): 8.

Weed, Steven. *My Search for Patty Hearst.* New York: Crown, 1976.

Weibgen, Frederick. "Compensating for a Childhood in Germany." *New York Times,* January 17, 1978.

Weinberg, Leonard, and Eubank, William Lee. "Italian Women Terrorists." *Terrorism* 9 (1987): 241–62.

———. *The Rise and Fall of Italian Terrorism.* Boulder, CO: Westview, 1987.

Weiser, Theodor. "Italy: The Terrorist War on the State." *Swiss Review of World Affairs* (December 1978): 11–13.

Wertham, F. "New Dimensions of Human Violence." *American Journal of Psychotherapy* 23 (1969): 373–80.

Whetten, Lawrence L. "Italian Terrorism: Record Figures and Political Dilemmas." *Terrorism* 1 (1978): 377–96.

White, C. A. "Terrorism: Idealism or Sickness?" *Canada and the World* 39 (1974): 14–15.

Whitley, Julian L. "An Examination of Terrorism from a Psychological and Historical Perspective." M.A. thesis, Pacific Lutheran University, 1981.

Wiener, Philip P., and Fisher, John, eds. *Violence and Aggression in the History of Ideas.* New Brunswick, NJ: Rutgers University Press, 1974.

Wilkins, J. L.; Scharff, W. H.; and Schlottman, R. S. "Personality Type, Reports of Violence, and Aggressive Behavior." *Journal of Personality and Social Psychology* 30 (1973): 243–47.

Wilkinson, Doris Y. "Political Assassins and Status Incongruence." In *Social Structure and Assassination Behavior: The Sociology of Political Murder.* Edited by Doris Y. Wilkinson. Cambridge, MA: Schenkman, 1976.

Wilkinson, Doris Y., and Gaines, Jerry. "The Status Characteristics and Primary Group Relationships in Seven Political Assassins in America." In *Social Structure and Assassination Behavior: The Sociology of Political Murder.* Edited by Doris Y. Wilkinson. Cambridge, MA: Schenkman, 1976.

Wilkinson, Paul. "Concepts of Terror and Terrorism." In *Political Terrorism.* New York: John Wiley, 1974.

———. "Pathology and Theory." In *The Terrorism Reader: A Historical Anthology.* Edited by Walter Laqueur. New York: Meridian, 1978.

———. *Political Terrorism.* London: Macmillan, 1974.

———. "Social Scientific Theory and Civil Violence." In *Terrorism: Theory and Practice.* Edited by Yonah Alexander, David Carlton, and Paul Wilkinson. Boulder, CO: Westview, 1979.

———. *Terrorism and the Liberal State.* New York: Halsted, 1977.

Wilson, Colin. *Order of Assassins: The Psychology of Murder*. London: Rupert Hart-Davis, 1972.

Winn, Gregory F. T. "Terrorism, Alienation, and German Society." In *Behavioral and Quantitative Perspectives on Terrorism*. Edited by Yonah Alexander and John M. Gleason. New York: Pergamon, 1981.

Wohlstetter, Roberta. *International Terrorism: Kidnapping to Win Friends and Influence People*. Santa Monica, CA: Arms Control and Foreign Policy Seminar, 1974.

Wolf, John B. *Fear of Fear: A Survey of Terrorist Operations and Controls in Open Societies*. New York: Plenum, 1981.

————. "Terrorist Manipulation of the Democratic Process." In *International Terrorism in the Contemporary World*. Edited by Marius Livingston. Westport, CT: Greenwood, 1978.

Wolfe, Tom. "The 'Me' Decade and the Third Great Awakening." *New York* (August 23, 1976): 26–40.

Wolfenstein, E. Victor. *Personality and Politics*. Belmont, CA: Dickenson, 1969.

————. *The Revolutionary Personality: Lenin, Trotsky, Gandhi*. Princeton, NJ: Princeton University Press, 1967.

Wolin, Sheldon S. "Machiavelli: Politics and the Economy of Violence." In *Politics and Vision*. Boston: Little, Brown, 1960.

————. "Violence and the Western Political Tradition." *American Journal of Orthopsychiatry* 33 (1963): 15–28.

Wollheim, Richard. *The Thread of Life*. Cambridge, MA: Harvard University Press, 1984.

Wolman, Benjamin B. "Psychology of Followers of Terrorist Groups." *International Journal of Group Tensions* 12 (1982): 105–21.

Worthy, W. "Bombs Blast a Message of Hate: An Interview with an Admitted Bomber." *Life* (March 27, 1970): 24-32.

Wright, Robin. *Sacred Rage: The Crusade of Militant Islam*. New York: Linden Press, 1985.

Wurfel, Seymour W. "Aircraft Piracy: Crime or Fun?" *William and Mary Law Review* 70 (1969): 820.

Wykert, John. "Psychiatry and Terrorism." *Psychiatric News* (February 2, 1979): 1.

Yates, Aubrey. *Frustration and Conflict*. London: Methuen, 1962.

Yong, Torado. "International Terrorism and Public Opinion Policy Processes." *Co-Existence* 8 (1971): 147–59.

Young, Robert. "Revolutionary Terrorism, Crime and Morality." *Social Theory and Practice* (Fall 1977): 287-302.

Zahn, G. C. "Terrorism for Peace and Justice." *Commonweal* (October 23, 1979): 84–85.

Zinam, Oleg. "Terrorism and Violence in the Light of a Theory of Discontent and Frustration." In *International Terrorism in the Con-*

temporary World. Edited by Marius Livingston. Westport, CT: Greenwood, 1978.

Zintl, Robert T. "Dream of a Bigot's Revolution." *Time* (February 18, 1985).

Zonis, Marvin. "Seminar on the Psychological Roots of Shi'ite Muslim Terrorism." Unpublished manuscript.

Zoppo, Ciro Elliott. "The Moral Factor in Interstate Politics and International Terrorism." Paper presented to the Conference on the Moral Implications of Terrorism, March 14–16, 1979, at the University of California at Los Angeles, Los Angeles, California.

_____. " 'Never Again without a Rifle,' by Alessandro Silj: A Review of a Book and a Situation." *Terrorism* 2 (1979): 271–81.

Zweig, Paul. *The Heresy of Self-love.* New York: Basic Books, 1968.

Index